BUSINESS STRATEGY

OTHER ECONOMIST BOOKS

Guide to Analysing Companies
Guide to Business Modelling
Guide to Business Planning
Guide to Cash Management
Guide to Commodities
Guide to Country Risk
Guide to Decision Making
Guide to Economic Indicators
Guide to Emerging Markets
Guide to the European Union
Guide to Financial Management
Guide to Financial Markets
Guide to Hedge Funds
Guide to Investment Strategy
Guide to Management Ideas and Gurus
Guide to Managing Growth
Guide to Organisation Design
Guide to Project Management
Guide to Supply Chain Management
Numbers Guide
Style Guide

Book of Business Quotations
Book of Isms
Brands and Branding
Business Consulting
Buying Professional Services
The Chief Financial Officer
Economics
Frugal Innovation
Intellectual Property
Managing Talent
Managing Uncertainty
Marketing
Marketing for Growth
Megachange – the world in 2050
Modern Warfare, Intelligence and Deterrence
Organisation Culture
Successful Strategy Execution
Unhappy Union

Directors: an A–Z Guide
Economics: an A–Z Guide
Investment: an A–Z Guide
Negotiation: an A–Z Guide

Pocket World in Figures

BUSINESS STRATEGY

A guide to effective decision-making

3rd edition

Jeremy Kourdi

PUBLICAFFAIRS

New York

Typeset in EcoType by MacGuru Ltd
info@macguru.org.uk

Library of Congress Control Number: 2015934934
ISBN 978-1-161039-476-5 (PB)
ISBN 978-1-161039-477-2 (EB)

First Edition

10 9 8 7 6 5 4 3 2 1

Contents

List of figures

List of tables

PART 1

Understanding strategy

1   What is business strategy?

BUSINESS STRATEGY is the plans, choices and decisions used to guide a company to greater profitability and success.

An inspired and clearly considered strategy provides the impetus for commercial success, whereas a weak or misunderstood strategy may lead to a company going out of business. Understanding what constitutes "strategy" is therefore crucial in developing a successful business, as is avoiding the tendency to label every plan and decision "strategic" when most are about implementing strategy rather than setting it. Equally important is for a strategy to be clear and effectively communicated to everyone with a role in implementing it, and to shareholders and other stakeholders.

A clear view

A focus on strategy will highlight where a unit or group of businesses can be more successful as well as those areas where it is weak, vulnerable or failing. It will show in detail where the business is making its money and why. This insight can be used to build profits, cash flow growth and shareholder value. Strategy indicates where resources (notably people, effort and finance) should be concentrated.

The process of developing and implementing strategy enables managers to understand their customers and competitors. Specifically, a sound strategy is grounded in an understanding of a business's customers. This understanding is dynamic – the company is able to develop its products and approach in line with its customers' changing preferences. Some of the strategies pursued by market-leading companies such as Microsoft and Apple involve anticipating what their existing and potential customers will like. Few purchasers of the Apple iPod were demanding a stylish new way to buy, download and play music before it was launched. Instead, Apple was able to combine developments in software, design, the internet and computer-chip miniaturisation with its understanding of what people would value to come up with a surprising product that caught the popular imagination.

Developing and implementing strategy strengthens a business in another important way. It makes sure that resources are devoted to the most important customers in order to retain their loyalty and get them to buy even more of the company's products or services.

Strategy helps to highlight how profits can be increased through the development of product extensions (new products based on existing offerings), changes to the product mix (the range of available products so that they complement each other), adjustments to prices or cuts in costs. The process of developing strategy also informs thinking about which products and markets to abandon.

Another benefit of strategy relates to developing and implementing a firm's internal organisation. A clear strategy shows managers where business skills need to be added or strengthened. It also highlights where productivity can be improved and why particular initiatives and activities have succeeded or failed. Above all, a clear strategy gives a company the impetus and focus needed to develop among its employees the culture, attitude and skills required to meet the needs of its customers profitably and in a rewarding way.

A business's strategy provides a guiding view of the future that influences employees' decisions, priorities and ways of working. People like to do work that is meaningful to them and that has a purpose. Strategy should provide that meaning and purpose. Those responsible for setting a business's strategy often lose sight of the intangible and valuable contribution it can make to employees' commitment, engagement, productivity and creativity. People work better and achieve more if they believe in what they are doing and have confidence in the direction they are going. Conversely, uncertainty or insecurity about the future breeds tension, lack of confidence and even cynicism, none of which are conducive to business success or personal achievement. A strategy that employees understand and believe in will help them develop their potential and attain new skills. In turn, this boosts self-confidence and increases self-awareness, both of which are qualities that intelligently managed companies need more of.

For owners or shareholders, strategy provides a way of measuring their business's progress. Events ranging from recessions to acts of God may obscure the reality of a firm's short-term performance, but what cannot be obscured is whether the right strategy and direction have been chosen, and the progress made in executing that strategy.

A strategy will not be successful if it does not provide benefits to customers. Indeed, they are more important than anyone. The crucial component of strategy is how it will result in greater appeal to customers. One business that has become adept in this area, growing steadily in a highly competitive and often turbulent market, is Cisco, which supplies networking equipment and network management for the internet. Its strategy is based on understanding what it can do to help its client achieve their goals, and then using this understanding to guide its decisions and focus its work. In short, customer success is the mantra behind client engagement.

Cisco and client engagement

At Cisco, people recognise that each client has different goals. Some are related to financial performance or market share targets; others are concerned with public-sector targets and governmental priorities.

Cisco places great emphasis on making sure that its approach focuses on helping customers to achieve their goals. Scott Brown, formerly vice-president, distribution for worldwide channels, says:

When we think about client engagement, the most important question we can ask is: What are we doing to deliver our clients' success and help them achieve their goals?

The challenge is to make sure that the focus is consistent globally and from top to bottom within the company. Cisco's experience shows that several things are essential.

Understanding what constitutes customer success

This requires an understanding throughout the organisation of what constitutes success for each customer so that everyone shares the same goal and is clear about what it is. For instance, the Cisco badge that forms part of every employee's security pass highlights the most important elements of the company's culture such as open communication, inclusion, trust and teamwork, but it also makes clear that all those attributes serve a single goal: customer success.

Getting the measurements right

If you measure things that are important to the customer and the company, it helps to reinforce their importance among employees – so it matters that you get what you measure and the way you measure it right. The old adage "what gets measured gets managed" holds true, and to determine customer success Cisco uses a wide range of measurements including customer satisfaction, customer loyalty and the number of franchises within a business.

Getting the compensation structure right

The size and nature of their remuneration or compensation package matters greatly to most people. Getting the compensation structure right helps generate positive behaviour and gives people the incentive to do the things that need to be done. At Cisco, a substantial portion (approximately 20%) of executives' pay is linked to customer satisfaction.

Managing performance effectively

At Cisco people get feedback on the measurement of results and know that their compensation depends in part on how good those results are. This reinforces the focus on the customer and benefits everyone involved.

Collaborating and sharing expertise

If a new Cisco client has a specific need and the experience or expertise to address this resides somewhere else in the business, there is an expectation that help will be forthcoming. Collaboration is fostered and managers communicate the standards of professionalism and integrity they expect.

Using technology to communicate

Cisco's focus on customer success benefits from a network-based approach in which communication includes videos from sales leaders, regular information about client successes, examples of how customers use technology, and details of what has worked and what has not. For a company selling networking equipment none of this is surprising, but this kind of communicating is standard in many big companies.

Developing skills and insight

Once the principles of client engagement are understood, practical aspects that a manager can develop include the following:

- Dialogue. The ability to question, empathise and listen is crucial for establishing rapport with customers and ensuring their success.

- Coaching. Encouraging people who have attained leadership positions because of their results and technical expertise to share their skills and experience is essential.

- Knowledge. A sufficiently deep knowledge and understanding of a client's industry, market, customers (and what they want and value), competitors and overall market position is crucial to being able to make a difference.

What strategy is not

Although it is important to know what strategy is and why it is important, it is also useful to appreciate what strategy is not. There is much confusion about the nature of strategy. Strategy is not:

- A vision or mission statement such as "Our strategy is to be a leading-edge provider/employer". This explains neither where the firm is going nor how it will make progress. Consequently, it is not a strategy.

- A goal, budget or business plan. Strategy is not a goal such as "We aim to be the best or number one". This is, at best, an aspiration. Also, strategy is neither a budget nor a business plan, although elements of these may contribute to how a strategy is implemented.

- Data analysis. Too often, data analysis leads to strategy, when what should happen is that strategic choices are made first and then refined and explored further using data analysis.

The choice of strategy

The development of strategy involves making decisions about:

- Who to target as customers (and who to avoid targeting).
- What products or services to offer.
- How to undertake related activities efficiently.

In every industry there are several viable positions that a company can occupy. The essence of strategy therefore is to choose the one position that a company will claim as its own. An example of the difference clear strategic thinking and decision-making can make is Nestlé's turnaround of Nespresso.

Clear strategic thinking: Nespresso

Nespresso is an espresso coffee-making machine consisting of a coffee capsule and a machine. The coffee capsule is hermetically sealed in aluminium and contains 5 grams (about one teaspoon) of roasted, ground coffee. The coffee capsule is placed in the handle, which is then inserted into the machine. The act of inserting the handle pierces the coffee capsule at the top. At the press of a button, pressurised hot water is passed through the capsule. The result is a high-quality cup of espresso coffee.

TABLE 1.1 **Nestlé's winning decisions**

Who	Who should I target as customers?	Target individuals and households, not restaurants or offices
What	What products or services should I offer?	Sell coffee, not coffee machines
How	How can I best deliver the product to customers?	Subcontract the manufacture of the Nespresso machine to prestigious manufacturers Take control of coffee side and focus on the production of high-quality coffee capsules Sell the Nespresso machine through prestigious retailers Educate retailers so that they can teach the consumer how to use the machine Sell the coffee capsules direct through the Nespresso Club

Nespresso was introduced in 1986 as a joint venture between Nespresso and a Swiss-based distributor called Sobal. The new venture, Sobal-Nespresso, purchased the coffee-making machines from another Swiss company, Turmix, and the coffee capsules from Nestlé. Sobal-Nespresso then distributed and sold everything as a system: one product, one price. Offices and restaurants were targeted as customers and a separate unit called Nespresso was set up within Nestlé to support the joint venture's sales and marketing efforts, and to service and maintain the machines.

By 1988, the business had failed to take off and headquarters was considering freezing the operation. However, in 1988–89 Jean-Paul Gaillard, Nespresso's commercial director, changed the strategy and made the business profitable. Gaillard decided that the coffee side of the operation had to be separated from the machine side. Since Nestlé was not in the machine business, he felt he had to focus on the coffee.

Production of the Nespresso machine was assigned to several carefully selected manufacturers such as Krups, Turmix and Philips. The machines were then sold to prestigious retailers including Harrods, Galeries Lafayette and Bloomingdale's. It was the retailers' responsibility, under the guidance and control of Nespresso, to promote, demonstrate and sell the machines to consumers. It was the responsibility of the manufacturers to service and maintain the equipment.

On the coffee side, the Sobal partnership was ended and the operation placed under Nespresso (later Nestlé Coffee Specialties). The target customer was changed from offices to households and the distribution of coffee capsules was organised through a "club". Once customers bought a machine they became a member of the Nespresso Club. Orders for capsules were taken over the phone or by fax direct to the club and the capsules were shipped to the customer within 24 hours. The club covers around 60 countries and employs more than 9,500 people, compared with 331 in 2000. Furthermore, there is a strong brand loyalty, with over 3 million Facebook fans and 180,000 customers visiting Nespresso's online boutique every day.

Avoiding pitfalls

All businesses need a strategy of some kind, and they should reconsider it as the business environment changes. But many get into trouble through lack of understanding or clarity about their strategy.

The first principle, therefore, is that strategy needs to be as clear, simple and compelling as possible.

There are other principles that can help a strategy to be successful.

Create a unique strategic position for the business

Focus on who your customers are, the attractiveness of your offer to them (known as the value proposition), and how you can connect the two as efficiently as possible. The benefits of a unique strategic position are highlighted by the concept of value innovation, developed by W. Chan Kim and Renée Mauborgne in their book *Blue Ocean Strategy: How to Create Uncontested Market Space and Make the Competition Irrelevant*.[1] This is the concept of defying conventional logic to either redefine or create a market. For example, for many years US TV networks used the same format for news programmes. They were aired at the same time and they competed on the popularity and professionalism of their presenters and their ability to report and analyse events. This changed in 1980, when CNN launched real-time 24-hour news from around the world for only 20% of the cost of the networks. Viewers, with their increasingly busy lives, valued news and analysis at a time that suited them, rather than having to fit around a TV channel's schedule.

Consider the availability or potential availability of resources

Money and other resources are limited, even though the balance can be improved through alliances to bring in other kinds of resources such as knowledge and skills. Realistic decisions must be made about how to use them to the greatest benefit. For example, if a company wants to retain existing customers but expand the customer base, it must widen its product range and the range of value propositions. Toyota, one of the world's largest car companies, has products ranging from small, economical vehicles to luxurious marques such as Lexus. This is in contrast to the UK car industry during the 1970s and 1980s, when one nationalised company, British Leyland, produced many more models than its competitors but failed to distinguish between any of them. The company's resources were spread too thinly, with product development and marketing weakening rather than strengthening each other. In time, these issues combined with other problems, such as poor industrial relations and weak quality assurance, to create a tidal wave of other troubles that eventually submerged the firm.

Understand the importance of values and incentives

Strategy must be based on reality about both the external and internal environments. The external forces shaping business strategy include regulatory developments, demographics, economic growth and political stability (see Chapter 4). Internal factors include skills, people's attitudes to their work, their commitment or "engagement", the way they operate and the overall culture of the business. If specific aspects of employees' work in achieving a company's strategy are measured and incentives are given, they will respond accordingly and the strategy will progress. The converse is also true: if a company ignores the need to get people working in a way that is consistent with the strategy, progress will be haphazard at best.

Gain people's emotional commitment to the strategy

Any strategy, however brilliant, will fail unless people understand it and are emotionally committed to its success. Therefore it is crucial to explain why the strategy is important to the organisation and the individual.

Be open to strategic ideas wherever they originate

Although the top people must decide a company's strategy, there is a mistaken view that only they can develop strategic ideas. Ideas can come from anybody, anytime, anywhere.

Keep the strategy flexible

All ideas are good for a limited time, not forever. Continually question the answers to the "who, what, how" questions. Strategy should not be changed too often, but it will require adjusting to altered circumstances. Give employees the freedom to respond and to adjust without waiting for permission or instructions.

Most major businesses recognise the need to empower their

employees and focus on their customers. Understanding how we have arrived at this way of thinking and the different views of the role of strategy is the focus of the next chapter.

Key questions

- What are the most profitable parts of your business? In particular:
  - What are the prospects in the short, medium and long term?
  - How precarious is the business? Does it rely on just a few products, customers, suppliers, personnel or distribution channels?
- What are the priorities when expanding? What must be done to achieve the benefits and avoid the pitfalls?
- What do colleagues see as the best options? What are their views on potential opportunities and difficulties?
- How well do your people-management policies reflect changing patterns of employment? In particular, are you co-ordinating the efforts and talents of all employees, enabling them to improve their skills and enhance the organisation's prospects?
- Are your operations unnecessarily bureaucratic? Could they be more flexible?
- Is there the commitment to act decisively and consistently? How can the culture of the business or team be enhanced?
- Do you understand how planned changes will affect people?
- What are your success criteria and performance measures? How will they be monitored?
- What is the medium- to long-term plan that will ensure the company's success is sustained?
- What are the priorities both within the organisation and externally?
- How will your planned strategy affect other aspects of the business and, in particular, the principal stakeholders (notably customers and employees)?

- How does your business involve customers? Are efforts made to understand what they want? Are you certain about what your customers value?

- Is any part of your planning weak or lacking clear direction? Do you lack confidence in your ability to make the right decisions to meet the strategy?

- Do you always consider multiple options before deciding? Is the quality of your strategic thinking narrow or uninspired?

- Is your organisation afraid of uncertainty or does it enjoy thinking about it? Do people see it as a threat or as an opportunity? Is it a potential source of competitive advantage?

2 What strategic thinking can achieve

THE PAST DECADE has been tumultuous by anyone's standards. It is understandable that many business leaders are feeling battered and are looking forward to the return of easier times, when countering a hostile takeover was simple compared with facing financial meltdown and market turmoil. This would be a mistake. Of course, it seems trite to say that the world is changing: it always has and always will. But the statement is not as simple as it may appear, as it comes with one important caveat: if you do not adapt, and quickly, you will be left behind. Like the inattentive wildebeest at the back of the herd, you will find that the result of not paying attention will, to be frank, be calamitous.

This simple fact has caught out many leading businesses – colossal firms such as Kodak, Bethlehem Steel, Chrysler, Daewoo, Firestone, Digital Equipment Corporation and others. In most of these cases, complacency and a commitment to the status quo escalated in a smooth, undisturbed fashion. The danger for any business is that lack of awareness and connection to the outside world will increase gradually, incrementally and sometimes almost imperceptibly, providing the foundation for most business difficulties. Firms that declined or failed did not do enough to understand or prepare for the future during the good times, and suffered as a result. In retrospect, countless business leaders recognise that good is the enemy of great; in other words, their firms were doing well, so they saw no reason to change. By the time they realised that the world around them had changed (notably customers, competitors and regulators, and sometimes even their employees) it was too late to respond.

Practical strategic thinking that connects "big picture" strategy with detailed, practical implementation is one antidote to this. In fact, no one ever moved from good to great – or sustained leadership in their sector – by being complacent or failing to move with the times. Having strategies that strongly feature innovation and organisational agility (which simply means being unbureaucratic, flexible and entrepreneurial) is one way of avoiding complacency, moving with the times and making sure that the strategy works in practice.

Creating value for customers

Some successful businesses, notably Google, Microsoft, Intel and Facebook, are fortunate to have had founders who created exceptional companies by conceiving a massively popular product with few initial competitors that could then be constantly improved and developed. However, among the lessons on strategy to be learnt from these giants of 21st-century business is a perennial truth that affects all businesses, first enunciated in the 18th century by Adam Smith, a Scottish economist, who wrote:

> The nature of things has stamped upon corn a real value, which cannot be altered by merely altering its money price.

In a rapidly changing world, the ability to create value will help to sustain success through even the toughest of turbulent times.

As Smith recognised, the ability to create value lies at the heart of successful business and commerce. For a price to be paid the object has to be valued; this underpins the theory of supply and demand that lies at the heart of market economics. Profitability requires that something is valued, and this is increasingly provided by the uniqueness of knowledge. The more abundant the supply of a good or service, the lower its price will be, even to the extent that it may not be profitable to produce and sell. But the more scarce the supply (or when competition is held back by barriers such as patents, expertise or other forms of knowledge), the more likely the good or service is to generate a profit. Where there are such barriers, the price of a good or service no longer relates directly to its cost of production but rather to its customer value, which in turn relates to its uniqueness or the costs that buyers would incur if the product were not available.

There are other important points about value. Every company's mission is to create and protect value. It is at the core of an organisation's purpose and, potentially, sets it apart from others. It is a source of competitive advantage and generates profit. The way to create financial value in a business is simple, well documented and unchanged since Smith's time: a company earns an appropriate return on the capital that has been provided. In today's global environment, shareholder value and total shareholder return (TSR – the total financial benefit that is generated for the owners of the business) are driven by market expectations of future cash flows, and these are based on a company's ability to sustain performance and grow over the long term.

To build a profitable organisation that can secure sustainable growth, you need to consider how value will be created – and value creation starts with an understanding of the organisation's purpose. Ask two questions:

- Why is the organisation here?
- What is it trying to achieve?

The answers will help you identify what it needs to do to achieve its aims. A vague idea is not good enough. An organisation's success depends on a clear understanding of why it is there.

Understanding your organisation's purpose

It is easy to frame business issues in terms of the activities to be undertaken. Although this is necessary, it omits one important ingredient: purpose. If you do not know the purpose of an organisation, it is highly likely that business plans and actions will miss the mark. Leaders need to step back from the day-to-day distractions and agree what the purpose is, and then look at all the business activities through this lens. This will ensure that everything from strategic development to managing operations will be focused on delivering real value and building a strong, resilient and successful business.

Essentially, business is about perpetually maximising profit. As noted earlier, to achieve this an organisation must offer something that other businesses or consumers want. Yet focusing on profit is only part of the equation. For some organisations profit is not their primary focus; for others, such as charities, it is of little or no concern. Looking at the motivation of these not-for-profit companies reveals how pivotal knowing the purpose of an organisation is for achieving its aims. An example of an organisation that blends the approaches of charitable and for-profit sectors successfully is Grameen Bank. Significantly, it reveals how much can be achieved by placing all business issues within the context of the organisation's purpose. This can be applied to any business in any sector.

Grameen Bank

Working as an economist at Chittagong University in Bangladesh in the 1970s, Muhammad Yunus witnessed the extreme poverty of the local population. He could see that the main reasons for people being trapped in poverty were that they had no access to credit, or the rates charged were so high that they were forced to live hand to mouth and were unable to grow their businesses or improve their standard of living.

The story began when Yunus visited a poor village with his students. A woman who made bamboo stools explained that she had to borrow money to buy the bamboo, and by the time she had paid back the loan after selling the stool, there was little money left for her to live on. This cycle continued, as the woman never had enough money to buy the bamboo and always had to get another expensive loan. It was clear that the exorbitant rates of interest being charged (often 10% a week) were preventing people rising out of poverty and building a secure future.

With no money to invest in their future, the cycle of poverty could never be broken. Yunus decided to use his own money and offer micro loans at affordable rates so that people were able to keep more of their revenue, thus enabling them to invest in the future, raise their standard of living and break the poverty cycle. The sums were small, amounts that other banks would not have been interested in – small returns on small sums would be considered not worth the effort. Moreover, the loans were given to people that other banks would have dismissed as too great a risk: they had no reliable credit history, no collateral and no obvious means of paying back the loans (the banks basically believed that poor people could not be trusted to repay the loans). Yet Yunus believed it could work. Not only did he feel that it was the right thing to do; he also believed he could minimise the risks and run the business successfully. Other banks and even the government advised him not to pursue this idea. He ignored them and, in 1983, formed Grameen Bank (which means village bank).

The reason for founding the bank was to help poor people escape from poverty by providing small, long-term loans at low interest rates. Key to making this work was trust and knowing who to lend to and on what terms. As a condition of taking a loan, borrowers were given financial advice. By insisting on this, it was more likely that ventures would be successful, which also minimised the risk to the bank. Yunus believed that poor people could be trusted to manage their finances, and he knew that it was the women who could be relied upon to run their business and personal affairs efficiently and responsibly and to repay their loans. Another important reason for its success is solidarity: 95% of the bank is owned by the borrowers themselves, giving everyone shared responsibility and commitment.

Today, the size of Grameen Bank is impressive: it has loaned over $9 billion through 2,564 branches to over 8 million borrowers in over 80,000 villages. It has the highest rate of successful repayments: 97% of loans are repaid. An important reason for this is the bank's policy of mainly giving the loans to women (97% of the total). It is at the forefront of a world movement that aims to eradicate poverty through micro-lending, and its methods have been used in projects in some 58 countries, including developed countries such as the US, France and the Netherlands.

Grameen has enabled many families to cross the poverty line. As well as giving business loans, it helps to improve people's lives in other ways. Housing loans have enabled people to build houses: almost 700,000 have been constructed. Loans for education have helped many to improve their chances of getting better jobs. The bank also awards educational scholarships to bright children, especially girls, as it is more difficult for them to get access to education in Bangladesh. It has been a lifeline for millions of poor people, proving that micro-credits work. These small loans have made all the difference, says Yunus, providing that "spark of personal initiative and enterprise" that helps get people out of poverty.

The bank provides something that so many people desperately need. Although most years have been profitable, its main purpose is to create something more than money – a better society – and it certainly does that. It is not surprising, then, that Yunus is known as "the banker of the poor". For his work in helping people to rise out of poverty, he was awarded the Nobel Peace Prize in 2006.

The example of Grameen Bank highlights an important theme: the need for work to have meaning, which is increasingly significant and links with the fact that successful organisations have a clear purpose and create value. It also shows that issues of value and purpose are as relevant in the not-for-profit sector as they are in the commercial environment, possibly more so.

Helping organisations to define their purpose is a crucial benefit of strategic thinking. The following steps are useful when seeking to agree on the purpose.

Understand buyers' motivations

Whatever product or service you are selling it is essential to know what motivates people to buy. Motivation and behaviour lie at the heart of creating value. People purchase a product or service for one basic reason: they expect it to improve their life. This is why they need to perceive the product or service as relevant. A successful product also adds something for the customer, such as freeing up time, boosting confidence, solving a problem, raising status, improving efficiency or making tasks easier. Clearly, the decision to purchase arises from the sense that the product or service will enrich a person's existence in some way. In short, it delivers extra value.

Focus on customers – the people you serve

Success, then, relies on a product's attributes adding value for the customer. This has implications for developing new products and repositioning or redesigning existing ones: a company must consider how it is adding value. Michael Raynor, a Canadian business writer, analyses the relationship between new products and purchasing decisions, arguing that when a product enriches someone's life, it represents a disruption from the past. This makes sense; if a product offers little extra advantage over what is already offered, there would be no obvious reason for customers to choose your product over a competitor's. Consequently, businesses can capitalise on this by aiming to disrupt customers from what they are used to, with products that break from the norm, giving them something that adds extra value to enrich their lives. In his book *The Strategy Paradox*,

Raynor calls this "disruptive innovation".[1] He adds that, because the future is uncertain, companies should remain flexible by developing a range of options to prepare for different situations.

Embrace uncertainty and change

The next step in finding a purpose is to embrace change. Many things affect a business's ability to respond well to change, not least a lack of information to help guide the correct course of action. If companies do not keep relevant data, are not looking for signs of change, or have never thought about how to deal with possible scenarios, their ability to remain profitable or even survive at all will be limited. In this instance mindset is critical.

Understand the difference between cause and effect

When embracing uncertainty and change, it helps to appreciate the difference between cause and effect. Causation means "if I can predict the future, I can control it", whereas effectuation means "if I can control the future, I don't need to predict it". Most people make decisions using causation, where they try to determine the best course of action; that is, they try to gain control of the future by predicting it. Successful business strategists, however, use effectuation, where they take action based on what they know, who they know and the resources they have available, rather than by analysing optimal courses of action. They evaluate opportunities based on whether the risk of the downside is acceptable, rather than the attractiveness of the predicted upside. Such strategists are confident that they can control the future so there is no need to predict it.

Creating value for the organisation

Establishing a purpose is an essential first step in creating value. Creating value is the lifeblood of an organisation; it is what connects it to its customers and differentiates it from competitors; it builds confidence among stakeholders and secures the organisation's long-term growth. Every organisation's mission is to create and protect value, but some do it better than others. Value is at the core of an organisation's being and what potentially sets it apart from others.

Creating value is a huge topic, but it is fundamental to what strategy can achieve. It is complex: prone to subjective judgments, easily and swiftly eradicated and subject to unexpected fortunes, good and bad. It is also manageable: managers have the skills and ability to stay in charge and direct the organisation's fortunes. There are common attributes that can help deliver value and secure long-term success, such as:

- connecting vision, strategy and business processes with what is needed for the business to succeed – above all, putting mechanisms in place to make sure that people work towards the same goal;
- positioning the organisation to deal with a range of possible scenarios, and then being able to hone in on what is needed when a particular scenario occurs;
- aligning the range of initiatives with the organisation's overall objectives and strategies;
- inspiring the actions required by leading others appropriately;
- focusing on the connections between stakeholders that will create value;
- using the strategies, and their value drivers, to present a credible picture of where the organisation is headed;
- making value creation central to evaluating and managing people and determining how performance is rewarded;
- appointing one person to align strategies, actions and performance management.

The next chapter looks at how strategy and strategic thinking have evolved, and how we can build on the lessons of the past to create value and thrive at a time of complexity and change.

Key questions

- How clear and compelling is the purpose of your organisation? What does it do?
- What more could your organisation achieve?

- What do your employees and customers want from your organisation? What would they value?
- How does your organisation help people? What value does it create?
- How scarce and valuable are the products or services provided by your organisation? How vulnerable are these to being adopted by others or undermined?
- How could your organisation strengthen and develop over the next 12 months? What could it achieve, and how might it be different?

3 The different views of strategy

IN FEBRUARY 1676 ISAAC NEWTON, a British scientist, wrote to Robert Hooke, another successful scientist with whom Newton was in dispute over optical discoveries: "If I have seen further it is by standing on the shoulders of giants." Historians believe that this was not a statement of self-effacing modesty from Newton but a sarcastic attack on the curmudgeonly Hooke, who was short and hunchbacked. Whatever the sentiment behind Newton's remark, the idea has lasted that in mathematics and science progress is made incrementally, by methodically building on the discoveries and insights of others.

The same is true of successful businesses and the strategies that drive them, even though business is often faddish, full of jargon, and lacking rigour, clarity and a methodical approach. Anyone can set up a business but there are fewer certainties in running one than there are in mathematics or science. So in business, strategic thinking requires learning from those who have gone before. They fall into several categories.

The classical administrator

Henri Fayol was a founding father of the classical school of management, which came into its own around 1910. He developed a set of common activities and principles, dividing general management activities into five sections: planning, organising, commanding, co-ordinating and controlling:

■ Planning involves considering the future, deciding the aims of the organisation and developing a plan of action.

- Organising involves marshalling the resources necessary to achieve these aims and structuring the organisation to complete its activities. Both roles remain crucial.

- Commanding may be a term that is out of fashion in the egalitarian, politically correct and empowered world of many Western organisations, but the concept remains significant. It is important to achieve the optimum return from people, frequently the most expensive component of a business.

- Co-ordinating involves focusing and, in particular, unifying people's efforts to ensure success.

- Controlling involves monitoring that everything works as planned, making adjustments where necessary and feeding this information back so that it can be of value in the future.

This classical-administrator approach to decision-making is largely concerned with measuring and improving skills and processes within organisations. It is characterised by hierarchy, usually in the form of top-down planning and control, formal target setting and performance measurement, structured programmes for functional improvements through "scientific" engineering and a formal organisation structure. Fayol was a forerunner of modern management theorists who take a prescriptive view of strategic decision-making. For example, Frederick Taylor, one of the founding fathers of management theory in the first half of the 20th century, introduced a scientific management approach to production department work; and Peter Drucker, a leading management thinker who died in 2005, can be categorised as a classical administrator, at least in his approach to strategy development and decision-making.

The classical approach really took hold once entrepreneurs such as Henry Ford realised that they needed to focus on the productivity of their new manufacturing plants. It led to the development of efficient production lines and a focus on production quality, which started in the 1950s, built up efficiency in the Japanese manufacturing industry and then took hold more widely in the 1980s. This quality revolution was championed by W. Edwards Deming, an American who helped the Japanese improve their production processes in the early 1950s, although it was not until the early 1980s that his contribution to improving quality processes and building a reputation for Japanese reliability was recognised in his native land. The emphasis on controlling and measuring foreshadowed the arrival of the total quality management movement.

The significance of Taylor's work was highlighted in a *Fortune* article in 1997:[1]

> It's his ideas that determine how many burgers McDonald's expects its flippers to flip or how many callers the phone company expects its operators to assist.

Taylor's ideas stemmed in part from his view that:[2]

> Nineteen out of twenty workmen throughout the civilised world firmly believe it is for their best interests to go slow instead of fast. They firmly believe that it is for their interest to give as little work in return for the money that they get as is practical.

It does not matter that attitudes have changed. The value of the classical-administrator approach lies in the structured framework for action that it provides. In an era of quickening change, unknown variables and global complexity, a simple framework designed to organise and focus activities remains as valuable for decision-making as it was in slower, more predictable times.

The design planner

The design-planning approach emerged in the mid-1960s, outlined by Alfred Chandler and Igor Ansoff, and later by Kenneth Andrews. It emphasises that the principal role of a leader is to plan the development of an organisation beyond the short term. This heralded the arrival of strategic thinking in organisations, as distinct from focusing on continuing management activities. In this approach, strategy results from a controlled and conscious thought process, achieving long-term competitive advantage and success through answering questions such as: Where are we now? Where do we want to be? How are we going to get there?

This recognised for the first time that organisations are beset with turbulent change. In 1965 Ansoff wrote:[3]

No business can consider itself immune to the threats of product obsolescence and saturation of demand ... In some industries, surveillance of the environment for threats and opportunities needs to be a continuous process.

Design planning requires expertise in two areas:

- anticipating the future environment, with the help of analytical techniques and models;
- devising appropriate strategies matching the external opportunities and threats to the organisation's resources, internal strengths and weaknesses.

Once the strategy is planned, it is simply a matter of using the techniques of the classical administrator to plan its implementation by, for example, having a master plan that schedules key tasks and budget-controlled activities.

The result was that strategic decision-making had been given a separate focus. Four decision types were identified, covering strategy, policy, programmes and standard operating procedures. The last three were already understood, with an emphasis on resolving recurring issues such as production efficiency. Attempting to shape the future through decision-making was in the ascendancy. Ansoff classified decisions as:

- strategic, focusing on the dynamic issues of products and markets;
- administrative, concerned with structure and resource allocation;
- operating, focusing on supervision and control.

These distinctions remain in the minds of decision-makers today, guiding their focus and actions.

The role player

In the 1970s, Henry Mintzberg, a leading management thinker and writer, started arguing that the models of the classical and design theorists did not reflect the reality about how leaders and organisations work. Decision-making had been flawed and was incapable of understanding what actually happens in organisations, leaving them poorly placed to face the challenge of change. Mintzberg advocated the need to prescribe through description, to observe and assess the reality of strategy in action.

The role-player approach views the job of the strategic decision-maker as more than that of a reflective and analysing planner and controller. What about the need for flexibility and swift responsiveness? What about the fundamental decisions made not at the top of the organisation but much further down? For Mintzberg, vision, communication and negotiation, as well as the need to be able to react quickly to disturbances and to change tactics at short notice, are of greatest importance. Moreover, an ad hoc approach balances short-term needs with a longer-term understanding of environmental developments. Such an approach can emphasise the benefit of learning-by-doing decision processes, where strategies emerge in the context of human interactions rather than resulting from deliberate and systematic planning systems. This is similar to the approach adopted by scenario planners such as Kees van der Heijden, emeritus professor at the University of Strathclyde Graduate School of Business, who favours the concept of a strategic conversation, outlined in Chapter 4. The decision-maker's role becomes one of learning, supporting and positively enabling rather than directing. The long-term result is incremental progress rather than a big bang, but it is no less real and over the long term may be more valuable.

The competitive positioner

The competitive positioner understands the power of the external environment and focuses almost exclusively on achieving competitive advantage. The underlying premise is the belief that market power produces above-average profits in a marketplace where competition is the defining characteristic. The main theorist behind this approach is Michael Porter, Bishop William Lawrence University Professor at Harvard Business School and director of the school's Institute for Strategy and Competitiveness. The competitive positioner's main tasks are to understand and decide where the organisation is competing and then align it so that it is able to gain advantage over its competitors.

Competitive forces include customers and suppliers, substitute products (which are increasing in significance because of the flexibility and choice provided by the online marketplace), and present and potential competitors. Future competitors may not be those that we recognise today, and new competitors may well enter the market by changing the rules of competition. To compete successfully against all this, the positioner may need to do any combination of the following: erect barriers to entry to its market; attract price premiums for its products; reduce operating costs below those of its competitors.

Core competencies are viewed as the key to achieving competitive advantage by those such as Gary Hamel and the late C.K. Prahalad, two leading management gurus.[4] And what is core needs to be competitive: those capabilities and sources of value that are scarce and cannot easily be replicated by competitors. Astute industry analysis also matters to enable the development of winning competitive strategies and their successful implementation. Lastly, this approach emphasises market differentiation and the need to make decisions that build customer loyalty as well as delivering higher quality and productivity.

The renaissance of Xerox

An example of competitive positioning is provided by the renaissance of Xerox during the 2000s. Having experienced challenges from Japanese manufacturers in the 1980s, by 1998 the US technology giant was doing well. A new chief executive was in post, the share price was rising and profits were strong. However, by the end of 1999 significant problems were emerging. There was too much change, too fast; new, opportunistic competitors emerged; economic growth was slowing; there were regulatory problems; and the company made a number of poor decisions. Revenues slumped, customers and employees left and the company's debts reached $19 billion.

Despite this, Xerox, led by CEO Anne Mulcahy, survived the downturn and made a comeback. Between 1999 and 2006 the share price doubled and costs had been cut by $2 billion. The company made profits in four consecutive years, rising to $1 billion in 2005. The foundation for this revival came from a strong brand with a loyal customer base, talented employees, recognition of the need to listen carefully to customers and greater responsiveness. Employees simply wanted a clear direction – no magic, just a focus on sound principles. The key was to win back market share with a competitive range of new products.

In Mulcahy's view, several factors lay behind Xerox's resurgence:

- Listen and never lose contact. This can be accomplished by creating a culture of good critics and being aware that managers can become out of touch, even within their own organisation.
- Learn and apply Six Sigma (see below).[5] At Xerox its use improved both costs and service for customers by providing a disciplined way to make process improvements.
- Recognise the need to be "problem curious". Constantly look for ways to differentiate and improve.
- Provide a clear, exciting, compelling vision of what the future will look like. People like a guiding light and a greater degree of certainty.
- Invest in the future and in innovation. In 2005, two-thirds of Xerox's revenues came from products launched within the previous two years.
- Remember that your business relies on its people. There needs to be a common set of goals and strong leadership; diligence in recruitment makes a huge difference.

For Xerox, factors that may determine future success are:

- The building of team cultures that are flexible, that understand what is happening and can move fast.
- Aligning resources and processes to ensure nimbleness and flexibility.
- Providing leadership that is not afraid to take risks, and setting priorities and communicating them.

Six Sigma

There are two main methodologies: DMAIC (define, measure, analyse, improve, control), which is used to improve an existing business process; and DMADV (define, measure, analyse, design, verify), which can be used to create new products or process designs.

DMAIC comprises five main steps:

1 Define the goals and the processes to be improved. These goals should be consistent with customers' demands and the business strategy.

2 Measure the main aspects of the current process and collect relevant data.

3 Analyse the data to understand cause-and-effect relationships. Determine what the relationships are and make sure that all factors have been considered.

4 Improve or optimise the process based on analysis of the data.

5 Set up a control system to make sure that any deviations from the target are corrected before they create defects. For example, set up pilot runs and beta tests before extending the approach and continuously monitor the process.

DMADV also includes five steps for setting up a new product or design process:

1 Define the goals. This is the same first stage as DMAIC. Set the goals and make sure they are consistent with customers' demands and the business strategy.

2 Measure and identify CTQs (critical to quality factors). Also identify and quantify the product's capabilities, the main elements of the production process and any significant risks.

3 Analyse the best design alternatives, then create a high-level design and select the best design.

4 Design the details and implement and improve the design. This phase may require simulations.

5 Verify the design, for example by using piloting and beta testing. Also implement the production process and make sure it is managed and improved continuously.

Typically, a company generates about 50,000 defects per million products – a 5% error rate. The Six Sigma method aims to reduce defects to less than four per million, that is almost zero. General Electric (GE) is an example of a company that has applied Six Sigma with considerable success.

In June 1995 GE got detailed information about Six Sigma from Motorola at one of the company's regular gatherings of global managers, and decided to start the first pilot immediately. In November that year, following positive pilot results, GE launched 200 Six Sigma initiatives. The next year it launched 3,000 projects, covering every business area from plastics and aircraft engines to financial leasing operations. Six Sigma implementation and expertise were quickly institutionalised, with more than 60,000 managers trained in the application of the method in 1997 alone, and global managers' bonuses were made dependent on Six Sigma results. GE, with revenues of $100.5 billion in 1998, enjoyed operating margins of 16.7%, compared with 13.6% in 1994 before the introduction of Six Sigma.

GE's success in applying a new working method so quickly and effectively was due to the quality of its 500 global managers, but it also highlights the power of the social network inside a company and between a company and its suppliers, customers and allies. GE's social network includes regular Corporate Executive Councils (or CECs, involving the company's top 30 executives), global management meetings (including the CEO and 500 global managers) and Town Meetings (each global manager with his business unit). By creating such a meetings "infrastructure", a new initiative can spread through the organisation from top to bottom remarkably quickly and effectively. The lesson is that it is wise to focus not just on the processes and objectives of development, but also on communication and its effect on stakeholders' perceptions.

The visionary transformer

The visionary transformer came to prominence in the 1980s, largely as a result of Tom Peters and Robert Waterman.[6] They considered vision to be fundamental for effective strategic decision-making, with regard to such issues as:

- Where should the organisation position itself in the market so that it can grow, continue to build shareholder value and keep ahead of its competitors?

- What type of organisation should it be? What are the brand values and aspirations of the organisation and what do they need to be to realise its aims?

- What guiding principles steer the organisation and how are they best assessed, communicated and applied? (This sense of mission is seen as essential; people who understand the core goals and values of the organisation are better placed to work towards these ends.)

- How should the organisation make sure that it is co-ordinated and working in concert? (This echoes Fayol's and Taylor's belief that co-ordination is a fundamental role of the classical administrator.)

Once these questions have been answered it is necessary to:

- develop and explain a powerful, compelling vision of the future that helps to guide people's decisions, as Xerox did;

- structure and lead the organisation in the most effective and appropriate way;

- control the skills necessary to implement and realise the vision. These include energy and drive, dogged determination, a capacity for hard work, exceptional communication skills and the ability to empower and motivate others and to act as a role model.

The success of a visionary approach depends ultimately on pragmatism: the ability to achieve a vision by listening, acting and learning rather than adopting plans or rigid approaches. In particular, it is essential that visions are achievable and that visionary transformers are able to make progress in achieving them.

It is not simply the clarity and relevance of a vision that matters but how that vision is developed and communicated and whether it routinely influences the way people in the organisation think and the decisions they make. Scenario planners can help an organisation keep in touch with reality, both internally and with the external competitive environment. An organisation that has an unrealistic view of its strengths and its market may find itself in trouble. For example, in the early 1980s IBM believed that future profitability in the computer industry would come from hardware, largely ignoring software, and mistakenly thought that it could dominate the hardware market. Business history is full of organisations that were sadly out of touch with their markets and lacked the vision and skills to make progress.

Too often businesses overlook two things that can be said for certain about the future: it will be different and it will surprise. These simple facts have caught out many leading businesses. An example is Lego.

Lego: transforming product development

Lego is a family-owned Danish company that in the 1930s invented the moulded plastic building bricks for children's play. The business was extremely successful for many years before sales started levelling in the late 1980s. Kjeld Christiansen took charge of the organisation in the 1990s; however, in the competitive world of children's toys, Lego's fortunes were far from certain. Profits peaked in 1997 and then fell precipitously. In 1999, Lego laid off 1,000 people, the first big lay-off in the company's history, yet in 2000 Lego still lost $120 million on sales of $1.1 billion.

Lego had reacted too slowly and inadequately to long-term changes in the marketplace. Products that were technologically sophisticated had quickly replaced plastic bricks as the preferred purchase – a sudden (and apparently unexpected) development, after Lego's years of steady sales growth and seeming invulnerability. It was caught in a constant struggle to keep up with changes in customer choice, even though the Lego brand remained consistently rated among the most powerful for families with children.

Since then it has transformed product development and design through a system called Design for Business (D4B), which emphasises collaboration and continual evaluation. As a result, Lego's sales have risen steadily in the past decade, reaching $4.6 billion in 2013. This prompted Jorgen Vig Knudstorp, the company's CEO, to comment on the company's website:

> In less than ten years, we have more than quadrupled our revenue ... In 2013 we successfully developed and launched products that children put high on their wish list all over the world.

The self-organiser

In a complex and fast-moving business environment, there is an advantage in being a "learning organisation" that adapts to change. Peter Senge, author of *The Fifth Discipline*, highlighted this in 2006.[7] Self-organising businesses need to be designed and led by people who can create an organisation where its constituent parts and, above all, its people continually self-organise around emerging strategic issues, fluidly developing the organisation. In this way, accepted formulas and perspectives are constantly challenged and revised.

To achieve this, organisations need the ability to develop learning communities (networks of people working together without traditional top-down management to improve effectiveness) to generate innovative solutions for commercial opportunities. Innovation and collaboration are crucial competencies for operating in environments that change rapidly and are difficult to control.

The turnaround strategist

This decision-making approach focuses on turning around the performance of an organisation in decline, perhaps when a visionary leader has failed. It is autocratic, ruthless and swift, and it is more context-specific. Invariably, the requirement is to operate when an organisation is in a state of crisis. Lou Gerstner turned around IBM after its dramatic decline by repositioning the business as a provider of services as well as a supplier of it products.

To achieve turnaround success, it is important to implement new control systems quickly, and to focus on the reasons for decline and reverse them while going for the easiest route to immediate growth. Short-term issues are critical, and a dramatic change of overall perspective is required. The IBM example also illustrates the importance of highlighting the causes of weakness, such as complacency, hubris and lack of vision, in order to change the culture and performance of the business.

The turnaround strategist faces several significant challenges. Many can be classed as cultural challenges that focus on the need to change not only what is being done but, crucially, the way that employees operate and how they work.

TABLE 3.1 **Challenges for turnaround strategists**

Challenges	Symptoms	Potential solutions
Focusing on priorities	The business is unable to define priorities	Establish a clear, practical vision
	Resources are spread too thin	Define and communicate clear priorities
	People spend large amounts of their time fighting fires	Review resources: are you getting the most from available resources?
Managing performance	Wide variations in performance of people and processes	Review reward systems: do they encourage the right behaviours?
	People fail to meet commitments	Lead by example: take action to resolve a performance issue
	Managers fail to resolve performance issues	
Innovating	The focus is internal, with processes, products or services developing slowly or incrementally	Find and reward ideas for improvement; encourage a questioning approach; challenge assumptions; listen to customers and generate ideas that benefit customers
	The emphasis is on stability, not for successfully developing the business	Establish an open, blame-free environment, where people are encouraged to take greater risks; remove obstacles to innovation and consider leading an improvement project
Teamworking	Competitiveness is directed in	Establish regular opportunities for colleagues to meet informally; allow time at team meetings for an open exchange of views; look for what people think, as well as what they say
	The business works in "silos" with managers failing to co-operate	Establish a project team with complementary skills and get them to work on a specific challenge; confront poor performance
Complacency or cynicism	Lack of focus on customers	Set goals that are challenging and SMART (specific, measurable, attainable, results-focused and time-constrained); this may help to force the business to take action
	The company is inflexible and fails to respond to customer needs	Challenge and remove sources of cynicism; consider revising reward systems to encourage effort, commitment and urgency

Choosing the right approach

Typically, there are six situations those heading a business face, each of which presents its own challenges:

- Business start-up – characterised by the need to acquire or develop the capabilities needed to launch a new business. These include people, funding, customers, technology and knowledge.

- Business turnaround – taking a business that is struggling, stabilising it and getting it back on track. It is resource-intensive as there is usually not much to build on. It requires determination and a capacity to make tough decisions quickly and to set clear priorities.

- Realignment – revitalising a business, product or team that is drifting, giving cause for concern or on a plateau rather than improving. Convincing people to change deeply ingrained and possibly outdated attitudes may require restructuring the top team.

- Increasing the pace – energising and enabling a business to move on to the next level. This requires focus and vigour.

- Maintaining growth and success – preserving and building on the best features of a business to take it to the next level. This requires finding ways to innovate and do even better. If people are wedded to the current business formula, it will require a change in their attitude.

- Winding down a business or part of one – a tough leadership task because it is associated with failure. The challenge is to maintain the operation so that it continues to achieve its short-term objectives while planning for a future that will be drastically different.

Choosing the right approach involves:

- gathering the right information;
- developing market awareness;
- deciding what action needs to be taken;
- assessing risk;
- thinking critically.

TABLE 3.2 **Choosing the right approach**

Situation	Description	Typical challenges	Benefits and opportunities
Business start-up	Developing the capabilities essential to starting a new business or project	Establishing new structures and systems without a clear framework or boundaries Building a collaborative, high-performing team Managing with limited resources	There is little rigidity in people's thinking and consequently the business can be made to work well from the outset. Also, people are energised by the possibilities and it pays to develop this enthusiasm
Business turnaround	Turning around a failing or struggling business that is either performing weakly or facing major challenges in the future	Revitalising the organisation, inspiring employees and reassuring other stakeholders Making a swift impact Making difficult choices (especially about people)	There is widespread recognition that change is necessary; consequently, those affected offer significant support. Also, there is a reserve of understanding and goodwill from the outset
Realignment	Ensuring that a once successful organisation is able to refocus and adapt to serious challenges	Leading change – starting with persuading employees of the need for change Reorganising the business and setting new priorities	The organisation has experience and resources that can be refocused and used. People want to return to (or maintain) their success
Increasing the pace	Improving the performance of a good-enough business with the aim of transforming it into a top ranking one	Overcoming complacency by creating such an urgent, compelling reason to change that it cannot be ignored Energising managers and employees Strengthening line management	Capabilities are already embedded in the business, they simply need direction. Also, quick wins can help generate momentum

Maintaining growth and success	Preserving and building on the best features of a team or business and taking it to the next level	Acceptance of new methods and priorities can be difficult Avoiding decisions that cause problems Finding ways to build the business	People are motivated to succeed and a strong team may be in place to capitalise on success. The foundations for continued success (such as the product pipeline) may already exist
Winding down	Closing down or divesting a business that is no longer strategically important or that no longer warrants investment	Maintaining a focused and engaged workforce Maximising cash flow and value in the short term Managing key internal and external stakeholder relationships	There is likely to be support from the centre to take the actions needed. Also, the agenda is clear, timescales are short and there is little need for widespread discussion before taking action

A pitfall in strategic thinking is "jumping to cause": making assumptions about the cause of a problem that are wrong. Fixing the wrong thing will not resolve the problem. At best, the problem remains; at worst, it will cause more difficulties.

Gather the right information

Ask the right questions and you will get the right information: What is the current situation? What has caused similar situations in the past? What, specifically, has caused this situation to arise? (It may result from a combination of factors.) If X is the cause, how does it explain all the facts? But be aware that too much information can create a fog and result in overanalysis.

A SWOT (strengths, weaknesses, opportunities and threats) analysis is a useful technique for gathering information (see Chapter 14). It can be completed either from the top or with each department or division conducting its own analysis, which is reviewed at a higher level. Some factors can be sources of both strength and weakness.

Develop market awareness

This means keeping up-to-date with what competitors are doing and how the company and they are perceived in the market – and why. Relative to competitors, consider:

- pricing policies;
- brand reputation and recognition;
- customers' perceptions;
- product quality;
- service levels;
- product portfolio;
- organisational culture and loyalty;
- customer loyalty;
- financial structure and reserves.

Decide what action needs to be taken

This is also essential. Major points in the data should be highlighted and the detail required to make decisions identified. It is important to keep people informed about relevant issues and trends with weekly updates, reports and discussions. Building informal networks with colleagues and others outside the organisation is useful. Mentors can clarify thinking when urgent decisions are needed. If there is concern that a decision may have the wrong effect, develop a worst-case scenario and prepare a contingency plan (see Chapter 5).

Assess risk

Assessing risk requires a solid understanding of the risks and benefits involved. This really comes down to market awareness and having the right information. Common problems include information paralysis – the result of gathering too much data and overanalysis. Determine how much data is really needed initially, and then fine-tune implementation with more data at a later stage.

Think critically

Think critically by asking "Why?", "What else?" and "What if?" questions to probe issues and current thinking skills. It is also useful to:

- challenge the thinking of others, even when they appear to be on firm ground;
- identify and challenge the assumptions or rationale that underpin decisions;
- get people to pinpoint the exact reasons for their views;
- challenge and provoke – look for radical change;
- play devil's advocate and go for the opposite of current practice;
- avoid acceptance of the status quo.

Understanding the different views of strategy

The different approaches to strategic decision-making outlined in this chapter and what will be most effective for an organisation will depend on circumstances; it is impossible to say that any one is more valid than another. The most effective approach depends on the issues faced by an organisation as well as the style and preferences of its leaders.

Management theories often build on earlier views. So the development of new thinking means not that earlier ideas should be discarded or are no longer valid, but that in certain circumstances they may no longer provide the best way forward, at least on their own.

In a complex world, a mix of styles is needed. The precise mix will depend on the personalities of those making the decisions and a good understanding of the strengths and weaknesses of the organisation, its environment and current position in order to establish, sustain and acquire the competencies that are required, and to adopt the most appropriate leadership style to see the overall strategy realised.

The underlying management themes of the past include the following:

- The need for leadership and sound decision-making to be present at every level.

- The need to manage uncertainty and get the best from new situations – problems as well as opportunities (the challenge of "leading change"). This requires intuition, creative insight and the ability to respond to events quickly, effectively and imaginatively. It is not simply what we know that matters, but how we react to what we do not know. In a volatile, competitive and international commercial environment, organisations must be alert and adaptable. Continuous improvement is always to be valued, but there are times when more dramatic change is needed.

- The need to manage in adversity, such as a market collapse or the failure of a product. An organisation's structure and its culture and control systems must be flexible enough to enable swift decision-making and action to get matters back on course.

Taking account of the unexpected

Although past approaches to strategic decision-making remain valuable, one issue now dominates the way that businesses plan and prepare for the future: change. In the early years of the 21st century, as the world displays the means, motive and opportunity to change further and faster than ever before, it is a truism to say that "the only certainty is uncertainty". However, this matters for businesses planning and organising for the future. There are two things that can be said for certain about the future: it will be different and it will surprise. Of course, the corollary of this is that if your world is not very different or is seldom surprising, you may be living in the past.

Change is endemic and rapid, and leads to huge uncertainties. In 2002 Donald Rumsfeld, then US defence secretary, drew attention to known unknowns, events that we know we cannot accurately forecast, and unknown unknowns, events that we cannot yet comprehend. Leaving aside his controversial personality and the clumsy, alienating description that he attempted to provide, he did have a point. His context for flagging "unknown unknowns" as a challenge for political, strategic and military leaders was the September 11th 2001 terrorist attacks in the US, but it is a framework that could be applied to other events. For example, no public-health planners could have predicted the Spanish influenza pandemic that between 1918 and 1920 killed 60 million people (around 3% of the world's population at the time). More contemporary unknowns include the cataclysmic Asian tsunami in 2004, as well as scares about viruses such as SARS in 2003 and Avian Flu in 2004. More recent sudden, unexpected events include Russian-sponsored actions in Ukraine in 2014 that resulted in international sanctions; the swift rise of Islamic State, an extremist, jihadist group controlling territory in Syria and other Middle Eastern countries, undermining stability in the region; and the world's worst outbreak of the Ebola virus in West Africa.

In commerce, as well as political and military affairs, unknown unknowns are a major cause for concern. For example, in 2010 BP and its CEO, Tony Hayward, paid a high price for the Deepwater Horizon oil spill in the Gulf of Mexico. The explosion that triggered the spill may have been a random disaster, but it is the engineering of simple processes, which are painfully obvious with hindsight and relate to areas as diverse as safety, business continuity planning and public relations, that could have partially mitigated the damage caused to BP's business.

Following the bankruptcy of Lehman Brothers, there has been an increasing focus on this aspect of volatility, which has come to be known as a black swan event (a term popularised by Nicholas Taleb in his book *The Black Swan*).[8] Also known as wild cards, these low-probability, outlier events have a huge impact if they do occur. Crucially, a black swan event (such as September 11th 2001, the 2011 Japanese tsunami or the collapse of Lehman Brothers) is rationalised with hindsight, as if it could have been expected. One reason for this is that people are so used to having the relevant information available that they assume it was simply overlooked or not taken into account.

Even when a potential disaster is clearly in sight, some people experience inertia or a sense of invulnerability, as if the looming event will not affect them. For example, at the end of 2008, it seemed that many financial trading firms were behaving like people picking up pennies in front of a steamroller – although they may have collected some money before getting run over, the upside value of this activity could not compare to the downside risk.

However, success does not rely on accurate predictions of black swan events, but rather on strategic awareness and readiness to respond to opportunities and risks arising from volatility and market disruption. This demands flexible, information-oriented leadership and strategic thinking that incorporates sufficiently robust processes. Critical to success in these circumstances is the type of thinking adopted by leaders (this is discussed further in Chapter 5). Those prone to focus only on selective history, to isolate themselves from reality or to display "groupthink" are less able to lead people successfully through periods of challenge and change.

The market disruptions caused by black swan events can, however, create great opportunities as well as potential disasters. Industries as diverse as bookselling, music and travel have experienced sudden, dramatic changes. These changes have enabled organisations that are flexible and ready to respond to prosper, regardless of their size and heritage, while the established and inflexible incumbents have collapsed. An example of how a business can flourish in changing times by finding new opportunities is that of HSBC, a multinational banking and financial services company. It describes itself as "the world's local bank", a proposition designed to highlight its size and strength but also to appeal to customers with banking needs across borders. With this in mind, HSBC's UK managers discovered a significant market among the rising number of east European immigrant workers, notably from Poland and other EU member states, following EU enlargement in 2004. These new customers were earning money in the UK and needed to send it to their country of origin, and for this purpose HSBC was able to provide them with a competitive banking service. This strengthened the bank's presence in several countries and among an increasing number of customers, as well as reinforcing its brand position.

Whether you are an incumbent wanting to protect your position or a newcomer wanting to assert your dominance, the battle will be fought over the ability to adapt, survive and dominate. For example, technological changes have changed the playing field, with new companies, such as Microsoft, Google and Facebook, coming to dominate markets and leave older companies behind.

We do not live in a fair, equal world, where we all have access to the same information and opportunities. Nor do we live in a world where we can rely on being the sole beneficiary of potentially lucrative information. We must anticipate the unlikely, the unexpected and the unfair. We must be ready, perhaps despite being the current top dog, to deal with better competitors wanting to usurp us, or new legislation that could undermine us, or technology that makes current practices obsolete. The only way forward, the only way to ensure our long-term survival, is to put in place the right processes, culture and leadership to equip us for the myriad changes that our companies will have to deal with. As discussed in the next chapter, firms that achieve this in their business strategy are capable of dominating their markets.

Key questions

Those taking a new leadership role should ask:

- How is your industry changing and, in particular, how are your customers' expectations evolving?
- What are the global developments (for example, increased migration, urbanisation or proliferation of mobile communications) that could benefit, threaten or generally alter the way that you do business?
- What are the political, economic, social, technological, legislative or environmental trends that could affect your business?
- What situation best describes the challenges and opportunities faced by the business? Is this clearly and widely recognised?
- What specific challenges are likely to be encountered? How can they be addressed?
- What are the major opportunities and what action is needed to realise them? Are there quick wins or low-hanging fruit that can be secured?

■ What are the greatest risks, threats and potential pitfalls? How will these be avoided or overcome?

■ What are the expectations of stakeholders? Are these expectations realistic – do they need adjusting?

■ What should be the priorities?

More generally, strategic decisions can be enhanced by considering the following questions at any time:

■ Should a range of approaches (such as classical, visionary, competitive) be applied to strategic decision-making? Is the approach to decision-making versatile and appropriate in various circumstances?

■ Are improvements needed in the ways that decisions are made or implemented, or both?

■ What lessons can be learnt from the use of technology? In particular, how can technology be used to improve decision-making?

■ How can increases and improvements be made in competitiveness, innovation and the way customers are served?

PART 2

Developing strategy

4 Forces that shape business strategy

TO SUCCEED, A BUSINESS'S STRATEGY needs to be relevant to its employees, shareholders and customers. As well as increasing its profitability and value and meeting any other goals that may be set, the strategy also needs to take account of present realities and future trends. The context in which strategy is developed and implemented will determine its success. This simple point is often overlooked, yet it is an important and recurring theme that may be called the "Goldilocks challenge": an organisation's strategy needs to be flexible enough to cope with changing circumstances and the unforeseen, yet specific, constant and consistent enough to guide people's decisions – a carefully crafted balance.

The problem lies in understanding the complex web of shifting priorities, aspirations, preferences and fears that people, institutions and societies quickly develop. They affect the way people work, as well as the wider environment in which firms strive to achieve their goals.

This chapter assesses the issues shaping business in the early decades of the 21st century and why they matter. Subsequent chapters describe some of the most effective and popular ways of linking strategy with these issues: scenarios (Chapter 5) and systems thinking (Chapter 7).

The past matters

Much of what needs to be known about the future is evident from the past, but there is a dangerous tendency to overemphasise the significance of broad trends without understanding their details, which can be crucial. This problem is often complicated by excessive emphasis on either the past or the future, when what is required is a balance between the two.

For example, for over a decade businesses in the developed world have been excited by the emergence of China, the world's most populous country, as a market for consumer goods. The belief is that a population of 1.3 billion people largely starved of these goods can be sold anything – and on a scale that will be highly profitable. In reality, the Chinese require investments in partnership with a Chinese enterprise, which limits profitability, and in some sectors, such as financial services, the level of foreign ownership is carefully controlled.

This lack of critical analysis is also apparent in the way senior managers can be seduced by the next big idea. Business people are competitive and aspirational, which is fine when it leads to innovation and progress, but the flipside is a tendency to overlook perennial skills and experience. History and psychology have much to teach about the future; little of it is new.

The 1803 Louisiana Purchase exemplifies the point subsequently made by President Calvin Coolidge that "the business of America is business". It also highlights many of the issues surrounding acquisitions. President Thomas Jefferson believed in reducing America's national debt, but when France's cash-strapped Napoleon Bonaparte offered to sell a massive slice of continental America, Jefferson believed that this was an opportunity not to be missed. It was a massive strategic acquisition that highlighted the benefits of boldness, flexibility and a readiness to spend. Although the problems of integration (and America's westward expansion) were significant, the deal laid the foundation for the nation's future.

So, before considering the implications of how the world is changing, it is helpful to look at some of the perennial issues that will continue to shape the success of any business strategy.

Leadership matters

Leadership is crucial. The challenge is to combine management skills and leadership ability in the right way at the right time. The skills that need to be covered are shown in the leadership spectrum (see Figure

FIG 4.1 **The leadership spectrum**

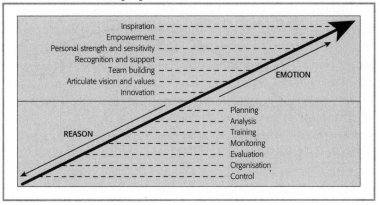

Source: This diagram is adapted from one used by the British Army at the Royal Military Academy, Sandhurst

4.1). This is not simply a scale of desirable activities and attributes; it shows the range of management skills and roles that every leader needs to master. This particular example is adapted from a version used by the British armed forces. New managers generally start their careers by focusing on the essentials of organisation and control. As they gain experience and develop their skills and confidence, they display greater reasoning and emotional attributes, and become more adept at empowering people. The most accomplished leaders display all the characteristics of the leadership spectrum, notably including the ability to inspire.

The skills and abilities featured in the leadership spectrum highlight several points about strategic decisions.

Emotion, integrity and empathy are crucial: what matters is not simply what happens but how people perceive events. They need to be involved and heard, and they need to be encouraged to achieve their potential if a strategy is to work. Strategists need to be flexible and ready to handle wild cards or black swan events: high-impact, low-probability events that are potentially dislocating and will shape the future. Because events such as the Ebola outbreak that caused havoc in West Africa in 2014 or the SARS epidemic that caused turmoil in Asian markets in 2002 and 2003 often move faster than people's ability to change track, it is crucial to be prepared and flexible. Businesses need to be guided by more than market research and think about the future as well as being guided by the past. As the 2008 global financial crisis showed only too clearly, all these factors mean there is a need to build trust and reputation – assets that are vital for future success.

Technology: always exciting, invariably hyped

It is a fallacy that the effects of technology are always immediate, dramatic and far-reaching. Usually they are evolutionary: from electricity and railways in the 19th century to genetics and the internet in the 20th. The significance of technology is often overestimated in the short term (less than five years) and underestimated over the long term.

The costs and risks associated with developing major technologies are often significant. If they are pitched as "a little bit better, but not much", they often sink without trace. It is better from the developer's perspective to make overstated claims that are later found to be flawed – but only after the development costs have been recovered.

In *The Shock of the Old: Technology and Global History Since 1900*,[1] David Edgerton says that many advances in such fields as aviation and nuclear weapons have been costly wastes of resources because of their relatively limited use for mankind as a whole. This contrasts with "smaller" technologies, such as the development of contraceptives, which have been more widely available and have had significantly more impact, and developments that have sprung from poorer parts of society, such as the spinning wheel, which have generated massive increases in efficiency. In addition, he argues, adapting existing technologies can spur innovation, such as the development of computers transforming communications, notably through the internet.

Competition: the beating heart of capitalism

Profitability depends on two truths. The first is the theory of supply and demand, which shows that in a competitive market, price will affect the quantity demanded by consumers and the quantity supplied by producers, resulting in equilibrium. The second is that profitability is linked to scarcity. The more abundant a product or service, the lower its price will be, even to the extent that it may not be profitable to produce and sell. The more scarce the supply, such as when competition is held back by barriers such as patents, expertise or other forms of knowledge, the more likely the product or service is to generate a profit. For example, if there is a high demand for a patented drug and no alternative exists, the future is lucrative, even if the research and development costs have been substantial.

Where does scarcity lie and where is it likely to develop? There will always be bottlenecks, blockages and needs not being met, but someone will come up with an innovative solution, so the scarcity will not exist for long. Having the insight and ability to deliver what the customer wants is crucial, but anticipating change puts you ahead of the competition.

So, to make the right strategic decisions, first understand why and where scarcity will occur, and then use people's skills and abilities to deliver new products and services that are difficult to replicate.

Competitiveness should always shape strategic decision, but many executives fall into the trap of thinking of business-as-usual (commonly called BAU thinking). Overcoming the dangers of BAU thinking is discussed in Chapter 5.

Globalisation's big effect

Globalisation brings both opportunities and challenges, creating an ever-bigger overall market but also with the possibility, because of industry consolidation, of reducing the number of players in the market. If the future creates more paradoxes, globalisation will spawn many of them.

What matters in the global economy is not simply size but also things such as scarcity or reputation. Companies offering something scarce and valuable are able to exert massive power and influence. Previously, that scarcity was competed for only within local or national markets; now the potential demand is much bigger. So either the price rises or the volumes increase: either way the business benefits.

Businesses such as Facebook and Google, founded within the past two decades, now provide services for millions of enterprises and individuals worldwide, and their revenues and profits dwarf the incomes of several countries.

The developments behind globalisation, notably in technology, require businesses to act swiftly and flexibly to stay ahead of the competition. People have been able to travel the world for centuries; the difference today is speed. The internet allows businesses to operate, unconstrained by geography, round the clock every day of the year. This has driven companies to organise themselves into smaller, more focused units. Logistics firms such as DHL, UPS and FedEx have responded to increasing competition by enabling their customers to track their packages. Large companies whose sheer size makes them more difficult to manage find it hard to become as flexible and responsive as smaller competitors. As Jack Welch, former CEO of General Electric, said:

> *What we're trying relentlessly to do is to get that small company soul – and small company speed – inside our big company body.*

The more global we become, the more tribal is our behaviour. In his book *Global Paradox*,[2] John Naisbitt argues that the more we become economically interdependent, the more we hold on to what constitutes our core identity. Fearing globalisation and, by implication, a homogenised Western (predominantly US) culture, countries such as Indonesia, Russia and France have passed laws to preserve their distinctiveness and identity. Matters are further complicated by the shift from traditional nation states to networks. The role of diasporas in developing the economic and political fortunes of many countries is significant, notably the Chinese diaspora in driving the economic development of many Asian states.

According to the World Bank, the top recipients of officially recorded remittances in 2013 were India ($70 billion), China ($60 billion), the Philippines ($25 billion) and Mexico ($22 billion). Other large recipients included Nigeria, Egypt, Bangladesh, Pakistan, Vietnam and Ukraine. However, as a share of GDP, remittances were larger in smaller and lower-income countries; the top recipients relative to GDP were Tajikistan (52%), Kyrgyzstan (31%), Nepal and Moldova (both 25%), and Samoa and Lesotho (both 23%). The World Bank also highlights the fact that remittances sent home by migrants to developing countries are equivalent to more than three times the size of official development assistance.

This change may be neither uniform nor as powerful as some believe. Human beings are gregarious; valuing community and the ability to share information and form allegiances across borders can reduce tribalism. But cultural issues run deep and must be taken into account in strategic decision-making. The 1998 merger of Daimler, a German automotive firm, and Chrysler, based in the US, involved huge cross-cultural problems of organisational and management culture, and also brought with it much tribalism. In 2007 the two companies demerged.

Globalisation means there are many opportunities beyond traditional geographic spheres of operation. In the past, poor countries remained poor and rich countries remained rich for generations. If a country's fortunes changed, they did so over many years. Now societies develop skills, wealth and commercial opportunity much more quickly. In 1945, Japan and Germany had been laid waste. Today, they are among the world's five largest economies. Conversely, at the start of the 20th century Argentina was a leading economic power, but in terms of GDP, in 2014 it ranked only 23rd in the world.

When considering which markets offer the greatest growth potential over the next decade, the likely prospects seem to be the BRIC countries (Brazil, Russia, India and China) and the N11 (the next 11 developing countries of Bangladesh, Egypt, Indonesia, Iran, Mexico, Nigeria, Pakistan, the Philippines, South Korea, Turkey and Vietnam). Early in the 21st century emerging markets grew at an average annual rate of 7%, well beyond the 2–3% achieved in the developed economies. Little wonder that so many CEOs rate emerging markets as their top priority, despite the political risks.

More customers – and they are more demanding

Globalisation, technological innovation and the end of the cold war have combined to deliver, in a relatively short period, sustained growth. Although the future remains uncertain and fragile, a huge number of new consumers have emerged in Asia, the Middle East, Latin America and central and eastern Europe. This is a major opportunity that figures prominently in companies' strategic decisions.

Combined with rising numbers of consumers in the developing world has been since the early 1980s an increase in customer expectations in the developed economies, encouraged by books such as *In Search of Excellence* by Tom Peters and Robert Waterman,[3] which emphasised the desirability of a greater focus on the customer. These greater expectations have been given an additional boost by the spread of the internet, which has provided customers with unrivalled access to information about their purchases and a taste for fast, flexible, tailored, cost-effective products and services. This has an escalating effect: the better the products and services customers receive, the more they expect in the future.

Yet while many business gurus have counselled that delighting the customer is everything, many customers regard innovations and service as routine. Stephen Brown, a professor of marketing research at the University of Ulster, argues that customers enjoy being tantalised and teased and are frequently repelled by strangers trying too hard to be their best friend. There are many instances of companies gleaning so much information about customer preferences from the internet and using it so poorly that they drive customers away.

Paradoxically significant

The modern world involves an increasing number of apparent contradictions. It has become ever more important for businesses to be both local (or regional) and global; to be centralised in some ways and decentralised in others; to rely on people to be innovative and use their own expertise, but also to collaborate, to plan for the long term, and yet remain responsive and flexible. Businesses rely on "hard" management factors such as finance, technology and processes, as well as "soft" factors such as leadership, communication and creativity. As Charles Handy, a British management thinker, says: "Everywhere we look, paradox seems to be the companion of economic progress."

Competitive pressure drives the need to excel in new ways. Ambition fosters the belief that we can benefit from doing things in ways that seem contradictory to the ways they have been done traditionally. Combining adventure and discipline may create extraordinary competitive advantage.

People and organisations are more able to reconcile paradoxes than ever before, partly because of technological progress. For example, in the 1950s and 1960s, marketing was concerned with mass coverage, and factors such as share of voice and column inches were important; if more people heard about the product, sales would increase. Computerisation during the 1970s and 1980s led to database marketing and customer profiling. In theory, only those customers likely to buy were targeted, reducing costs and increasing marketing efficiency. Holding data on individual customers became a source of competitive advantage and led to data-protection legislation. Then, in the 1990s, widespread use of the internet allowed companies to combine mass marketing with niche targeting. In this way the online bookseller or travel agent can combine the mass appeal of a major retailer with a personalised service.

This increasing rate of change is highlighted by three paradoxes:

- In a fast-changing world, leaders must establish and communicate a consistent set of values and principles to make the process of change sustainable. They must ground themselves in the certainty of a specific perspective before leading people into a shifting, uncertain world of possibilities.

- Leaders need information to understand the complexities of their environment. Yet the amount of information available is overwhelming, offering the potential for "paralysis by analysis". Again, traditional leadership values are important. The solution is often to follow a consistent set of principles that enables the capture and filtering of relevant knowledge that is then turned into effective action.

- Leaders need to manage both planned and emerging issues successfully. This is a difficult juggling act. Too often, businesses either focus on a long view that may be undermined by events, or are fire-fighting, reacting to circumstances with little prospect of achieving sustainable growth.

Understanding and managing apparent paradoxes depends on timing. Contradiction only emerges over time because at any one moment, one factor or the other is in the ascendant, like a seesaw.

Similarly, a team undertakes some tasks together while others are completed individually. None of this is new. The difference is the increase in the number and heightened significance of apparent conflicts.

The undiscovered country: the future

Although perennial issues continue to affect business strategy, there are other, far-reaching developments that shape the context in which businesses operate and have implications for business strategy. They include demography, health care, politics, international relations and the environment.

Demographic trends

The world's population has more than quadrupled from 1.6 billion in 1900 to 7.2 billion in 2014. The largest annual population increase in human history took place (a 2% rise) in 1969, and the shortest doubling of global population occurred between the administrations of US presidents John Kennedy and Bill Clinton. This took place at the same time as significant international migration and increased urbanisation, resulting in the emergence of megacities.

That was just the 20th century. The big increases in populations today are in India, China, Pakistan, Nigeria, Indonesia and Bangladesh. In 2006, the UN estimated that six and a half days of India's population growth equalled a year's population growth among the 25 members of the European Union. While Europe's population is likely to remain largely static in the century from 1950 to 2050 (around 500 million–700 million), Africa's is expected to increase from 250 million to 2 billion (see Figure 4.2). Demographers estimate that by 2050 the global population will have risen by about 2.5 billion to about 9 billion.

For businesses, demographic change offers a massive opportunity by helping people adjust to its implications. For example:

- Demographic developments are changing family composition in the developing world, increasing the influence of women.
- Populations are ageing throughout the developed world with profound implications for pensions, taxation, welfare, employment and spending.

FIG 4.2 **Population of Europe and Africa**
Millions, 1950, 2000, 2050

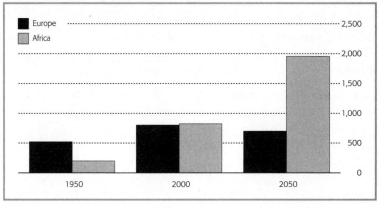

Source: Centre for Migration Studies, New York

■ Urbanisation is increasing. In 2007, the global urban population exceeded the world's rural population for the first time. This will alter consumers' behaviour and expectations.

■ Lower fertility rates are spreading from Europe through Asia and Africa; international migration is rising and population concentration is growing in less developed regions but declining in many developed countries. This has implications for the way businesses are run, skills are acquired, people are recruited and knowledge is managed.

The world's developed economies are facing population changes with far-reaching consequences. For example, Japan's population seems likely to fall by 30% by 2100, the result of a low birth rate and a very low level of immigration; by 2020, Italy will have more than 1 million people aged 90 or over; and both the Russian and German populations are falling well below replacement levels. The US is the only developed country with a rising population, largely as a result of migration. By 2050, it will have around 400 million inhabitants.

How demography will affect the labour market and potential customers is shown by the change in support ratios: the number of working taxpayers supporting each retired person (see Table 4.1).

Fewer taxpayers and more retired people will mean increases in taxation, reductions in public services and people working for longer.

TABLE 4.1 **Support ratios in selected countries**

Country	Support ratio	
	2000	**2050**
China	10.0	2.7
France	4.1	2.1
Germany	4.2	1.8
Italy	3.7	1.5
Canada	5.4	2.4
US	5.4	2.7

Retirement age in 2050 needed to maintain current support ratios

China	78.7
France	74.0
Germany	76.2
Italy	76.5
Canada	75.2
US	73.1

Source: Centre for Migration Studies, New York

Managers rarely discuss demography yet it will affect a company's plans. Too often companies focus on the next quarter or the next 12 months when strategy requires a much longer perspective, such as that of multinational banking company HSBC. Its investments in China are regarded as the foundation for a much stronger, larger presence in the country over the next 25 years.

The implications of these demographic changes will vary according to a company's circumstances, but several aspects will affect them all. First, more women are employed and many want flexible careers. Men also want greater flexibility. The populations of developed countries are ageing and increasingly some people are choosing to continue working beyond traditional retirement ages, often part-time.

During the second half of the 20th century, the prevailing view was that, as their economies expanded, countries such as India, China, Brazil and others in Asia, Latin America and central Europe were ready sources of cheap labour and potentially profitable new markets. However, globalisation means that these countries offer pools of talented people who companies are increasingly keen to employ, not only because they are less expensive, but also because they are often better at doing the work for which they are employed and more reliable. The new sources of labour also mean new markets for products.

Health care – getting fit for purpose

Health care matters to business because it is important to people. For example, in September 2007, General Motors averted a strike by 73,000 United Auto Workers Union members by setting up an independent trust to meet more than $50 billion in health-care liabilities for its retired workers. The 2003 outbreak of SARS in China caused global disruption, and many African economies and firms remain hampered by the devastating effects of HIV/AIDS.

Businesses will continue to be affected by three overriding health-care issues in the early 21st century:

- The existence of a large and growing gap between people's health-care expectations and their experience. This is a major source of political and social instability, as highlighted by the GM example above.

- The threat from pandemics in which the speed and scale of transmission could result in unprecedented consequences. AIDS and drug-resistant tuberculosis are major threats to the stability of the business environment as well as to specific businesses. This is highlighted in South Africa, where workers and skills in some sectors are in short supply as a direct result of the AIDS pandemic.

■ Inefficiencies and haphazard health-care provision. At present, resources are focused on meeting the health-care needs of ageing, wealthier people in the developed world; this will continue, together with the need to provide health care to poorer people in the developing world. But health-care inequalities affect businesses in new and diverse ways. For example, health-care reform in the US may require businesses to pay new or increased taxes, and Western shareholders, customers and employees increasingly believe that businesses trading with the developing world have a responsibility to improve the quality of life for people there.

Political and social influences on business strategy

The anti-globalisation movement has a direct effect on business and must be taken into account when deciding and implementing strategy. Anti-globalisation is widespread and disparate, with protesters coalescing around a concern about political, economic and social exclusion and a perception that governments do not make sure that corporations act in a responsible way. Protesters seek to force corporations to change the way they do business through direct action, legal redress, negative publicity and product boycotts.

Significantly, the forces arrayed against multinational corporations can affect their ability to attract employees. Some surveys suggest that as many as 50% of university graduates would not work for an "unethical" business.

Five anti-globalisation forces affect multinationals' operations:

■ Trusted NGOs (non-governmental organisations) such as Greenpeace run increasingly effective campaigns. The turning point came in 1995 when a small group of protesters forced Royal Dutch Shell to abandon sinking the obsolete Brent Spar offshore oil platform. Eventually, it was put to other uses.

■ Social activists perceive a widening gap between "haves" and "have nots" in developed and developing countries. They take direct action and also mount legal campaigns to force companies to match standards of care in their operations abroad with those demanded in their home countries. Examples include the campaigns against the use of cheap Asian labour by Nike and Gap.

- Grassroots activists use film, posters and the internet to ridicule brands. An example is the Rainforest Action Network (RAN), a Californian pressure group that gained celebrity support for a television advertising campaign against Citigroup, an international financial conglomerate, which RAN claimed was funding groups destroying tropical rainforests. Citigroup altered its policy to take these concerns into account.

- Political shoppers act by removing their custom.

- Governments are pressed to legislate to address environmental, social and ethical concerns. There is also increasing regulation from supranational bodies such as the EU on corporate governance, data protection and employment. For example, in 2002 the US introduced the Sarbanes-Oxley Act requiring CEOs to formally vouch for the accuracy of their companies' accounts. The law covers directors of overseas companies whose shares trade on US stockmarkets. Other countries, notably China, are recognising that an efficient capital market can operate only if there is intelligent and effective company regulation, and unethical practices such as copyright infringement are weeded out.

It is possible, however, to be commercially driven and to meet social concerns. For instance, microfinanciers lend small sums to entrepreneurs in the developing world, targeting the bottom of the wealth pyramid. Muhammad Yunus and the Grameen Bank that he founded were jointly awarded the Nobel Peace Prize in 2006 (see Chapter 2). Grameen lends amounts as small as $50 at a commercial rate of interest to help develop a product or realise an idea. This stimulates a self-sustaining cycle of wealth creation. Crucially, it also provides a commercial return for the lender.

In one example, some Guatemalan farmers were each lent $50 to buy seed or fertiliser. As their crops were sold over the course of a season, the farmers repaid their loan in instalments, with small amounts of interest. This meant they were able to save for future supplies and make a profit to support their families.

In another example, a Ugandan mother of nine children convinced her village bank to lend her enough money to buy a basket and pay her bus fare. She then collected wild fruit and vegetables and sold them at the local market. This started a cycle of development and the woman now owns a restaurant, which she runs with four of her daughters.

The environment

Divisions of opinion about the environment and the impact of climate change are often a result of differences in timescales and vested interests. However, it is widely acknowledged that the impact of human-induced climate change will increasingly affect businesses during the 21st century. They will face both costs and opportunities that will become harder to ignore, such as those already arising in the automotive, travel and energy industries.

The risks resulting from climate change are complex. They include the direct impact on capital and profits; the risk of punitive taxes and emission caps; damage to brand reputation and sales if a company is viewed as environmentally irresponsible; and the spectre of heavy penalties if companies are sued for the consequences of their activities on the environment.

The factors affecting business strategy are diverse and prone to change. They include perennial challenges as well as concerns and opportunities that are significant temporarily before fading. A 2008 survey of 600 executives worldwide by the Economist Intelligence Unit identified a diverse range of potential risks. The most severe combine a medium to high level of severity and likelihood with a medium to low level of preparedness. According to the survey, the greatest risks were:

- retrenchment of globalisation/increase in protectionism;
- oil price shock;
- asset price collapse;
- emergence of disruptive business model;

- international terrorism;
- unexpected regulatory change;
- global recession;
- instability in the Middle East;
- increased competition from emerging-market companies;
- talent shortages;
- climate change;
- increased industrial pollution.

The significance of each depends on a business's individual position, but it is important to be aware of them and to relate them to a specific decision or strategy.

People change

People know that there are no longer jobs for life and that they are likely to have several employers during their careers. They are also changing their attitudes to work. Studies by the EU Commission and the US Department of Labour found that people work longer average hours than they used to and are often prepared to work flexible hours. In return, they expect greater job satisfaction, higher rewards, more personal recognition and a more flexible work environment.

Semco: changing patterns of employment

Ricardo Semler, a maverick Brazilian businessman, transformed Semco from a struggling machine business into an innovative, profitable company through adopting employment policies and procedures that recognised how patterns of work were changing.

Semler believes that people are valuable and unique: they can participate in local and national democracy, contribute to the community, raise children, express themselves through hobbies and other activities, and have the knowledge and potential of the internet at their fingertips. But when they go to work they are treated as robots. Consequently, he set about finding ways to liberate and reward his employees. Workers were empowered to find out about, discuss and help set the direction of the business and implement the plans.

They could set their targets and salary levels as well as deciding other issues traditionally left to senior managers. This approach allowed talent to flourish throughout the organisation. Furthermore, employees were paid not according to hierarchy or status, but to reflect the real value, the scarcity, of what they did. The business prospered.

Charismatic leaders such as Henry Ford, Alfred Sloan, Akio Morita, Harold Geneen, Sir Richard Branson, Jack Welch, Herb Kelleher, Warren Buffett and Bill Gates will always inspire, but their organisations are likely to succeed only if there is a coherent, well-organised and imaginative team supporting them. These teams need to understand the markets they serve and how they are changing; they also need to use this understanding to inform their plans and decisions. This is discussed in the next chapter.

Key questions

- What are the greatest non-customer influences on the business such as regulation, shortage of talent and political risk? What are their implications?

- How susceptible is the business to black swan events or wild cards – high-impact, low-probability events? How prepared are the employees? Can the business compensate for its weaknesses and vulnerabilities?

- Trust, integrity and involvement are valuable assets, especially during uncertain times. How strong are these attributes? What can be done to strengthen them?

- What do customers value about the company's products and brands? What makes it competitive and successful? How secure are these sources of advantage, and how can the business remain competitive and appealing to customers?

- How can the company use technology to benefit customers or increase profits?

- How is the company responding to the opportunities and threats of globalisation?

5 Scenarios

WHY DO SOME GREAT BUSINESSES decline while others go from strength to strength and what difference can be made by strategy? The previous chapter outlined some of the main influences on strategy and strategic decisions; this chapter shows how to connect an understanding of the future with plans and decisions being made today.

Taking the right road

There are two things that can be said with certainty about the future: it will be different and it will surprise. This has caught out many leading businesses, as the examples of Bethlehem Steel and Xerox illustrate. The reason is often that complacency and a commitment to the status quo gradually become embedded in a company's culture and behaviour such that it loses awareness of and connection to the outside world. Companies that decline or fail usually do so because they do not do enough to understand or prepare for the future and so suffer when the wind changes. With the benefit of hindsight, many managers recognise that when their businesses were doing well they saw no reason to change. By the time they realised that customers, competitors and regulators and sometimes even their employees had changed it was too late to respond.

Two factors should be considered. First, every organisation is affected by perceptions of the business or brand, and these views can be altered by the action (or inaction) of only a few people. Second, no one ever moved from good to great – or sustained leadership in their sector – by failing to move with the times.

The long goodbye: Bethlehem Steel

In his book *Good to Great*,[1] Jim Collins highlights the example of Bethlehem Steel (1857–2003). At one time it was the second largest steel producer in the United States, one of the biggest shipbuilding companies in the world and one of the most potent symbols of US manufacturing. Bethlehem provided the steel that helped to win the Second World War. During the war, its 15 shipyards produced 1,121 vessels, more than any other shipbuilder, and the company employed 300,000 people.

Bethlehem Steel's high point came in the 1950s, when it produced 23 million tons of steel each year and forged a wide range of products, notably for construction, defence and power generation. In 1958, the company's president, Arthur B. Homer, was the highest paid businessman in the US.

After the devastation of war, the steel industries in Germany and Japan were rebuilt incorporating efficient technology, which enabled them to increase productivity. While German and Japanese steelmakers developed their businesses largely within their domestic markets, the US steel industry faced little significant foreign competition and used its earnings to increase wages and benefits rather than invest in new technology.

Imports of cheaper foreign steel began arriving in the US in the 1980s, sharply reducing Bethlehem Steel's domestic market share. In 1982, the company lost $1.5 billion and was forced to close many of its operations. Profitability returned briefly in 1988, but restructuring and shutdowns continued through the 1980s and 1990s.

In the mid-1980s, the market for Bethlehem's structural products began to shrink as new competition arrived. Added to this were developments in core markets, such as construction. Buildings required lighter styles and different materials rather than the heavy structural grades produced by Bethlehem. After 138 years of metal production at its Bethlehem, PA, plant, Bethlehem Steel ceased operations in 1995. The firm had left the railroad car business in 1993 and stopped building ships in 1997 in an attempt to preserve its core steelmaking operations.

These actions failed and Bethlehem filed for bankruptcy in 2001. In 2003 its remaining assets were sold to International Steel Group, which merged with Mittal Steel in 2005.

Bethlehem Steel's demise is often cited as an example of the US economy's transition away from industrial manufacturing and its inability to compete with cheap foreign labour. However, Collins argues that cheap imports were not the cause of decline and suggests that the main reasons for the firm's failure were the absence of a long-term perspective and a lack of desire to renew and innovate.

Things to avoid copying: the mistakes of Xerox

A classic example of flawed thinking and lack of awareness is provided by Xerox, which in the early 1970s held a 95% share of the global copier market.

In 1956, Chester Carlson, the inventor of the electrostatic process that spawned the copier industry, sold his patents to the Haloid Corporation, which changed its name to Xerox in 1961. The 914 machine (named because it could copy documents 9" × 14" in size) was introduced in 1959 and heralded Xerox's emergence as the dominant force in copying. The first of its kind to be able to make multiple copies and also capable of making the most copies per minute, the 914 opened up the era of mass copying.

Xerox seized the initiative with a business model that targeted large businesses needing to copy in large volumes. The results were spectacular: by 1961, only two years after the introduction of the 914, Xerox became a *Fortune* 500 company. *Business Week* featured the 914 on its cover and *Fortune* said it was "the most successful product ever marketed in America". In 1968, Xerox achieved $1 billion sales, achieving that landmark faster than any other company at that time. Its customers were large corporations and Xerox provided them with a complete service package. The word Xerox was synonymous with copying: people did not copy documents, they Xeroxed them.

Xerox's customers cared less about price than they did about reliability, and the company's success was underpinned by the substantial barriers that deterred competitors from entering its chosen market. These included patents, and the high costs of its sales force and of providing a 24-hour service network. Along with its powerful brand, these barriers were simply too great for a new entrant to overcome; even IBM tried and failed. Xerox developed a strong sense of invulnerability.

Then along came Canon, a Japanese multinational and a newcomer to the industry. It systematically attacked every aspect of Xerox's business: technology, service levels, customer base, pricing and distribution network. Canon adopted an approach of value innovation (see Chapter 13) years before it was formally identified as a business strategy.

Canon focused first on overcoming the problem of patents. It had dedicated its research during the 1960s to developing an alternative to Xerox's patented technology. In 1968, it invented the New Process (NP), which used plain paper to photocopy but did not violate Xerox's patents. Canon used two of its existing skills to develop NP technology: microelectronics (from its calculator business), and optics and imaging (from its camera business).

The next line of attack was to redefine the customer base. In the late 1970s, Canon designed copiers targeted at small businesses and individuals. These copiers, which made 8–10 copies per minute, cost between $700 and $1,200. In contrast, Xerox's high-speed machines, which produced 90–120 copies per minute, were priced from $80,000 to $129,000.

Then Canon focused on rethinking distribution. Because the target market included millions of customers, it could not effectively use the direct-sales approach. Instead, it chose to distribute its personal copiers through traditional office-product dealers, computer stores and retailers. This not only eliminated the need for a huge cash outlay but also allowed rapid market entry.

Tackling servicing was the next challenge and the next area of innovation. Because of the inverse relationship between product reliability and the need for service, Canon designed its copiers for maximum reliability. Each copier had just eight units that could be assembled on an automated line by robots. It made replacement parts modular so that customers could replace them when they wore out, removing the need for a service network. The copier drum, charging device, toner assembly and cleaner were combined into a single disposable cartridge that the customer could remove and replace after 2,000 copies. The design was so simple that traditional office-product dealers could be trained to make repairs. Lastly, because the Canon approach enabled firms to buy copiers for different departments rather than rely on a central copying service, people could use other machines when theirs needed attention.

Canon's effect on the copier industry was similar to its earlier, redefining effect on the camera industry, and it used its reputation for high quality and low cost in that sector to great effect when it went into the copier market.

One of the benefits of scenario thinking is that it helps avoid conventional thinking that may be outflanked by a competitor, inventing new ideas and ways of working. An important factor is reaction time and the need to get there before anyone else.

Avoiding business-as-usual thinking

Business-as-usual thinking is dangerous for companies because it:

- prevents managers from sensing problems;
- delays changes in strategy and tactics;
- leads to action that is disconnected from customers and reality;
- frustrates clients and employees.

The need to avoid business-as-usual thinking is highlighted by Xerox's delayed response. There were probably several reasons for it not responding quickly enough to Canon's attack. It did not see Canon as a serious threat because the Japanese firm was not perceived as competing head-to-head and Xerox did not expect low-end copiers to become a huge market segment. Xerox believed it was safe in its dominant position, but it had inherent vulnerabilities. These included:

- an inability to see potential threats and relying on business-as-usual thinking;
- a lack of courage or commitment to changing its business model and approach;
- an absence of vision to consider how the external environment was changing, and how these changes might affect its future.

Where did Xerox go wrong?

- It sat and watched while its customer base was redefined, thinking it was safe behind the barriers to entry it had built round its market.
- It failed to identify potential new customers in an evolving industry, preferring instead to stay with tried-and-tested products, customers and approach.
- It allowed competitors to develop new, better products.
- Its focus on a single way of doing business was dangerously inflexible.
- It did not take seriously a smaller, unfamiliar competitor with an established track record of redefining an industry (cameras).

The underlying themes include: complacency, lack of flexibility, absence of awareness and imagination about how the market would develop and an inability to remain innovative relative to competitors. The same potential pitfalls exist for any business in any industry at any time.

Xerox's experience gives rise to the question: how is corporate success developed and sustained? One of the most significant techniques for answering these questions – an approach that is both practical and proven – is scenario planning.

Scenario planning

When establishing a strategic direction and the priorities that will guide strategists and decision-makers, few techniques are as powerful as scenario planning. Scenarios are perspectives on potential events and their consequences; they provide a context in which managers can make decisions. By contemplating a range of possible futures, decisions are better informed and a strategy based on this deeper insight is more likely to succeed.

Scenario planning enables organisations to walk the battlefield before battle commences so that they are better prepared for it. Scenarios do not predict the future but they do illuminate the causes of change. This, in turn, helps managers to take greater control when market conditions shift.

In his book *Competitive Advantage*, Michael Porter defines a scenario as:[2]

> *An internally consistent view of what the future might turn out to be – not a forecast, but one possible future outcome.*

Scenario thinking has been used by the military for centuries and by organisations such as Royal Dutch Shell since the 1960s. Kees van der Heijden of the University of Strathclyde Graduate School of Business says:[3]

> *Scenario planning is neither an episodic activity nor a new technique: it is a way of thinking that works best when it*

permeates the entire organisation, affecting decisions at all levels. However, unlike most popular management initiatives, it does not require major investment in resources or restructuring, simply a commitment for people to take time away from their routine activities to come together to reflect and learn.

The benefits of scenario planning

The first benefit of scenarios is greater understanding of the way in which the world is changing. Scenario planning helps provide a better insight into how different factors affecting a business affect each other. It can reveal linkages between apparently unrelated factors and, most importantly, it can provide greater insight into the forces shaping the future, delivering real competitive advantage.

This improved understanding of the present and the direction of the future helps firms to overcome complacency and business-as-usual thinking. Scenarios should test both established strategies and new ideas. Seeing reality from different perspectives mitigates the pitfalls of groupthink (the suppression of ideas critical of management or the direction the company is taking), fragmentation, procrastination, hindsight bias, shifting responsibility and bolstering commitment to failing strategies. (These and other potentially hazardous pitfalls for strategists are discussed in Chapter 18). The example of Shell highlights the fact that much forecasting is little more than optimistic or pessimistic views of the future from the present position. This "tyranny of the present" leads managers to overlook a large number of threats and opportunities.

A further benefit of scenarios is to sound a call to action and generate greater ownership of the strategy process. Scenario planning helps to break the constraints on traditional strategic practices, enabling ideas, plans and perspectives to be discussed in a wider context.

Scenarios stimulate creativity and innovation. Considering different possible futures encourages minds to open to new possibilities and generates a positive attitude about achieving the desired outcome. Scenarios also help people to understand their environment, share knowledge, consider the future and assess strategic options. Information is better evaluated and integrated in the scenario planning process because it enables those involved to recognise and react to emerging circumstances.

Lastly, scenario planning allows discussions to be more uninhibited and creates the conditions for a shared sense of purpose to evolve. This should mean that the strategic decisions reached through scenario planning have widespread support.

Saving billions with scenarios: Pierre Wack and Shell

One of the first companies to use scenarios was Royal Dutch Shell in the 1960s. The process was largely driven by Pierre Wack, head of group planning, who said:

> Scenarios help us to understand today better by imagining tomorrow, increasing the breadth of vision and enabling us to spot change earlier … Effective future thinking brings a reduction in the level of crisis management and improves management capability, particularly change management.

Shell created a unit, managed by Wack, to overcome problems of cash flow management and to forecast future cash requirements. Wack recognised that the company was trying to apply statistical techniques to variables that were fundamentally unpredictable. Fundamental uncertainties had to be distinguished from what could be predicted. So the team started to discuss what was predictable, in this case the future of the global oil price and issues of supply and demand. Since global demand for oil had grown consistently by 6–8% per year since 1945, it was assumed that demand was predetermined. This led the team to focus on supply. Engineers assured the group that availability would not be a technical problem, so most people at Shell assumed that traditional price trends would continue.

Wack was not satisfied. He wanted to know if factors other than technical availability affected supply. By listing stakeholders, the team quickly identified governments in oil-producing countries. Wack asked if these governments would be happy to continue to increase production year on year. Would this be in their interest? Through role-play it became apparent that many oil-producing countries did not need extra income and that it was logical for them to reduce supply, increase prices and conserve their reserves.

When Wack outlined this to his superiors, he was told that the oil-producing countries were not united and consequently the oil companies were, in practice, able to control supply. His response was to refine the scenario to include growth in demand and the increasing realisation by the members of the Organisation of Petroleum Exporting Countries (OPEC) of the strength of their position if they acted in concert. As Wack commented:

Participating in the scenario-building process improves a management team's ability to manage uncertainty and risk. Risky decisions become more transparent and key threats and opportunities are identified.

His scenario became reality. The 1973 Israeli–Arab war had the effect of cutting the supply of oil and prices rose fivefold. Fortunately for Shell, Wack's work had encouraged the company to be prepared for such a change, and when it happened, Shell was far ahead of its competitors, enabling it to climb from seventh to second place in the league table of oil-company profitability.

Scenarios remain a crucial part of Shell's approach. They help it to understand the dynamics of the business environment, recognise new opportunities, assess strategic options and take long-term decisions. For Shell, scenario thinking is an essential strategic tool, which is not surprising given that the energy and resource industries deal with projects with long lead times. For example, a large gas project might require an investment of $10 billion, take six years from the decision to invest to come on stream, and have a life of at least 20 years. Thus the review of such a project requires thinking over at least 25 years.

Shell's experience demonstrates that scenarios are an effective way of assessing existing strategies and developing and assessing options. The scenario planning process helps underpin and develop the strengths of an organisation and makes it more sensitive to early signs of trouble.

Using scenarios

Scenario thinking does not provide a single snapshot; its effectiveness lies in stimulating decisions, what Van der Heijden in his book *The Sixth Sense* calls "the strategic conversation".[4] This is the continuous process of planning, analysing the environment, generating and testing scenarios, developing options, selecting, refining and implementing – a process that is itself refined with further environmental analysis. Steps in the scenario process include:

- planning and structuring the scenario process;
- exploring the scenario context;
- developing the scenarios;
- analysing the scenarios;
- using the scenarios.

Planning and structuring the scenario process

The first stage is to identify gaps in a company's knowledge that relate specifically to business challenges whose impact on it is uncertain. It must then create a team to plan and structure the process. The team members should be noted for their creative thinking and ability to challenge conventional ideas. This makes an external team better placed to provide objective views, free from internal agendas or tensions. In discussion with the team, the next step is to decide how long the project should take; ten weeks is usual for a big project.

Exploring the scenario context

A few employees should join the team exploring scenarios. They should be interviewed separately by the external team to identify their views, which should then be assessed and explored by the whole team. Questions should focus on crucial issues including sources of customer value, the current success formula and future challenges. They should identify how each individual views the past, present and future aspects of each factor.

George Cairns, professor of management at RMIT University, Melbourne, says:[5]

> The interview statements should be collated and analysed in an interview report, structured around the recurring concepts and key themes. This now sets the agenda for the first workshop and should be sent to all participants. It is also valuable to identify the critical uncertainties and issues, as perceived by the participants, as a starting point for the workshop.

Developing the scenarios

The workshop should identify several significantly different possible outcomes, and the forces that could lead to each of them should be listed. The next step is to consider how these forces are linked (if at all), and whether they will have a low or high impact and a low or high probability. With different outcomes and the driving forces clearly presented, the team can then develop the likely histories, or scenarios, that lead to each outcome.

With two opposite outcomes and the driving forces clearly presented, the team can develop the likely scenarios that lead to each outcome. These histories of the future can then be expanded through discussion of the forces behind the changes. The aim is not to develop accurate predictions but to understand what will shape the future and how different events interact and influence each other. The discussions focus on each scenario's effect on the business.

This makes the team members alert to signals that may suggest a particular direction for the organisation. The outcomes of different responses are "tested" in the safety of scenario planning before a strategy has to be implemented.

Analysing the scenarios

The analysis stage examines the external issues and internal logic. What are the priorities and concerns of those outside the organisation who may affect the main decisions in the scenario? Who are the other stakeholders? Will they change and would they really act and make decisions in the way described? Systems and process diagrams can help answer these questions, as can discussions with other stakeholders.

Remember that the aim is not to pinpoint future events; rather it is to consider the forces that may push the future along different paths.

Using the scenarios

Working backwards from the future to the present, the team should formulate an action plan that can influence the organisation's thinking. Then it should identify the early signs of change so that if and when they occur they will be recognised and met with a timely and effective response. The process continues by identifying gaps in the organisation's knowledge. For Van der Heijden, the continuation of the strategic conversation and its integration into people's routine thoughts reduces risk and promotes success:[6]

> *The participatory and creative process sensitises managers to the outside world. It helps individuals and teams learn to recognise the uncertainties in their operating environments so that they can question their everyday assumptions, adjust their mental maps, and truly think outside the box in a cohesive fashion.*

Scenarios are tools for examining possible futures. This gives them a clear advantage over techniques based on a view of the past. In a rapidly changing and largely unpredictable environment, assessing possible futures is one of the best ways to promote responsiveness and direct policy. Scenario planning makes understanding and preparing for the future possible.

Important points to consider about scenario planning are as follows:

- It works best when it involves people at all levels of the organisation.
- Scenarios must be relevant.
- Critical assessment of each scenario keeps the process focused and relevant.
- The process involves understanding the forces that will shape the future but not predicting it; understanding why things might happen in a certain way; and relating those insights to the organisation's future.
- Creative thinking is crucial; existing biases must not be allowed to guide the process.
- The organisation must be genuinely committed to scenario planning. If day-to-day operational pressures are allowed to overshadow the process, they will limit the individual energy and creativity put into it.

Key questions

The following questions should be considered when using scenarios:

- Do the current strategic approaches typify traditional, business-as-usual thinking? Is the company prepared to accept that a strategy is failing or is vulnerable?

- Is the organisation in touch with market developments and the needs of customers? Is it prepared to challenge its confidence in existing orthodoxy?

- Is any part of the organisational planning weak and lacking clear direction? Is there confidence in the ability to engage in strategic debate?

- Does the decision-making process routinely consider multiple options? Is the quality of strategic thinking limited, narrow and uninspired?

- Is the organisation afraid of uncertainty or does it enjoy thinking about it? Do people see it as a threat or an opportunity? Is it recognised as a potential source of competitive advantage?

6 Involving and engaging stakeholders

COMPANIES THAT GROW for the sake of growth or that expand into areas outside their core business strategy often stumble. On the other hand, companies that build scale for the benefit of their customers and shareholders more often succeed over time.

Stakeholders include anyone with a stake in an organisation, notably shareholders, customers, employees and suppliers, and they have a decisive influence on the success of the organisation's strategy. Their support, whether active or passive, is essential for success. Their actions and engagement can decide the speed of progress and success, and their criticisms and concerns may undermine the directors and the strategy. If the business takes the wrong path, the stakeholders may be adversely affected; but if it prospers and succeeds, they are the people likely to benefit. It makes sense, therefore, that they should at least be aware of the strategy and, ideally, active contributors to its success. Increasingly, this is also their duty, at least for employees and shareholders, as Eliot Spitzer, a former New York Attorney General, observed: "Shareholders have the right and obligation to set the parameters of corporate behaviour within which management pursues profit."

When seeking to involve an organisation's stakeholders with the business strategy, it is useful to map the stakeholders and then work with each group.

Mapping an organisation's stakeholders

At the start of the mapping process, ask:

■ Who are the principal players and influencers?

- What are their roles?
- How do they participate in the business process and interact with one another as well?

Stakeholder maps:

- help you understand the holistic, big-picture view of an organisation's principal influencers;
- identify sources of power and interest, both inside and outside the organisation;
- include internal functions and teams, as well as those outside, such as:
  - clients, targets, alliance/strategic partners, potential recruits;
  - academics, analysts, government/non-government organisations;
  - industry groups, trade associations, lenders, shareholders, suppliers/vendors;
  - media/press, opinion leaders, communities/public at large, special interest groups;
- record stakeholders' effects on and interactions with the system and each other;
- help you identify potential sources of support and conflict, giving clues about whom to engage and how;
- enable you to plan and manage initiatives, campaigns and change-management programmes.

Building a stakeholder map

The value of stakeholder maps becomes apparent as soon as you start developing them, as they will help to fine-tune your strategic thinking skills. There are two notable points about stakeholder maps:

- Internal players, such as employees, play a crucial role in a business. Stakeholder maps define and illustrate the functions and interdependencies within an organisation's "social" system. They are therefore invaluable; nothing else you do will matter if you do not fully understand, manage and steer the internal players effectively.

■ The stakeholders identified as clients (or customers, purchasers, patrons, patients) are the next most significant group, as they buy the organisation's products or services and provide revenue for the business.

There are several steps in building a stakeholder map:

■ Work with colleagues to list the organisation's principal stakeholders, who may be internal and external.

■ Understand and map their relationships and linkages with each other, specifically how, when and why they interact, and with what results.

■ For each group determine what they value, what they need, their motivations, their contributions and their role (either actual or potential) in supporting the strategy.

■ Determine what the possibilities are, what more can be done, and what new actions can be taken.

If implementing a business strategy is a journey, stakeholder maps are a good way of understanding the people that need to be with you on that journey.

Managing an organisation's stakeholders

The role of the customer or client

The centrepiece – and main focus of attention – of an organisation is its clients. Many questions must be answered if an organisation is to succeed in client relationships. For example:

■ Who are our current and potential clients and what do they want?

■ How are their needs and preferences evolving?

■ How do we attract and retain customers?

■ How do we acquire them from competitors?

■ How well are we serving them?

■ How can we sell them more? Specifically, how can we shape relationships that ultimately influence buying behaviour?

■ Does one isolated event create and maintain deep-rooted client loyalty?

This process of identifying and understanding stakeholders shows ways of delivering value and how to strengthen those relationships to create more value. What may have initially seemed a routine exercise of plotting the principal players on a flat, two-dimensional diagram can reveal a complex, multi-dimensional world of possibilities.

Organisations have much to consider about stakeholder relationships. They generate opportunities as well as challenges and they profoundly shape almost everything that organisations are trying to accomplish: from selling to teamworking; customer service to innovation; engagement and energy to customer loyalty and competitiveness.

This applies to both internal relationships, including employees and other stakeholders, and external relationships, including those with customers, distributors, the media, opinion leaders and vendors. It is important to develop strong relationships with all stakeholders, as success depends on the quality of those relationships.

Understanding internal relationships

It is easy to see why internal relationships matter, typically those with employees but also those with suppliers. It is less easy to know how to ensure these relationships are positive. An organisation whose strategy is to be among the best at something needs to attract and retain the best talent; and talented people look for talented colleagues, a positive working environment and interesting challenges. Unfortunately, there are many barriers hindering good working relationships, such as competitiveness and rivalry, guarded behaviour, an unwillingness to open up, and seeing others in terms of their job title rather than as individuals. This way of working is symptomatic of a lack of any real connection between people and can lead to limited, potentially damaging relationships. Where there is a poor level of connection, it is likely that people's motives and behaviours will not be understood and conflict may result. To avoid this, organisations should promote a way of working where people feel connected.

This may sound like another touchy-feely fad, but feeling connected to colleagues is the foundation upon which strong relationships grow. Everything springs from this: trust, certainty, confidence, comradeship, decisions. These qualities in turn underpin other business activities: teamworking, collaboration, innovation, knowledge-sharing, selling and serving customers, and improving operational efficiency.

People are essentially social creatures, so relationships matter. They make us more effective in what we do, helping us form ties that transcend boundaries, such as geography, culture and personal differences. These linkages forge loyalty, commitment and high performance. They create value and protect us, which is especially helpful in times of crisis.

Using the corporate lattice

If the workforce has changed, so has the workplace, and this affects relationships at work. In particular, the previously accepted linear mode of employee advancement has been challenged. The one-size-fits-all approach that focused on offering a bigger office, a bigger pay cheque, and greater power and prestige needs re-examining. Today, if we were to look for the corporate ladder, we would be in for a surprise: it has gone. It has been replaced by what Cathleen Benko and Molly Anderson refer to as the corporate lattice, which, they say, has arisen because:[1]

> *Globalisation and technology are creating organisations with fewer rungs and more options for how, when, and where work gets done. And these are only two of many major shifts that have occurred.*

A major advantage of the corporate lattice is that it enables people to work more flexibly and productively. It is better able to tap into each individual's own motivation and offer them the working conditions and opportunities that they are looking for. Organisations are realising that less hierarchy and better connections between people release large amounts of potential, greatly improving productivity and employee retention.

This way of working has profound implications for relationships in the workplace. No longer constrained by the hierarchical structure of the past, relationships improve in every aspect, from better collaboration to the flow of internal communications. Given the changing nature of many workplaces it is sensible for organisations to review how to:

- engage the workforce – for example, use an intranet to facilitate communications, including blogs, and remember to include past employees and those who have retired;
- help people grow and develop – for example, use mentoring, coaching, a company university and a training allowance;
- provide flexibility – consider using virtual working to ensure that employees are better able to maintain a healthy and productive work–life balance;
- recognise and reward – for example, "spot" rewards, performance-related pay, contests and recognition in a company-wide newsletter;
- build trust – surveys and town-hall style meetings can be useful as they make people feel that they are valued, and that they are being listened to and can contribute.

Organisations should encourage and facilitate relationship-building activities with their internal stakeholders. But this is only half the story: building relationships with external stakeholders is the other half.

Developing external relationships

Too often, business thinking and analysis assess an issue from the organisation's perspective using internally generated measurements and conclusions. Yet some of these conclusions miss one obvious source of information: the clients. If a company wants to be successful in the marketplace, it must improve its relationships with external stakeholders. To do this, it must directly, and regularly, engage with customers; and communications must be meaningful.

Relationship capital is the gold standard for building relationships with external stakeholders. Quite simply, it drives a business. By investing in relationships the capital and goodwill accumulates over time, providing companies with a valuable cushion against future difficulties.

Building brand relationships brick by brick: Lego

Founded in 1932, Lego is one of the world's most popular children's toys. In 2004, the company faced financial difficulties and, for the first time in its history, someone from outside the family was appointed CEO. Jorgen Vig Knudstorp took charge and set about rebuilding the company and revitalising the brand. To do this, he devised a seven-year strategy known as the "Shared Vision". Central to his plans was the need to build strong relationships with customers and employees.

Knudstorp's relationship with employees grew from this shared vision and his leadership style. In the early years, the focus was on surviving and turning the situation around. This demanded a top-down style of management, often frowned upon in business literature. However, the financial situation left little room for manoeuvre, and Knudstorp was successful because he built the right conditions for good relationships to develop. He gave people a shared vision, so that everyone was working together towards the same goals. In short, the certainty and purpose of this shared vision was the glue for good working relationships. Indeed, all working relationships benefit from having a purpose.

The mission statement was a call to arms: "We are here to make money." This was about more than simply communicating the company's aims; it was about building the right relationship with employees. When there are clear goals and a sense of purpose, relationships are more collegiate. By creating a bond between everyone, people work better with each other. Everything leaders do and say has an impact on relationships in the workplace.

Also, Knudstorp made sure he was visible and approachable by, as he puts it, "managing at eye level". It seems obvious but it is often overlooked: it is easier to have a relationship with someone who is there, someone you can approach and have a conversation with. Being visible and approachable and promoting a sense of shared challenges built camaraderie, trust and commitment. Once the financial tide turned, Lego could move towards a looser, ground-up corporate structure that empowered managers, unlocking creativity and ideas.

Forming strong relationships depends on what people think of their leader; they will judge whether he or she is worth following or not. At Lego people trust Knudstorp: he takes responsibility and makes things happen. Interestingly, Knudstorp's belief that leadership should have "less talk and more action" also sets the tone for other relationships in the company. The emphasis is on each person taking responsibility and delivering results, and because everyone knows this, it creates an environment where people work well together to get things done.

One of the main reasons for the crisis at Lego was its lack of attention to customer relationships. In the main, it ignored its customers. Instead of learning directly from them and discovering what they really wanted, Lego relied on the information provided by retailers. And that was not enough. With sales falling dramatically, Lego needed to learn more about its customers if it was to turn the situation around; and relationship and community marketing helped it do just that.

As part of the turnaround, Lego developed the notion of a "creative platform", engaging in two-way conversations with customers. It now has direct contact with consumers through its own sales channels, clubs and collaboration programmes. The backbone of the customer communications exercise is the Lego Club, which has almost 3 million members. The Lego community is certainly one of the company's core assets. It actively encourages fans to interact with the company, including sharing their ideas for new products. Lego has only 120 staff designers, but it can potentially access 120,000 volunteer designers to help develop new products. An additional advantage is that Lego knows what its customers want, removing the uncertainty of "Will customers buy it?" that surrounds all product development.

This two-way communication really does get customers to invest psychologically in the company. When people feel part of something and that they are contributing to it, they want to stay with the group. By listening to customers, acting on their suggestions, and encouraging them to share their ideas and thoughts with each other, Lego has built a loyal customer base. Building such a two-way relationship gave the company the information it wanted, and its customers felt valued and part of a community. Lego was turning ordinary customers into loyal customers. The result was swift: sales increased and customer retention grew. The company went from making a $327 million net loss in 2004 to a $232 million net profit just four years later.

That is the difference developing strong customer relationships makes: Lego had learnt to put all the pieces together.

Developing trusted client relationships

For success in business and other relationships, trust is imperative. Andrew Sobel studies how to manage trusted client relationships, and in his book *Clients for Life*, written with Jagdish Sheth, he offers a model built upon seven attributes.[2] These principles are applicable to all who serve clients in all fields and industries. Organisations must have:

- empathy – specifically, ask great questions and listen;
- selfless independence – balance dedication with detachment and objectivity;
- depth as well as breadth of knowledge;
- synthesis – combining ideas as well as analysing them;
- judgment that incorporates their own and their clients' values and beliefs with their clients' organisational capabilities;
- conviction to communicate recommendations with belief and energy;
- integrity and competence – built through mutual familiarity with the client.

A common trait of trusted adviser relationships is that the adviser places a higher value on maintaining and preserving the relationship itself than on the outcome of the current transaction. The adviser makes a substantial investment in the client, without guarantee of return, before the relationship generates any income, let alone any profit.

David Maister, Charles Green and Robert Galford address the subject of trust in their book *The Trusted Advisor*.[3] Their research has highlighted the following points:

- It is essential to focus on the client's needs rather than your own. In this regard, it is also important to the client as an individual rather than a job title.

- A focus on problem definition and resolution is more important than technical or content mastery.

- A strong competitive drive should not be aimed at competitors; instead, it should be aimed at constantly finding new ways to be of greater service to the client.

- The focus should be on doing the right thing rather than on achieving specific outcomes. In other words, the means are as important as the ends.

- You should do the right thing for the client rather than be led by your organisation's rewards and dynamics.

- View methodologies, models, techniques and business processes as means to an end – if they prove effective for a client, keep them; if they don't, discard them.

- Always value the quality of contact with clients – successful client relationships depend on the accumulation of high-quality contacts.

- Dedication to helping clients lies at the core of a good relationship – the client will know if this is genuine and will value it when it is.

Developing relationships with current and potential customers: Starbucks

Starbucks began life with one small outlet in Seattle. It was hugely popular and soon became an internationally successful coffeehouse chain. When revenues fell during an economic downturn, the founder, Howard Schultz, admitted that past success had made the company complacent. Customers had drifted away, partly because they no longer felt a connection with Starbucks. The close relationship with customers that the company had always valued and worked at had disappeared, and, along with it, customers were disappearing too. Starbucks set about reversing this situation, aiming to win customers back. Getting customers through the door was the priority, and that would only happen by successfully rebuilding all relationships, with both customers and employees.

Everything rests on building relationships. This simple truth is summed up by Schultz's belief: "The best way to deliver the greatest customer experience is to deliver the best employee experience." So before looking at how Starbucks builds excellent customer relationships, we will consider the employee experience.

The inclusive, connected approach is evident from the outset, as employees are known as partners; and they are not just called partners, they are really considered partners. It is an attitude that promotes good relationships, as people feel equal and that their opinions matter. This means that they are more confident, they value what they do and they work well with colleagues, which ultimately results in an excellent customer experience. Furthermore, a number of policies (from corporate health care to staff stock options) make a clear statement that partners are valued. The small-company atmosphere is highly conducive to partners being able to connect with each other and work well together, promoting trust, responsibility and dependability. Staff training is high on the company's agenda, not only teaching basic skills and product knowledge but also encouraging a genuine enthusiasm for coffee and customers.

Relationship building does not stop there. Starbucks builds trust further through its responsible, we-all-share-the-planet approach to doing business, with community-minded and environmentally responsible policies. This attitude of a shared planet is reflected in its sense of shared community in the workplace. This matters: for relationships to grow, there has to be a point of connection, they need shared experiences. Of course, this also helps to build strong relationships with customers.

If one idea dominates Starbucks' approach, it is being totally customer-centric. Starbucks was conceived as a place for conversation with a sense of community. It was designed to be a third place – not home, not work – where people could relax and enjoy a different, special experience during their day. From the outset, building great customer relationships was central to the company's approach. It is not just a place to have a cup of coffee; it is a place where you share a portion of your day with Starbucks. Having an easy, relaxed atmosphere, establishing rapport and gaining trust means customers enjoy a connection to Starbucks. As soon as customers walk through the door – probably the reason they walk through door – they feel that they belong, that they are sharing the space with like-minded people. Being able to develop such a close relationship with its customers is a crucial reason for Starbuck's success. This connection helped the company rebuild its stock of relationship capital that it had previously depleted. As Starbucks found out: you should never let the coffee cup run dry.

Moving beyond transactions

For a business to generate sustainable earnings and profit it needs to move relationships with stakeholders beyond transactions to understanding, engagement, affection and respect, if possible. Those businesses that convert interactions with stakeholders into experiences and value are much more likely to see their strategy succeed. For businesses that use social-media tools to connect with people – keeping them informed, asking for their support, giving them special insights or things of value – the benefits in terms of relationships are powerful.

One final point about relationships is that even the most successful can hit a sticky patch. After all, no one is perfect and every relationship, even the most successful, has moments of tension or difficulty. What matters is how these challenges or concerns are addressed and, more generally, how readily companies learn about the best way to improve the relationship. This requires them to evaluate their capabilities and address any weaknesses: the crucial skill of managing resources when focusing on business strategy, which is the focus of the next chapter.

Key questions

- Which stakeholders are the most significant for your organisation? Whose input will be valuable when the strategy is being developed, and who will be decisive for its implementation?
- How do your stakeholders relate to each other, and how could these relationships be strengthened or leveraged further?
- What do your stakeholder groups value? What do they want and how effectively are they getting it?
- How are you going to strengthen your stakeholder relationships?
- How should you communicate with stakeholders, with what frequency, message and channel?

7 Resources and strategy

ORGANISATIONS ARE DYNAMIC ENTITIES, linking their activities through a set of connections that can be both complex and simple. Emphasising one aspect or resource in the business has profound implications for the rest of the organisation. Understanding how to assess and manage this web of interactions lies at the heart of systems thinking, and is central to developing a flexible and robust strategy and then implementing it successfully.

The benefits of a resource-based view

Kim Warren, a management writer, highlights the fact that possibly the greatest challenge facing managers is to understand how to build their business's performance over both the short and long term. Warren says:[1]

> When the causes of performance through time are not understood companies tend to make poor choices about their future. They embark upon plans they cannot achieve, failing to assemble what they need.

He calls this "the critical path" – the journey the business takes in seeking to improve its performance and value.

There are three main problems with existing approaches to developing and implementing strategy. First, the approach businesses take is often backward looking, relying on established business formulas and making only incremental change, believing that "if it isn't broken, don't fix it". Second, businesses use their appraisal of the past to help them focus on the present – the next quarter's results or the daily stock-price fluctuations. Third, projections and longer-term plans turn out to be flawed or simply wrong, failing to take adequate account of variables and undermining the whole strategy.

The problem is not that existing tools are wrong: it is that there is an overreliance on a few simple techniques. Management tools fall into several categories:

- Simple principles open to wide interpretation – for example, vision statements and some strategic plans.
- Substantial changes to business configuration – for example, re-engineering and outsourcing.
- Major changes to management processes – for example, value-based management (increasing the sale value of the enterprise) and the balanced scorecard (which sets objectives in finance, customers, innovation and learning, and guides internal processes linked with the strategy).
- Problem-solving processes – for example, five forces (see below).

All these tools have their merits and limitations. The challenge for leaders is to work out which are best suited to developing and implementing their business's strategy. A study of strategy analysis tools shows that relatively few possess sound methodological foundations.[2] There is a tendency to favour qualitative methods over quantitative ones when both are needed. Worse still, many qualitative methods seem to work well only in the hands of their developers and can be limited in their ability to provide confident, fact-based analysis.

Another particular weakness of most existing approaches to developing strategy (with the notable exception of scenarios) is that they are largely static, offering little explanation of what is driving an organisation's performance through time. They are also approximate, relying on sound leadership to make the course corrections.

A better approach is to adopt a rigorous, dynamic and time-based view of resources, the factors driving success or failure. Success is determined by whether resources strengthen or decline, complement or undermine each other, take from competitors or are eroded by them. When the causes of performance through time are not understood, organisations make poor choices about their future. They embark on plans they cannot achieve, failing to assemble the resources they need to achieve even those plans that might be feasible. Organisations are often capable of far more than they imagine, provided they understand the factors and resources driving their success so that they can set objectives that are challenging but grounded in reality.

It is crucial to make sure that the quality and quantity of resources are sufficient and then manage them well. Resources often fall into two basic categories: those that drive demand for the product and those needed to create the supply of product.

Vendor lock-in is one example of a resource-based approach to strategy whereby firms develop products that are only compatible with other products in their range, making it likely that they will get a steady flow of repeat business from customers. Gillette's razor handles are only compatible with its brand of razor blades; consequently, its blades are the primary source of income. Philips's Sonicare toothbrushes have an electronic base that requires a Sonicare replacement toothbrush head. The higher the switching cost, the less likely a customer is to switch.

Many businesses seek to lock in their customers. For example, Hewlett-Packard provided proprietary cartridges for its printers and Nespresso controlled the supply of coffee capsules for its machines (see Chapter 1). This provides a strong position as long as the firms' patents last. One of the challenges, however, is preparing for the time when patents expire and new entrants arrive in the market. This is most obviously the case in the pharmaceutical industry. Barriers to entry, superior service and product innovation are some of the answers.

Where many attempts at vendor lock-in fail is in viewing the reusable component as just an add-on. It is not. It is the product, the benefit for the customer and the profit for the business. Another example of the success of a resource-based approach pursued over time is that of easyJet.

---

easyJet: a resource-based approach

easyJet is a low-cost UK airline. Its success came at a time when the global airline industry faced increasing costs combined with static or declining passenger numbers. There was sympathy for Sir Richard Branson's comment that "the safest way to become a millionaire is to start as a billionaire and invest in the airline industry."

Stelios Haji-Ioannou, the founder of easyJet, followed in the footsteps of another low-fare European operator, Ryanair, when he launched the airline in November 1995. He created an efficient operating system, built brand awareness and maintained high levels of customer satisfaction, factors that would reinforce each other and make sure that easyJet was distinctive. In his view:

> If you create the right expectations and you meet or exceed those expectations, then you will have happy customers.

easyJet's success was initially similar to the model developed by Southwest Airlines in the US, with one type of aircraft (Boeing 737), short-haul travel, no in-flight meals and a rapid turnaround time resulting in aircraft utilisation 50% greater than the industry average. easyJet took this approach further, cutting out travel agents, not issuing tickets, selling food and drink on the plane and building sales through the internet. These actions developed and reinforced the strategic priorities of efficiency, awareness and customer satisfaction – and they made easyJet popular, distinctive and successful in a highly competitive market.

Avoiding pitfalls

Analysing competitive conditions within an industry has dominated efforts to understand and develop a firm's performance. This approach says:

■ We try to make profits by offering products for which customers will pay us more than they cost us to provide.

■ The more powerful are our customers, the more they can force us to cut prices, reducing profitability.

- The more powerful are our suppliers, the more they can charge us for the resources we need, again reducing our profitability.
- If we make profits, this will attract competitors, new rivals and firms selling alternative or substitute products, all of which will try to take business away from us – again depressing profitability.

These "five forces" – buyers, suppliers, rivals, new entrants and substitutes – partially explain why companies are unable to sustain performance over time. The boom and bust of the dotcom era was a classic illustration of the five forces at work. By eliminating the substantial costs of conventional supply chains, e-businesses could offer products at low cost, while still – at least in time – generating attractive profit margins. It was anticipated that buyers would face few switching costs in taking up these alternatives, so by getting very big, very quickly, the new providers would establish considerable buying power over their own suppliers and erect substantial competitive barriers against rivals or would-be entrants. The established suppliers' bricks-and-mortar investments would weigh them down and prevent them from competing in the new business model. An example of this approach is provided by Amazon during its early years (from 1995), when many commentators believed that conventional bookselling would become almost obsolete.

The five forces also describe neatly why so many of the new businesses were doomed. Buyers who were able to switch to the new offering faced low barriers to switching among the host of hopeful new providers and did so for even the smallest financial incentive. The new business model was often transparent, requiring little investment in assets, so rivals and new entrants could copy it quickly. Worst of all, since so many enterprises saw the same opportunity for the same high returns from the same business models, there was a rush of new entrants. In anticipation of great future profits, many gave away more than the margin they ever expected to make in the hope that, as the survivor, they would be able to recapture margin in later years. Significantly, those firms that prospered during the dotcom boom and have continued to develop and grow (for example, Amazon, Expedia, Google, eBay and others) understood their resources, how they interrelate, how they contribute to the business's success and how they need to be managed.

Understanding resources

Resources can be classified into two of four categories: direct or indirect; tangible or intangible.

■ Direct resources include staff expertise, cash or intellectual property which can be developed and nurtured by the business. Customers are, perhaps, the biggest direct resource. (Viewing customers as a resource focuses thinking on how to accumulate and retain them.)

■ Indirect resources have a bearing on the quality, strength and value of direct resources. For example, effective training and development policies are an indirect resource as they build staff expertise.

■ Tangible resources are physical, such as cash and stock.

■ Intangible resources include service quality, brand reputation or staff expertise.

Determining which resources are most important and how they should be managed requires a clear understanding of the nature of each resource, specifically:

■ **The fragility of resources.** Cash, quality, customers, staff and reputation can all disappear with remarkable speed. It is, therefore, important to monitor and control the factors most likely to damage or undermine resources. For example, quality can be eroded by suppliers, service can be undermined by the attitudes of employees and brand reputation may be damaged by the actions of distributors.

■ **The interaction between resources.** Resources can combine in a cycle to accelerate their growth. For example, rising sales volumes may generate more cash and extra market share, both of which can be used to generate increasing sales, perhaps by entering new markets and so on. Similarly, product quality (an intangible resource) may lead to increased sales, and in turn generate sufficient cash to continue to improve product quality (and to increase sales further). In the same way that resources can interact to reinforce each other, they can also limit each other. For example, sales demand may rise, but if the trade-off for increasing production to meet demand is to reduce quality, brand reputation and long-term sales may suffer.

■ **The value of resources.** Businesses should always seek to extract more value from their resources. For example, the value of a customer base might be increased by encouraging customer loyalty by, for instance, introducing a loyalty scheme.

Identifying resources

Generally, when managers seek to identify the most important resources on which their business relies, they focus on strategic resources: those few, special items that might explain why one firm is more profitable than its rivals. Resources can be divided into three: demand, supply and financial.

■ The obvious demand-side resource is customers. This may not, though, be all that is needed to create demand for a product. In many cases, customers can only be reached through dealers or other intermediaries – that is, other demand-side resources.

■ Supply-side resources include the products and services that organisations offer in order to satisfy demand. A restaurant has its menu, a car manufacturer has a range of models and a law firm has the range of legal services it can provide. Next is a firm's capacity to produce the product or service; for example, the capacity of a restaurant's kitchen to produce meals or a car manufacturer's factories and equipment enabling vehicles to be produced at a certain rate. Making the whole system work requires people, who are crucial resources. In certain cases, the production capacity itself may be people. The capacity of a law firm, for example, is made up of the professional staff doing the work.

■ Financial resources include cash and receivables – but against them have to be put any financing costs and payables. Debt is a "negative" resource even though it helps to produce positive cash.

FIG 7.1 **A time path of performance**

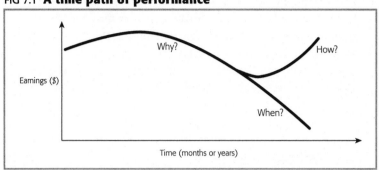

Assessing performance over time

Drawing up a time path of past and future performance is helpful in focusing managers' minds on current performance and how it can be sustained or improved (see Figure 7.1).

When preparing a performance time path:

■ Ask relevant questions. Why is performance following its current path? Where is it going if the company carries on as it is? How can a robust strategy be designed to radically improve performance in the future?

■ Chart the resource that would ultimately signal success or failure (this may include profits or revenues). Include a numerical scale and a timescale, including enough history to cover the explanation for the present situation. Use absolute numbers rather than ratios.

■ Display three important characteristics for each resource:
  - a numerical scale (such as the number of customers);
  - a timescale;
  - the time path – how the position changes over that timescale. This should be done for both the preferred and feared futures.

■ Support the main performance chart (such as profits or revenues) with one that measures contributions to that outcome (such as unit sales and customers). This can indicate where the main source of the challenge is likely to lie.

■ Understand how resources affect performance. Managers know that it is crucial to build and conserve resources, both tangibles such as staff, cash and customers and intangibles such as reputation and investor support. They also understand that resources are interdependent – a winning product range is of little value if poor delivery performance damages reputation. Resources are the foundation of success. Leadership, capabilities, vision and all the other subtle and complex concepts brought to bear can only improve performance if they help to win and retain the necessary resources.

Resources grow and shrink over time. Since a firm's performance at any time directly reflects the resources available, it is essential to understand how those resources develop over time and how that process can be controlled. But just knowing that resources are growing or shrinking is not enough to allow managers to take control. It is also necessary to know:

■ how many customers, staff and other resources are present in the system;

■ how fast these numbers are changing;

■ how strongly these factors are being influenced by other controllable factors and by other forces.

Managing and developing resources

To manage resources and make sure that they drive performance in the desired direction, start by understanding how resources work together. The logic is clear: the resources in place drive performance at every moment, so a manager must know how the quantity of each resource changes through time. The only means of controlling performance through time is to manage the flows of resources into and out of the system.

Several factors move resources into and out of an organisation including its own decisions, for example spending money on marketing, offering discounts or hiring new staff. There are also outside forces such as changes in customers' needs, shortages of suitable staff or price cuts by competitors. Then there are resources already in place, for example sales people to win customers, service teams to deliver service and retain clients, and researchers to develop products. Understand what is happening over time to the quantity of resources by examining how their flows change.

To understand the scale of potential resources being developed, ask the following questions:

- How many of these potential resources are there?
- Does this scarcity put any constraints on the rate at which the resources can be developed?
- Is anything happening to the potential resources pool itself – is a shortage looming or is an increase likely?

Competitors and other factors also affect the flows of resources into or out of a business. External influences fall into four categories, collectively known as PEST (political, economic, social and technological):

- Political changes include deregulation, which opens up entire industries.
- Economic changes can create new customer groups. Fast-developing economies can create conditions in which the inflow to the potential customer pool grows quickly. The opposite occurs when economies contract.
- Social changes also drive the migration of consumers, employees and others into and out of the resource base of different industries. Demographic changes bring new young consumers into a potential market each year and take them out when they age.
- Technological progress changes how products are used and reduces the unit cost of offering them.

Benefiting from the interdependence of resources

The use of current resources controls the rates at which resources grow or shrink in a business. It is necessary to analyse the interdependence between resources and to use this information to manage their development:

■ Chart the history for a resource, the growth of which needs understanding and controlling.

■ Identify the history of inflows and outflows by gathering data on all aspects of a resource.

■ Review and quantify the most likely factors driving a flow. This will reveal the factors behind changes in resources, allowing more effective management of them.

Gathering this information will clarify what has been happening and why. However, it may be necessary to go further. Use statistical methods to see if the expected reasons really do explain the resource flow rate. If the initial list of causes does not explain how resource flows have changed, investigate what might be missing. When the explanations are coherent, analyse each factor to highlight how the flow of resources might be improved.

Assessing why performance has followed a particular path

How healthy are the resources? For example, are there low-value customers and marginally valued products, with staff working unproductively to support these poor-quality resources? If so, consider reconfiguring to a smaller but more powerful and competitive core.

Developing strategy needs an understanding of all the elements making up the business, together with information that explains why it has performed as it has. These are as follows:

■ A time-chart of one or more performance measures, with scale and timing (for example, profits, sales, service levels).

■ A list of likely resources involved (for example, customers, clients, staff, products, services, cash and capacity).

■ A chain of immediate causes for that performance, often with simple arithmetic relationships (for example, gross margin, revenue, labour costs, demand).

- At the head of those causal chains, the resources driving demand, supply and performance (for example, customers, staff, products, services, cash).
- Flows of resources into, through and out of the system (for example, customers won and lost per month, staff hired, promoted or leaving per month, products added or discontinued per year).
- The immediate causes for those flow rates.
- The dependency of each resource flow on existing resources, for either the same resource or others.

Upgrading your resources

Look beyond the quantity of resources the business has or can win and focus on their quality.

First, consider the existing resources. What is the quality of each and how is this quality distributed? Is there a valuable group of staff, products or customers, for example, or does the business rely on a handful of stars? Find out how those qualities are changing. Are the customer base and revenue growing only by adding low-value business, or are inroads being made into good-quality customers?

Next, consider potential resources. Is the focus on building business with new resources leaving the potential of existing ones undeveloped? Is there an opportunity to build a new resource – new markets or products, for example – that will bring with it the chance to attract new customers?

Is any potential resource in danger of running out? Are resources declining in quality? Is there a danger of resources cannibalising each other? If one or more of these problems is looming, can anything be done to counteract it or should the organisation recognise the resulting limits and reconfigure itself? The only way to understand the significance of these phenomena is to work the numbers.

Resources are useful items an organisation owns or can access; capabilities are activities it does well. Capabilities determine how effectively an organisation builds, develops and retains resources.

If the supply of any resource is inadequate, the performance of the entire system will suffer. So the organisation must be capable in all resource-building and maintenance activities. Capabilities influence performance by improving the organisation's success at developing resources, whether winning them, developing them or retaining them.

Key questions

- Is the resource durable? A resource that quickly deteriorates or becomes obsolete is unlikely to provide sustainable advantage. The more durable the resource, the better.
- Is the resource mobile? Many resources, such as employees, can move easily between firms and so provide little sustainable advantage.
- Is the resource tradable? Resources are particularly mobile if they can be bought and sold. The less tradable the resource, the better.
- Is the resource easily copied and thus offers little competitive advantage? The less easily copied the resource, the better.
- Can the resource be substituted? Computer systems supplier Dell's direct supply system is a substitute for not being in retail stores. The less easily substituted the resource, the better.
- Are existing resources complementary? Could the way they interact and support each other be improved?

Such questioning will uncover detailed information about the organisation's resources. This, in turn, will enable continued development of resources and assessment of their effectiveness over time.

To understand the scale of potential resources being developed, ask:

- How are the flows of each resource changing?
- How many of this potential resource are there?
- Does scarcity constrain the rate at which the resource can be developed?
- Is anything happening to the potential resource pool itself – is a shortage looming or is an increase likely?

For any resource that develops from state to state, ask:

- What are the exact stages?
- How many of this resource are in each stage now, and at what rate are they moving between different stages?
- How have rates changed in the past, and how may they change in the future?
- What is the organisation doing that influences these flows, and by how much?

8 Strategies for growth

AMONG THE MOST IMPORTANT strategic decisions are those relating to growth, specifically how to grow a business. It is tempting to believe that continuing to do what has been done in the past will lead to continued growth. But although it may lead to continuing success, it may lead off a cliff. If managers are to make the right decisions, therefore, a strategic direction and set of guiding priorities are needed together with an assessment of the most effective strategy for growth.

The different routes to growth are:

- organic growth;
- mergers and acquisitions;
- strategic alliances, partnering and joint ventures (integration activities);
- diversification;
- specialisation.

They are not mutually exclusive and can overlap. They are, however, limited by the resources available and each requires a clear focus on objectives and a sustained level of commitment.

Organic growth

This occurs when a business grows by using its existing resources. Organic growth can take place because the market is growing, or because a company is doing increasingly better than its competitors or is entering new markets. Exploiting a product advantage can sustain organic growth; examples are a law firm with a star partner or a software company with a unique program. But there is only so much growth that one person or one product can generate. People retire and products mature, so organic growth normally requires launching new products or product extensions, entering new markets or establishing wider distribution networks and sales agency agreements, or licensing or franchising.

Organic growth depends on a firm's available resources and capabilities as well as its planning, time and cash.

- Core competences and capabilities. Organic growth depends largely on what an organisation is good at and capable of. It is helped by identifying and exploiting synergies across different parts of an organisation's activities; by structuring the organisation to take advantage of "priority" opportunities; and by creating a culture that is able to spot opportunities when they arise and make the most of them.

- Planning. Growth can be achieved quickly and unexpectedly, but for it to be sustained a co-ordinated plan of action is needed among business functions such as marketing, production, finance and human resources. Organic growth gives an organisation total control over the process of development and relies on the experience and expertise within the firm.

- Time. Growing organically can be a slow process. It requires patience, application and strong, focused leadership to keep the strategy on course and maintain support for it.

- Cash. This is essential for organic growth, preferably cash generated from within the business being used to develop other parts, or cash provided as a loan or in return for an equity stake in the business. Cash is needed to pay for taking on new staff, buying in new resources (such as IT systems), developing and producing new products or undertaking marketing initiatives.

IKEA: growing organically

IKEA is a highly successful business that has grown organically. Established in Sweden in the 1940s, today it is a global business with stores in countries as diverse as Russia and Kuwait, Canada and Malaysia. National websites demonstrate the individuality of the dispersed business units, yet in its corporate literature the organisation emphasises:

> *It is no accident that the logo is blue and yellow. These are the colours of the Swedish flag.*

Building upon its success in its home market, IKEA expanded rapidly across Europe during the 1970s and 1980s. It sold the same products in the same way and broke some key principles of retailing. Some of these rules are now broken universally, such as telling the customer: "We flat pack our products because it is easier and cheaper for us to transport and store them."

IKEA expanded into North America in the 1980s but in contrast to its experiences in Europe, the new stores did not rapidly become profitable. IKEA learnt the hard way that a universal solution is unlikely to work in global markets with varied cultures.

In North America, IKEA realised that it had to blend its traditional Swedish design and low-cost products with context-specific responses to customer needs. For example, IKEA supplied chests of drawers with deeper drawers in the US market to accommodate the larger amount of knitwear favoured in that part of the world. King- and queen-sized beds were offered, with dimensions given in inches rather than centimetres. By 1997, nearly half of IKEA's products sold in the US were sourced locally and almost one-third of its total product range was designed exclusively for the US market.

IKEA is not alone in applying a mix of generalisation and localisation to its products and services. As the giants of the motor industry seek more standard components (such as engines and transmissions) across models, brands and countries, they also recognise the need to cater for local tastes. In developing the Focus as an international model, Ford has addressed the failings of its earlier attempts to offer the Escort as a car with universal appeal. The model may be the same, but the product has differences – such as trim and suspension settings – to suit different tastes across markets and different environmental conditions. Similarly, MTV has moved from being a universal provider of 24-hour music on television to exploiting local market differences. In Europe, MTV provides different language stations; this allows it not only to meet local demand but also to tap into local advertising markets and to generate additional revenues locally.

In a world of global brands such as Sony, McDonald's, IKEA and CNN, successful business strategies are based on core values and standards implemented with local sensitivity and awareness. This aligns organisations with local needs and demands that are largely driven by cultural differences; it also requires them to engage with local communities to understand their tastes and expectations in order to design products that will be acceptable and that people will want to buy. This generates productive relationships, based on mutual understanding and respect, in which there is an overt acceptance of divergence and a willingness to "agree to differ" in a state of "creative conflict".

Mergers and acquisitions

One of the fastest routes to growth is through an acquisition or merger, but it is also one of the hardest and riskiest. There are two views about mergers. One is that mergers between titans will result in an even larger titan, too cumbersome to operate as flexibly and efficiently as it needs to. According to this view, a merger results in:

- more bureaucracy;
- diminishing returns negating the benefits of increases in size and capacity for production;
- diseconomies of scale, swallowing huge quantities of capital and causing organisational lethargy;
- a lumbering giant that will be outpaced and outsmarted by smaller rivals.

The second, more optimistic, view is that mergers result in:

- economies of scale and efficiency;
- stability and greater potential for growth resulting from a broader base of customers and products;
- an intellectual capital and management infrastructure to deal with market change.

There are differing views on the value of mergers, and although they often hold a great deal of promise, negotiating the many pitfalls inherent in such deals – from cultural issues to communications – can be hazardous and difficult. Furthermore, the forces that drive firms to merge in the first place might place strains on the union over the long term. For a merger to succeed, prudence, diligence and sound leadership are essential.

Researching cross-border mergers and acquisitions (M&A), Michael Hitt of Arizona State University found that the successful ones benefited by gaining access to new and lucrative markets; expanding the market for a firm's current goods; acquiring new knowledge and capabilities; gaining access to valuable and complementary resources, and enhancing a firm's ability to innovate.

Joseph Bower, Donald K. David Professor Emeritus at Harvard Business School, concluded that mergers and acquisitions typically represent five types of strategic activities with different motives:[1]

- To deal with overcapacity, through consolidation in mature industries (for example, the 2007 merger of Corus with Tata Steel).

- To acquire competitors in geographically fragmented industries (for example, Bank One acquiring local and regional banks).

- To expand into new products or markets (for example, General Electric buying Nuovo Pignone, an Italian company, from ENI).

- As a substitute for research and development (for example, Cisco buying companies in an effort to dominate the internet server and communication equipment fields).

- To exploit eroding industry boundaries by inventing an industry (for example, entertainment company Viacom buying the Paramount films studio, the MTV and Nickelodeon cable networks and the Blockbuster video distributor).

Some mergers are defensive. McDonnell Douglas merged with Boeing because its main customer, the Pentagon, slashed expenditure by half. Mergers can also result from intensified globalisation. Chrysler merged with Daimler-Benz because it was worried about its ability to prosper in a global business environment. The threat may arise from a single foe. Bayerische Vereinsbank merged with Bavarian rival Hypobank to avoid being taken over by Deutsche Bank. Such mergers are rarely positive. Mergers that are more likely to work are those with clear advantages in mind, rather than those aiming to minimise disadvantages.

The greatest test of the success of a merger or acquisition is the extent to which it provides a platform for future development and growth. The challenge of finding the right business to merge with or acquire is complicated by the difficulty of constructing the best deal and then seeing it through. Many deals look good on paper, only to fail because of weak execution.

Decisions on whether to merge with or acquire a business are complex and usually involve a high degree of risk. If the decision to merge is well judged and the implementation of the merger is well executed, it can generate large-scale, rapid growth. The reverse is also true: a misguided or poorly implemented merger can be hugely damaging. There are three stages in the merger or acquisition process:

- planning and preparation;
- due diligence;
- post-acquisition planning and integration.

Planning and preparation

This involves several decisions:

- Decide your strategy. The first step includes a top-down strategic vision based on the advantages of acquisition versus other approaches such as joint ventures or organic growth. Soundly based knowledge of the sector and the strengths and weaknesses of all the players involved will also help inform the strategy. This vision determines how the business approaches the deal: what is to be gained, likely targets or partners, and the rationale for it. Coupled with this is the bottom-up approach, in which lower-level managers or, in the case of a group, senior managers at subsidiary level are involved in the strategic process as they can highlight potential pitfalls as well as more positive developments that may be overlooked. They may also provide useful information, such as a target's strengths and weaknesses or specific opportunities.

■ Identify and select targets. When seeking a suitable acquisition or merger target, consider:
- the target specification – attributes that are either essential or desirable in a target company;
- the opportunities available in the sector and a list of potential candidates, ranked in priority order;
- what each target offers and how it will fit with the business;
- who to approach, how and when.

■ Decide specific objectives and understand how issues affect them. Be clear about the deal's objectives, which may include gaining access to intellectual properties or new markets, providing synergies with existing activities, increasing capacity or simply removing a competitor.

■ Assess the current and potential value of the target business, taking into account factors such as tangible and intangible assets (notably property and intellectual property), the expertise of its personnel and the likelihood that they will remain. Investigate the target business's management expertise and organisational culture, the way that the business is run and decisions are made, as well as its culture and values. Then assess what benefits these would bring and what difficulties they may cause in the integration process. Consider what you might have to pay to win support from the target company's (and your company's) shareholders and other interested parties. Work out who else's support you need, for example managers, the media and stockmarket analysts. All this affects the ease with which the company can be acquired as well as the depth of long-term support and the cash that may be available for future developments, such as costly restructuring.

Due diligence

This is the process of investigating a target company in detail. The purpose and value of due diligence are to make sure that the target business is fully understood and the acquisition proceeds successfully, and to provide a financial and legal audit. Due diligence involves examining the target's accounts, contracts and all other commercial aspects. It provides a basis for identifying and avoiding risks, ensuring accurate valuation and preparing for post-acquisition integration, and, in particular, understanding the many people issues that invariably determine the ease and success of the merger.

For these reasons due diligence is often conducted in parallel with contract negotiations, although some advisers recommend that it follows negotiation and is completed as the final stage before the deal is concluded. As with the planning and preparation stage, due diligence also involves several important decisions:

- Price is paramount. It will depend on whether it is a buyer's or a seller's market, and requires a judgment about the minimum price the seller will accept. A decision must also be made on the buyer's maximum price, which should take into account the additional costs on top of the purchase price: for example, fees paid to legal and any other advisers; the cost of raising capital and financing the acquisition; tax considerations; integration costs to realise the full potential of the acquisition; and legal completion costs. Once due diligence has been completed and any surprises it has uncovered have been taken into account, contracts can be drawn up.

- Negotiations often take place at the same time as due diligence, but there will be a final stage when matters such as warranties and indemnities, designed to protect the buyer against surprises not revealed by the due diligence process, are agreed.

Post-acquisition planning and integration

Whatever precedes this stage can be rendered worthless if successful integration of the target is not achieved. An effective post-acquisition strategy is crucial and post-acquisition planning needs to start before the deal is finalised.

The key to success with post-acquisition planning is to realise the benefits of the deal as quickly as possible, generating momentum and support for the deal. Post-acquisition integration decisions should take into account:

- the overall strategy of the business;
- the culture and management styles of the two organisations;
- issues of presentation, communication and understanding;
- customer-focused market issues (how will customers, current and potential, react, and can this be turned to the acquirer's advantage?);
- people issues, including motivation, empowerment and innovation;
- management procedures and systems, especially for information technology and finance;
- the need to inform shareholders.

An interesting example is Pernod Ricard's purchases of Seagram's drinks division in 2001 (jointly with Diageo) and Allied Domecq in 2005 (again jointly, this time with Fortune Brands). These deals transformed the French wines and spirits producer from fifth position in the global league table to second, behind Diageo, and greatly broadened the global reach of its products. This was followed in 2008 by the purchase of Sweden's Vin & Sprit, including Absolut vodka, the third-best-selling premium spirit worldwide after Diageo's Smirnoff and Johnnie Walker brands. At the time, this put Pernod Ricard in joint first place with Diageo in terms of sales volume. The integrations were completed and the planned synergies achieved ahead of schedule, allowing the French group to pay down debt quicker than planned.

Strategic alliances, partnering and joint ventures (integration activities)

Another way to grow is to work more closely with other businesses through partnership deals, joint ventures or strategic alliances. Integration can be vertical, involving organisations in the same industry but at different stages of the value chain (for example, PepsiCo linking up with restaurants that will sell its beverages). Vertical integration can provide businesses with greater control over the process of creating goods or services and getting them to the customer.

In contrast, horizontal integration involves collaboration between organisations in the same industry; for example, a law firm in the US may link with law firms in many other countries to provide a more global service. Horizontal integration can provide economies of scale as well as enhancing the size, expertise and credibility of both businesses. But to grow successfully through strategic alliances the aims of everyone involved need to be similar and clearly understood. The alliance must be structured so that it does not fall foul of antitrust laws and competition regulations, notably in Europe and the US.

Nokia: a fruitful alliance

When Nokia, a Finnish mobile phone manufacturer, decided to enter the US market it was relatively unknown, and as Kari-Pekka Wilska, head of Nokia's US operations, recalled: "We didn't have the money to do it all ourselves." So Nokia formed an alliance with Tandy, which enabled its phones to be sold via 6,000 Radio Shack outlets in the United States. It was an inspired pairing. Nokia had learnt its skills in Scandinavia where technological innovation was imperative. Tandy brought a new set of priorities. "For Tandy, the first priority was cost, then it was cost, and then it was cost, and then came something else," said Pekka Ala-Pietila, president of Nokia's mobile phones division. Nokia learnt how to cut manufacturing costs to the bone.

Nokia proved a quick learner. For example, it quickly learnt from Tandy the importance of high volumes and low cost, two factors that proved crucial to its growth and success. One of Nokia's strengths was that its new portable phone was designed for large-volume production. Nokia recognised that it needed to sell enormous volumes to make money and give it a competitive advantage.

Tandy benefited from access to popular technological products and association with Nokia's brand as well as learning a lesson about the importance of innovation.

With commercial partnerships, firms can pool resources and achieve complex goals that may otherwise have been out of their reach. Such deals can be negotiated either by giving partners a share of profits or by arranging a mutual relationship that allows them to use your resources in return.

Oneworld, an airline alliance – whose members include American Airlines, British Airways, Cathay Pacific, Finnair, Iberia, Japan Airlines, LAN Airlines, Malaysia Airlines, Qantas, Qatar Airways and Royal Jordanian – gives customers the chance to organise more simply trips encompassing over 650 destinations in 134 countries through any one of the airlines. None flies to every destination but the alliance provides a means of complying with the restrictive rules governing ownership of airlines in a way that benefits customers.

For a strategic alliance to work successfully those involved need to:

- steer clear of illegal practices such as price fixing;
- assess the terms and implications of the arrangement so as to be sure it is in their best interests and will work fairly;
- structure and plan the way the alliance will work with great care, doing as much as possible to anticipate potential problems and making sure everyone shares the same view of how it will work;
- be ready to expand the alliance to other companies when it makes sense to do so and will help drive growth.

The motives for entering into an alliance with another company are similar to those for mergers and acquisitions. For example, to consolidate their commercial strength in Europe, Mobil and British Petroleum formed an alliance in 1996 which involved operating refineries, buying crude oil and other raw materials for refineries, refining and converting downstream products (such as lubricants), and marketing them in western and eastern Europe as well as in Turkey and Cyprus.

Alliances are sometimes used for specific reasons that are not valid for mergers or acquisitions. For instance, if a company seeks to divest a non-core business that may have intangible resources or ties to other businesses, potential buyers may hesitate to make a deal since it is difficult for them to value the business. In these circumstances, an alliance can be used to provide the potential buyer with a call option. For example, Philips wished to leave the large domestic appliances market, so it entered into a joint venture with Whirlpool in 1989. Whirlpool was given the option to acquire the joint venture within three years, which it did. The joint venture gave Whirlpool time and experience to assess the value of this business. Other specific drivers of alliances include:

- the desire to reduce risks in uncertain markets;
- the need to share the cost of large-scale capital investments;
- the hope of injecting fresh entrepreneurial spirit into maturing businesses.

Diversification

Diversification involves a business moving into an additional area of activity. This can be either a new product in an existing market, for example an airline starting a low-cost service, or a new product in a different market, for example a bus operator buying a rail franchise and running train services. Diversification can be achieved with partners, as well as through new finance, and can provide several benefits, including:

- removing overreliance, or even dependence, on a small group of customers and spreading risk;
- making the existing business more attractive, enhancing perception of the brand, customer service and market share;
- improving market share in both businesses as synergies and marketing offers can be exploited;
- protecting against changing conditions in traditional markets that can result in short-term difficulties or long-term terminal decline;
- minimising the damage created by leaving a market if you operate in other profitable markets.

Diversification can provide new opportunities for existing skills as well as spare capacity. For example, an advertising agency may set up a unit to make corporate videos because it has the necessary skills and resources. This is known as concentric diversification because it is based on existing skills, customers and sales channels but the applications broaden in concentric rings.

Specialisation

The opposite of diversification, specialisation involves dropping non-core activities, or even redefining and focusing on core operations. The main advantages are a clear focus and strength in depth, with all available resources channelled into one endeavour. It also means that any cash available from the sale of non-core operations can be used to grow the business.

Reliance on specialisation requires doing what you do sufficiently better than your competitors and successfully anticipating and adapting to market changes.

Balancing core and context

Core activities are the unique skills that differentiate an organisation from its competitors and persuade customers of its superiority. Context activities are the processes needed to meet the industry standard without surpassing it. Getting the right balance between the two is surprisingly tricky.

Core activities are known as business idea factors, while context activities refer to "hygiene" factors – those essential to the success of any business. For example, a core activity for Microsoft might be its ability to develop new software, whereas context factors include its ability to process orders and dispatch products. Both are crucial, but the real value of the business lies in the core.

Shareholders typically want to concentrate on core activities as these generally increase share prices. But sometimes businesses become too involved in context activities and lose focus on the core, which is where the potential for growth and any competitive advantage lies.

Geoffrey Moore, a Silicon Valley consultant and business strategist, recommends balancing core and context activities by outsourcing or automating context activities. This means that context activities are handled competently and cost-effectively by a specialist company. A further benefit is the ability to devote increased investment to gaining a competitive edge.

Many companies, including Cisco, Dell, General Motors, IBM and Kodak, have outsourced their context processes to allow their organisations to cope with both core and context demands. Sabrix, a leading provider of software for managing taxation that was acquired by Thomson Reuters, outsourced its context processes. Its president and CEO, Steve Adams, says:

> *Outsourcing human resources and parts of our financial IT system has allowed us to keep the right people focused on the right things – things that differentiate our company.*

In Sabrix's case, this was on reaching new levels in tax research, software development and customer support.

When deciding how best to balance core and context:

- Be clear about what is core and what is context. Recognise that some of these activities might be dynamic, moving between categories.
- Be prepared to overcome possible resistance to outsourcing initiatives and rearranging managers' responsibilities.
- Delegate core activities from senior managers to middle managers, as they will have a better view of market trends. Delegating responsibility helps ensure that no level within the organisation becomes overwhelmed.
- Encourage top-level support for outsourcing and managing context activities.

The perils of growth

Growth is difficult to manage and depends on having clear objectives, the necessary cash and capable leadership. Because of the time lag between making an investment and it starting to repay, it is crucial to maintain the support of financial backers.

Growth can disrupt existing processes, organisational structures and working methods. If growing pains are not remedied quickly, they can have serious consequences. The solution is to identify all those things about the current business that work well and must be retained, as well as what needs improving. Explaining plans to customers and suppliers will help to allay their concerns.

Competitors may see a change in strategy or structure as an opportunity to attack, perceiving it as a sign of weakness or as possibly heralding a period of strength that requires a pre-emptive strike. Growth can also signal that the sector is doing well, encouraging competitors to enter the market or broaden their activities. The solution is to monitor the market and act decisively to counter competitors' moves.

Cost control is crucial in a strategy for growth. Rising costs, most frequently administration costs, occur if there is duplication (in the case of M&A) or if the administrative function is badly managed. Another reason for rising costs is too much stock.

Depending on its speed and scale, growth will affect everything from innovation to decision-making and team-building, so employees may need additional training and support. Integrating workforces with broadly similar roles but large differentials in pay and conditions may prove difficult.

Key questions

When determining a strategy for growth, ask:

- Where do the most profitable parts of the business lie?
- What are the prospects in the short, medium and long term for other potentially profitable parts?
- How precarious is the business? Does it rely on too few products, customers, suppliers, employees or distribution channels?
- Is the business clearly focused? Does it have too many products, markets and initiatives, or are there too few opportunities on which to capitalise?
- What is likely to be the best method of expansion? Is it affordable in terms of money, other resources and time?
- What are the advantages and disadvantages of expanding? What must be done to achieve the benefits and avoid the pitfalls?
- What do people in the organisation see as the best options? What are their views of potential opportunities and difficulties?

■ Is there the commitment to act decisively and consistently? Once set, the course needs to be followed rigorously. One of the greatest obstacles to growth is inertia.

■ Do you understand how the changes will affect people? If employees feel threatened, disregarded or insecure, no matter how sensible the decision and its implementation it will probably fail through a lack of commitment.

■ What are the success criteria and performance measures? How will they be monitored?

When considering a merger or acquisition, ask:

■ Does it fit the business strategy?

■ What are the main issues faced in making the deal a success?

■ What decisions are needed and how will they be reached?

■ How will the best target be identified?

■ How well is the deal structured?

■ Is the price acceptable and likely to provide a realistic return?

■ On what can you compromise and what is non-negotiable?

■ What are the main priorities and intended benefits and how swiftly will they be realised?

■ How might issues of organisational culture affect the deal?

■ How can you limit any negative effects or, ideally, build on the cultural fusion?

■ Who is responsible for planning and communicating the deal, promoting its benefits and establishing the identity and focus of the new business? How will they achieve this?

■ Is the leadership ready to make the decisions that will make or break the deal?

9   Developing a business strategy and thinking strategically

THE ABILITY TO PLAN AHEAD and succeed in the short term is essential. Thinking strategically enables managers to map the route to success as well as developing their skills of analysis and leadership. This chapter explains:

■ the essence of successful strategies;
■ how to develop a business strategy;
■ strategic thinking techniques.

Owners and managers can benefit from developing a business's strategy. It helps managers see where and how change is needed to make the business successful. It shows where it makes the most profits and how this can be continued and developed, for instance by changing the product mix, reallocating resources, reviewing prices or cutting costs. Above all, strategy enables the business to develop so that it can be more successful than its competitors at meeting its customers' needs.

The essence of successful strategies

Successful strategies:

■ Are flexible. This point was highlighted by one of the world's richest entrepreneurs, Warren Buffett, in his 1999 chairman's letter to Berkshire Hathaway's shareholders:

> Our carefully crafted acquisition strategy is simply to wait for the phone to ring. Happily, it sometimes does so, usually

because a manager who sold to us earlier has recommended to a friend that he think about following suit.

In his 1994 book *The Frontiers of Excellence*, Robert Waterman says:[1]

Strategies that succeed are organic. They evolve. They wrap themselves around problems, challenges, and opportunities, make progress and move on.

■ Guide the way people work and make decisions. A strategy has a trajectory; its future is linked to its past. This was recognised by Peter Drucker in his 1980 book *Managing in Turbulent Times*:[2]

Long-range planning does not deal with future decisions. It deals with the future of present decisions.

■ Constantly guide development of the business. A business without a strategy (or with a flawed one) is like a traveller without a map. This was recognised by Andy Grove, a former chairman and CEO of Intel, in his 1996 book *Only the Paranoid Survive: How to Exploit the Crisis Points That Challenge Every Company and Career*:[3]

A question that often comes up at times of strategic transformation is, should you pursue a highly focused approach, betting everything on one strategic goal, or should you hedge? ... Mark Twain hit it on the head when he said, "Put all of your eggs in one basket, and WATCH THAT BASKET."

■ Focus on customers. Philip Kotler, professor of international marketing at Kellogg School of Management, Northwestern University, commented:[4]

There is only one winning strategy. It is to carefully define the target market and direct a superior offering to that target market.

Michael Porter, writing in *Harvard Business Review*, said:[5]

Competitive strategy is about being different. It means deliberately choosing a different set of activities to deliver a unique mix of values.

■ Recognise that the journey is as important as the destination. Strategy is not simply the structure of a company's products and markets but also the way it works and the decisions it makes.

Strategies succeed by being simple and compelling, routinely guiding decisions. They are considered as well as aspirational; they are distinctive and play to a firm's strengths.

Strategic decisions are the keys to the future. They provide reassurance; they reduce sources of stress; they turn problems into opportunities; and they can create benefits out of very little. Too often they are given too little thought before they are made.

Developing a business strategy

The task of strategy is to make a business more valuable. This means moving it from A to B and guiding people clearly on how to make this journey.

The development of business strategy involves three distinct phases:

■ analysis;
■ planning;
■ implementation.

Analysis

When analysing a business's strategy there are no constantly right answers, but there are some constantly right questions. As the business and the business environment change, the best answers will change over time. The solution is to question rigorously, decide the best approach and then check the course of action through further questioning (see Table 9.1).

Analysis reveals much information. The next step is to extract the elements that will have the greatest effect on your strategy and then summarise and share them. A summary of strengths, weaknesses, opportunities and threats is a useful way to present this information.

TABLE 9.1 **Analysing a business strategy: issues and questions**

Issues to analyse	Questions to ask
Understand your market	
What opportunities and threats might you encounter? How might your market develop in the future (see Chapter 4)? Issues shaping strategy highlight some of the main considerations, and Chapter 5 outlines scenario planning.	What changes are affecting your customers and competitors? What are the trends and likely developments? What are customers' priorities and preferences? How will these affect your business?
Decide on your business	
Segment your business according to your customers and competition (see Chapter 14). Make sure the focus is on customers' needs.	What business are you in? How and why should the new plan differ from your previous approach? What would make your approach distinctive and competitive? What does the history of your business (and your market) teach you about the future?
Focus on profitability	
Analyse profitability by segment, by customer and by product. Where is money made, where is it spent and where are there opportunities to increase profitability? This will entail deciding the level of risk you are willing to accept. Managing finance and risk highlights techniques to meet this challenge (see Chapter 17).	Where does the business make or lose money? How can you improve profitability? How accurate were previous forecasts and plans? What did the business learn from these experiences? Where are your competitors most profitable? What would it require to double your growth rate and profits?

How strong is your competitive position?

Nothing highlights the dynamic nature of the market like customers and competitors. Take a close look at your competitors.

What are your competitive strengths and weaknesses?

How will you build on them?

Can you improve your monitoring of competitors?

Where will growth come from?

Which competitors do you admire and why?

Which of your competitors are admired and why?

Assess strengths and weaknesses

Understand what you do well, why you are successful and how you need to improve.

What skills, capabilities and resources underpin your success?

How can you play to your strengths?

How can you address areas of weakness?

Which resources and capabilities do you need to acquire, and how?

Understand your customers

What do customers think and what does that mean for the way you do business (see Chapter 14)?

What do customers want?

What are their needs and priorities?

How are your customers changing?

How can you encourage them to stay loyal, buy more, pay more or leave your competitors?

Can you target new groups of customers?

How well do they know your products and brand?

What do they think of you?

Innovate

Making progress is difficult without change, improvement and innovation. The challenge is to understand what can be done differently and better.

Where can you innovate in your business?

What innovations do customers want?

What would they value (even if they don't know it yet)?

How will you make innovations pay?

Can you prioritise potential innovations in terms of their ease, impact and return?

Planning

There are several stages in the strategy planning process, each relying on rigorous analysis:

- Define your purpose. Summarise where you are now, where you want to be and how you will change. People will want to know what the business will do and what they will be expected to do. Present a clear statement of goals as briefly as possible.

- Explain your advantage. People will want to understand how the business will succeed and what success will look like. Explain briefly why customers will buy from you rather than anyone else. These competitive advantages must be clear and convincing.

- Set the strategy's boundaries. Be clear about which products and markets you will deal in, and which you will not. Too many boundaries will make the strategy inflexible and cause frustration; too few boundaries will lead to a lack of focus.

- Prioritise. Emphasise the most profitable or significant products, customers and markets. Give employees specific responsibilities, objectives and resources so that the potential of these priorities can be realised. Encourage debate about priorities to foster focus and commitment, and regularly review the priorities as circumstances change.

- Budget. Recognising the financial requirements of a strategy is fundamental to its success. Estimate costs, revenues and the cash implications and prepare a budget to meet the strategic objectives. Measure results against the budget and make changes that will either maximise opportunities or take corrective action.

  Remember to:

- budget early and recognise that it is dangerous to prepare budgets without consulting widely;
- seek advice and communicate;
- include a cash flow forecast;
- be realistic;
- consider different scenarios;

- make sure that budgets are consistent with the business's plans as well as the present realities;
- act on the information provided by analysis of the budget;
- explain the process to gain commitment and focus attention.

Implementation
Integrating the strategy
The strategy needs to take account of the realities of the business. To succeed, it must be consistent with the work of other departments, the capabilities of employees and suppliers and the expectations of customers. The challenge is to avoid confusion or conflict.

Communicating
Clear communication is crucial in developing and implementing a strategy, but communication skills are often overlooked and leaders frequently forget they can always be improved to benefit the organisation and everyone within it.

Several techniques can help to develop skills as a trusted communicator:

- Watch the body language, both yours and theirs. Keeping eye contact shows trust and interest and observing posture indicates how people feel. Reflecting someone's body language sensitively helps to show you are listening.
- Ask questions not only to improve your understanding but also to test assumptions and show that you are listening. When asking questions, signal for attention to let the other person know that you want to comment. Respond to their point and allow them to pause and switch their attention to you before you speak.
- Summarise what you want to say at the start and finish by summarising what has been agreed. This helps to prevent misunderstandings.
- Be professional and control emotions. Do not interrupt, embarrass people or be rude. Even if you feel it is the only way

to make your point, consider whether it would undermine your position. Controlling emotions helps you stay in control.

■ Maintain trust and avoid rumours, misunderstandings and unnecessary complications by respecting confidences. Being critically aware when communicating requires:
  - reacting to ideas, not people;
  - focusing on the significance of the facts and evidence;
  - avoiding jumping to conclusions;
  - listening for how things are said and what is not said.

■ Be aware of people's concerns and reactions by fostering an honest and open environment. Even then, some people will still not say how they feel or what they think, or they may not be able to express themselves adequately. The leader needs to ask open, probing questions to indicate what the person is thinking.

Other crucial aspects of implementing strategy include:

■ Achieving short-term goals. Quick wins help to generate momentum, as well as demonstrating the strategy in action.

■ Agreeing clear objectives. They should be specific, measurable, achievable, relevant and time-constrained. People also need to be held personally accountable for achieving their objectives. This means setting milestones, agreeing limits of authority and discussing how best to proceed.

Successful implementation will also depend on:

■ testing aspects of the strategy;
■ coaching people so that they have the required skills and confidence;
■ making sure that people are motivated, engaged and committed to the strategy – for example, reward systems may need adjustments to encourage specific actions and behaviours;
■ assessing and monitoring the risks with new initiatives (see Chapter 17);
■ monitoring performance and reviewing operational targets.

How strategic thinking shaped Sony

The Sony story began in the 1950s when Akio Morita and Masaru Ibuka were introduced to the tape recorder. Japanese companies did not make them so they decided that tape recorders would be their first product. From the beginning, Sony's founders were more pioneering than traditional Japanese companies, developing their own machine and magnetic tape without outside help. Crucially, they were ambitious and they were willing to be unconventional.

Initially they thought their product would sell itself, but prospective customers said the price was too high. So Morita researched the market and realised that high-value items sell only if the consumer understands their value. As the public was not familiar with its product, Sony had to educate people about it. Morita realised that the fewer links in the chain of communication the better, so instead of relying on third parties for distribution, which was normal in Japan, Sony set up its own sales outlets.

Japan's economy was unstable so Sony realised that to offset regional and national business risks it needed to target international markets. Instead of dealing through trading companies, however, it set up its own marketing system.

Sony quickly improved its products' quality and reliability because defective products exported from Japan were expensive to repair. This also boosted its productivity and cut costs. While Western companies were choosing between product differentiation or competing on price, Sony was doing both simultaneously.

With sales increasing and its reputation growing, Sony began production outside Japan. In 1970 it opened its first colour television factory in the US in San Diego. Production facilities spread through the US, Europe, Brazil and Venezuela and Sony invested heavily in market development, creating a worldwide brand. The growing market share generated further process improvements and lower costs.

To exploit the investment in its brand, Sony developed a portfolio of products by putting together project teams. As Morita explained:

> We always have an image of how an ideal product would look and perform in our minds. This is not wishful thinking on our part, but a concrete plan for which exact product specifications have been drawn up, including a target price. Management then carefully selects and challenges a small taskforce, or design team, to produce a prototype with step-by-step creative engineering.

Sony launched the first home video recorder in 1964 and the solid-state condenser microphone in 1965. The Trinitron colour TV tube triggered a decade of explosive growth when it was introduced in 1968, and in 1979, Sony launched the Walkman personal stereo.

Morita gave the go-ahead to the Walkman design team, overriding objections from the sales and marketing departments, which were not convinced that a portable tape player would sell. After launching the Walkman, Sony immediately made improvements and introduced new versions, believing that since the prototypes had been developed, flexible marketing was all that was needed. With 85 Walkman models on offer, Sony took 40% of portable tape player sales in the US and 50% in Japan in the late 1980s.

By the end of the 1980s, Sony had become the world's leading consumer electronics company.

The company's strength and flexibility meant that it was able to withstand making significant mistakes. Sony's Betamax video system lost the battle to become the industry standard to Panasonic's VHS version; and the digital audiotape Sony launched in 1990 to rival the compact disc sold a fraction of what was planned and had to be retargeted to the professional market.

Faced with a rising yen and intensifying competition, Sony began to diversify beyond consumer electronics hardware. In the late 1980s, it bought CBS Records and Columbia Pictures Entertainment, two of the largest media companies in the US. Sony recognised the external factors shaping its industry, notably the international battle over high-definition TV standards, and decided that the music and the films themselves rather than the machines on which they were played offered the best route to future profitability. These high-risk takeovers took years to succeed and taught Sony the need to first lower the risk by forming media alliances when breaking into new markets.

That is how Sony entered the markets for semiconductors, home video games and laptop computers. It manufactured Apple's highly successful PowerBook and joined Intel to develop PC desktop systems. With Nintendo it created a games console with the graphic capabilities of a desktop computer, and when Nintendo pulled out, Sony introduced the PlayStation. By the end of the 1990s, Sony was challenging Nintendo and Sega as the leading producer of game computers, which are now its largest source of profits.

A flurry of other alliances and partnerships enabled Sony to expand its portfolio of low-cost options and hedge its bets against the uncertainties created by the fast-changing and increasingly overlapping consumer electronics, personal computer, software and media industries.

Sony's history illustrates the importance of achieving the right emphasis between evolutionary and revolutionary strategies and how the most profitable approach is determined by the level of uncertainty in the business environment. If it can be managed effectively, revolution such as an acquisition in a new sector may work. If it cannot, a cautious, evolutionary approach is preferable, emphasising internal improvements to quality and cost and the value of alliances.

Thinking strategically

Successful business strategists consistently:

- Solve problems and make decisions that are fast, reliable, informed, predictive, responsive and responsible; inevitably, this increases the likelihood of mistakes (see Chapter 18).

- Avoid subjective or irrational analysis. Flawed analysis can result from prejudice or being unduly influenced by the "halo" effect, where past successes blind people to current risks. It may be connected with false expectations or assumptions about behaviour or circumstances, or it may be a result of complacency, arrogance, laziness, tiredness or overwork.

- Are aware and sensitive. Not appreciating the sensitivity of a situation often undermines strategic thinking. Pressures of work, lack of time and too little or too much information are common reasons for not recognising important nuances. Communicating, trusting and empowering people as well as seeking and analysing information can help to develop and demonstrate awareness. Calculating in advance the consequences of decisions is also crucial. For example, under Lord Weinstock, GEC, a British manufacturing conglomerate, had a reputation for efficiency and increasing shareholder value and built up sizeable cash reserves. Shortly after Weinstock retired, the company altered its strategy to focus on the booming telecoms market. Failing to realise that the boom would be short-lived, GEC bought an equipment supplier, Marconi, at the top of the market and rebranded itself under that name. Almost immediately, the new group was hit by the effects of overcapacity and overvalued businesses and franchises. The share price fell by more than 80% because of insensitivity towards customers, employees and shareholders.

■ Establish clear priorities and objectives. People need to know what to do and how to do it, and to be given the skills and resources needed to do it successfully. Jean-Cyril Spinetta, who became chairman and CEO of Air France in 1997 and later chairman and CEO of Air France-KLM Group (he retired in 2013), guided Air France through the aftermath of the September 11th 2001 terrorist attacks in the US and the subsequent industry downturn. His strategy was to secure the airline's viability by emphasising cost control. To do this he stood firm against unions, reached partnership deals with suppliers and, eventually, allied Air France with KLM.

■ Foster creativity and innovation. It is crucial to develop an innovative and creative culture to help people adapt their thinking and decisions to new circumstances.

■ Understand substantive issues. Insufficient information or analysis or being overwhelmed by a difficult, sensitive or highly complex problem often means people waste time on smaller issues, rather than solving the big one. Work out what is happening – and why – what are its consequences and how the problem can be resolved.

■ Focus on the relevance and potential of the business idea. Many failing organisations focus inadequately on their markets, customers or products. Regular reviews of strategy and a forward-looking approach can counter these difficulties.

In his book *The Mind of the Strategist*, Japanese management consultant and theorist Kenichi Ohmae says:[6]

The strategist's method is very simply to challenge the prevailing assumptions with a single question: "Why?"

Key questions
About your business
- Who are your customers?
- Which markets do you serve?
- Do your customers have anything in common?
- Which products and services do you provide?
- What do customers value about your products and your business and brand generally?
- What are the main external threats, such as regulation or demographic change, affecting your business? How are they significant?
- What plans need to be put in place to address these issues? What are the opportunities and threats?
- What does your business do well? What do you need to improve, and how will this achieved?

Profitability
- Which are the most profitable activities now and over the period of the strategy?
- What are the financial goals?
- What is a challenging but realistic expectation for the business's profitability? How much money should the business make?

Resources
- What are the business's most important resources?
- How do your resources affect each other? For example, cash affects the ability to market a product, another resource, so that customers, a further resource, can be acquired and used to generate cash.
- Which resources are strengthening or accumulating, and which are weakening or draining away?

PART 3

Implementing strategy

10 Vision

PRESIDENT JOHN KENNEDY made a speech at Rice University in Houston, Texas, on September 12th 1962, in which he said:

> We choose to go to the moon in this decade and do the other things – not because they are easy but because they are hard. Because that goal will serve to organise and measure the best of our abilities and skills, because that challenge is one that we are willing to accept, one we are unwilling to postpone, and one which we intend to win.

Many of Kennedy's speeches contained stirring calls to action, such as the one in his inaugural address to "ask not what your country can do for you – ask what you can do for your country". Kennedy's objective was to inspire the American people. In business, leaders need to inspire those who work for their company or who have a stake in it. They must set out a vision that guides the business's strategy.

A clear and meaningful vision of the future to which a business is aspiring will help to engage people and unlock energy and commitment. It also guides actions and decisions at all levels of the organisation and helps to promote consistency of purpose so that everyone works towards the same goal.

It is often the case that managers focus on the immediate priorities of meeting customers' needs, resolving problems, managing and leading others. They may be effective at managing for today but unable to prepare for tomorrow. That is why at the heart of a leader's role is the ability to set the right course for a successful future and take people with you. This is likely to involve organisational change or, in some cases, transformation.

There are typically three distinct types of vision, each with a different purpose, value and characteristics. Clearly, using the right approach at the right time and being explicit about what you mean by "vision" is valuable but is often neglected by many managers and leaders.

TABLE 10.1 **Vision: purpose and value**

Type of vision	Purpose and value	Characteristics
Vision for the organisation (corporate vision)	Provides a clear direction and aspiration for the business Inspires and engages people Guides behaviour and decisions at all levels (providing a starting point for other business visions)	Inspiring and aspirational, clearly setting the direction, tone and priorities for the whole organisation as well as informing suppliers, customers and shareholders
Vision for a business unit, department or team	Provides a clear, guiding direction for the business unit, department or team Supports the overall vision by translating it into a realistic aspiration for the smaller team, sustaining commitment and energy	Inspiring and directly relevant to the work of the team, it engages and mobilises people so they work together, contributing to the overall success of the business
Vision for a specific task or outcome	Provides a clear focus for action in a specific area or for a particular task Used when delegating, or when forming or re-forming a team	Guides the way that the task or role is approached, providing a clear view of what success will look like

Guiding visions at work

Vision of a specific task or outcome

In 1935 Allen Lane, a British publisher, was returning from visiting Agatha Christie, an author, in Devon. He was looking for something to read on his journey back to London, but found only popular magazines and reprints of Victorian novels at the station. This triggered the idea that good-quality contemporary fiction should be made available cheaply and sold not just in traditional bookshops, but also in railway stations and chain stores. Paperbacks were available then, but poor production often mirrored the quality between the covers. From Lane's experience, the vision of the popular paperback was born and used to guide the development of Penguin as an inventive, mass-market publisher. The first Penguin paperbacks appeared in 1935 and included works by Ernest Hemingway, André Maurois and Agatha Christie. They were colour coded (orange for fiction, blue for biography, green for crime) and cost just sixpence, the same price as a packet of cigarettes. The paperback revolution had begun.

A corporate vision

An example of the power of a corporate vision is provided by HSBC. Within ten years, it moved from being an established mid-range bank operating predominantly in Asia to the world's second largest financial services corporation. In the 2014 strongest global brand survey by Interbrand, an international branding consultancy, it was ranked 33rd, despite the worldwide reaction against banks for their perceived role in causing the economic recession from 2008 to 2013. There are many reasons for the rapid development of this long-established bank, but foremost among them is the direction set by successive chairmen Sir John Bond and Stephen Green in the early 2000s.

HSBC'S vision is "To be the world's leading financial services company". This vision and the strategy to achieve it were set out for employees, shareholders and analysts in "Managing for Growth", which highlights how the vision will be achieved. Selected extracts are as follows:

> At HSBC we aim to be the world's leading financial services company.
>
> "Leading" means being preferred, admired and dynamic. It also means being recognised for giving the customer a fair deal, and developing a leadership position in each of our markets.
>
> There are several other responsibilities that we all share if we are to become the world's leading financial services company. These include: meeting the challenges of corporate governance, recognising our corporate and social responsibilities and focusing our philanthropic activities on education and environmental initiatives.

Also, customers and staff must be aware of our core values. These include: maintaining long-term, ethical client relationships; increasing productivity by improving team work; setting and achieving high standards, and developing our international character and prudent orientation.

The characteristics of a compelling vision

People respond best when they understand what they are doing and why they are doing it. An effective vision is convincing, realistic and powerful enough to excite and inspire. It encapsulates a set of values that will guide decisions and action. It is also easy to explain to everyone, specific enough to provide guidance for decision-making and flexible enough to allow for individual initiative as well as changing conditions.

Developing a guiding vision

Some leaders adopt a consensus approach to formulating a decision. Others make their own (hopefully informed) judgment of what it should be. There is no single way to develop visionary thinking, but the following actions will help you to get started:

- Decide for yourself what will be important in the future.
- Trust your intuition. If you feel that a situation is changing or if you have an idea that makes sense to you, explore it further.
- Test your assumptions. Insights do not readily come from old information, so look for trends and try to understand why things are changing, not just how.
- Get people to understand and support the vision.
- Remember that progressive visions are powerful, communicable, desirable, realistic, focused and flexible.

Communicating the vision

When communicating the vision, powerful, emotive but simple language is the most effective. Less is normally more and without clarity and succinctness the attention of the audience will be lost.

President Kennedy and his speechwriter, Ted Sorensen, also used various devices to reinforce the message.[1] One is known as the "reversible raincoat", which is also used by those such as Bill Clinton and Barack Obama. An example of this is the phrase: "Let us never negotiate out of fear but let us never fear to negotiate." The same words are reversed and reused for effect. Kennedy also organised his words to simplify, clarify and emphasise, recognising the need to have a coherent and consistent theme that listeners find easy to follow.

Kennedy also understood the need to use language that is elevated but not grandiose. According to Sorensen, Kennedy believed in elevating the sights of his listeners ("We choose to go to the moon") while keeping his language as simple as possible. He kept his sentences short and his words comprehensible. He understood the importance of avoiding terms so esoteric they could not be understood easily by the average listener.

Lastly, a vision needs to deliver substantive ideas. In Sorensen's view:

> A great speech is great because of the strong ideas conveyed. If the words are soaring, beautiful, eloquent, it is still not a great speech if the ideas are flat, empty, or mean-spirited. The effectiveness of your message will ultimately rest on the power of your ideas.

Using the vision

The vision needs to guide actions and plans across the organisation and at all levels, and leaders must demonstrate that it is guiding their actions and decisions. What matters most is that acting in accord with the vision produces results that will help see off the sceptics and get everyone committed to it.

Getting commitment to the vision

Obtaining commitment to the vision involves:

■ explaining the context and the vision so that people know what it is and what it means;

- getting people to understand why the vision is important to both the organisation and themselves;
- making people believe the vision is attainable – as stated above, it will make a big difference if it is seen to be producing results;
- making people believe it will be attained. To do this it helps to lay down a route map with milestones so that everyone can see the way ahead. It also helps to celebrate when milestones are achieved.

Avoiding pitfalls

The vision needs to be flexible and capable of coping with changing circumstances. When developing a vision, questions to ask include:

- What are the weaknesses with this approach?
- What are others doing and how is the situation likely to alter over time?
- Are the people involved prepared (in terms of attitude) and skilled (in terms of ability) to react to changing circumstances? How can this be measured? What remedial action might be needed?
- What may prevent the vision from being achieved?
- How will the organisation minimise the risks that could threaten the vision and how will it deal with unforeseen problems?

Key questions

- Do the business strategy and vision reinforce each other? In particular, does the vision help to generate commitment and engage people with the strategy?
- Is the vision relevant, continuing to guide people's thinking given emerging trends and changing events? Does the vision anticipate a broad range of changes in the business environment (including the market, economic, sociological, technological and regulatory environment)? Have you evaluated the impact of these factors on your business?

- Do people support the vision and use it to guide their actions?
- Is the vision compelling and engaging?
- Does everyone understand the vision – what it is and why it matters? Are there practical examples of how the vision can guide people's work?
- Is the vision sufficiently different and stretching – even audacious? Is it sustainable and will it bring major success?
- What are the principal milestones or steps that need to be taken to help people move towards the vision?

11 Leading people through change

THE CHALLENGES OF IMPLEMENTING business strategy and leading people through changing, turbulent times raise two crucial questions:

- What are the lessons from the changes of the past 20 years in general and the past decade in particular?
- How can a successful strategy be implemented and sustained?

Leadership lessons in an era of volatility and change

There is a fortune to be made (or at least not lost) by the person or corporation that answers the question of how to thrive in times of complexity, volatility and change. So, unsurprisingly, many have tried. The best answers, described briefly below, appear consistently and display common sense.

Avoid active inertia

Donald Sull, author of *Revival of the Fittest*,[1] believes managers become trapped by success, a condition he calls "active inertia". This occurs when managers respond to disruptive changes by repeating (and usually accelerating) activities that succeeded in the past. This often results in the firm digging itself further into a hole.

Active inertia can be overcome by focusing on changing, even transforming a business's strategy – and consequently its processes and priorities and its values and commitments. However, such a change or transformation is not without risks: making it work depends

FIG 11.1 **How active inertia works**

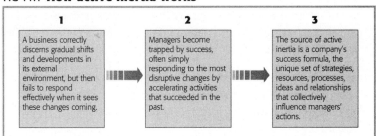

on a company's financial security, competitors' likely responses and management ability.

To understand the extent to which an organisation is at risk from active inertia, two questions need answering:

- Could external developments threaten the core business?
- Is there a better alternative to the status quo?

Understand the limits of current success

Managers and other employees become used to operating within a specific frame of reference, using a formula that is familiar and has worked well in the past and has become embedded. This is fine in a stable environment, but when the external competitive environment changes, strengths can become weaknesses and assets can become liabilities. For example, Xerox's expensive sales force had been a major asset until the market shifted and customers started buying copiers direct from office-equipment suppliers. Similarly, the focus on centralised corporate print departments blinded Xerox to the possibilities for departmental copying and the potential for emergence of the smaller business market.

Recognise that revolutions fail, flywheels succeed

In *Good to Great*,[2] Jim Collins argues that dramatic change-management programmes and restructurings may save the day, but they do little to sustain or develop success. There is no single action that can achieve this. Collins likens the process to relentlessly pushing a heavy flywheel in one direction, steadily building up momentum until a breakthrough is achieved. No single push makes the breakthrough; success comes from the cumulative effort. Collins's research shows that:

- moving from good to great is a cumulative process – it happens step by step, action by action, and leads to sustained and spectacular results;
- good-to-great companies have no name for their transformations – there is no launch event, no tag line, no programmatic change, no miracle moment;
- a process of continuous improvement coupled with achieving tangible results helps companies to transform; people can see and feel the build-up of momentum and their resulting enthusiasm helps sustain the process;
- great companies artfully manage the process of changing, gaining commitment from employees without having to emphasise it; under the right conditions, the problems of commitment, motivation and resistance to change melt away.

Deal with difficulties

Managers must maintain unwavering faith that they will prevail regardless of the difficulties, and at the same time have the discipline to deal with and not ignore or underestimate any tough realities they face.

Keep in touch with reality

Among the causes of decline is an inability to understand or adapt to change. In retrospect, people identify changes that passed unnoticed at the time. Typical examples include new products and new substitutes arriving; changes in product technology, demography, income distribution and fashion; and a cyclical fall in demand that was not taken seriously. The most significant sources of change were highlighted in Chapter 4. Any organisation must answer the question: what are the most significant changes affecting us?

Develop a culture of discipline

All organisations have a culture, some have discipline, but only a few have a culture of discipline. This matters because, for example, people who think and act in a disciplined way do not need hierarchy or bureaucracy, and when discipline is combined with entrepreneurship it is more likely to lead to great performance. Often, companies that excel in stable markets struggle in turbulent ones. Sull notes an example in the steel industry. Lakshmi Mittal established a steel mill in India in the 1970s and thrived by selling in the most turbulent markets he could find – such as Kazakhstan, Mexico and Indonesia – where his competitors found it difficult to operate.

Develop peripheral vision

For everyone – from start-ups to established corporations – opportunities and threats often begin as weak murmurs in markets. In their book *Peripheral Vision*, George Day and Paul Schoemaker explain how to stay aware and cope with turbulence.[3] They believe that what determines success is peripheral vision, and in their research they found that less than 20% of firms have developed it sufficiently to remain competitive. Developing peripheral vision is a crucial step in building a vigilant organisation, one that is constantly aware of changes in the environment. Their point is illustrated through a number of case studies, including how the BBC dealt with the digital challenge, Anheuser-Busch's early response to the low-carb diet revolution, Mattel's struggles with its Barbie franchise and lighting manufacturers' strategies for addressing the threat from LED technologies.

Day and Schoemaker explain that vigilant organisations win by using the following techniques:

- setting the right scope;
- using different ways to scan their environment;
- avoiding common traps;
- knowing when and how to probe;
- understanding how to act proactively.

Most people have selective vision, seeing only what they hope to see. This means that there is a vigilance gap, a failure of both individuals and organisations to act on weak signals from the periphery before it is too late. This echoes the view of Peter Drucker, who said: "There is surely nothing quite so useless as doing with great efficiency what should not be done at all." Day and Paul Schoemaker then explain the value of a "strategic eye exam", an approach that helps readers to audit their peripheral vision.

The global financial crisis of 2008 was not caused by subprime mortgages, credit default swaps, or failed economic policies, but by a failure of leadership. New and increasing regulation cannot heal wounds created by leadership failure.

Provide leadership – especially during times of crisis

Bill George, in his book *Seven Lessons of Leading in a Crisis*,[4] argues that there are several lessons leaders should learn from the latest recession:

- Face reality – which starts with those in charge acknowledging their role in creating problems that have to be solved. Widespread recognition of reality, even if painful, is crucial before problems can be solved. Myopia suffocates organisations' ability to respond to emerging threats and opportunities. As Jamie Dimon, chief executive of JPMorgan Chase, comments:

  It's not sufficient to have one person on your team who is a truth teller. Everyone on the team must be candid in sharing the entire truth, no matter how painful it is.

  How can we solve problems, if we don't acknowledge they exist?

- No matter how bad things are, they will get worse. Faced with bad news, many leaders cannot believe that things are really so grim, and they try to convince the bearers of bad news of this. They think that swift action will make the problems go away and underestimate the work needed. It is far better for leaders to anticipate the worst.

- Build a mountain of cash and get to the highest hill. In good times, leaders worry more about earnings per share and revenue growth than about their balance sheets. In a crisis, cash is king. The main question in a period of volatility is: does your organisation have sufficient cash to survive in the direst circumstances?

- Get the world off your shoulders. In a crisis, many leaders act like Atlas, carrying the weight of the world on their shoulders. They think they can solve the problem themselves. In reality, they need everyone's help to devise and execute solutions.

- Before asking others to sacrifice, volunteer yourself. If there are sacrifices to be made, leaders themselves should make the greatest ones. People are watching to see what their leaders do, so if leaders want others to get on board, they must be willing to lead by example.

- Never waste a good crisis. This adage is attributed to Benjamin Netanyahu, an Israeli politician. When things are going well, people resist major changes or try to get by with minor adaptations. A crisis provides the leader with the opportunity to foster change.

- Be aggressive in the marketplace. This may sound counter-intuitive, but a crisis offers an excellent opportunity to gain market share by finding new strategies to boost profitability. Many people look at a crisis as something to get through before going back to business as usual. But business as usual never returns because markets are irrevocably changed – that is the difference between turbulence and uncertainty. It is better to create the changes that move the market in your favour, rather than waiting and reacting to the changes as they take place.

Overall, George argues:

Optimistic, forward-thinking leaders are sitting on a rare opportunity, and they must be systematic in how they take advantage of it if they want to make positive changes.

Another valuable, proven perspective on managing in turbulent times is provided by Andy Grove, a former CEO and chairman of Intel, one of the world's leading manufacturers of computer chips and a driving force behind the technological revolution of the late 20th century. In his book *Only the Paranoid Survive*,[5] Grove describes the lessons learnt from building a profitable firm in a market characterised by disruptive innovation and turbulence.

He highlights the concept of a "strategic inflection point", a time in the life of a business or project when its fundamental situation is changing significantly. The term "point" can be confusing, as it may be a longer event. It is important to distinguish between change and a strategic inflection point. Change is routine; in contrast, strategic inflection points are seismic events, and Grove provides a framework for determining whether one is near. A useful technique is to consider who the main competitors are. If this is unclear, it may be a sign the marketplace is approaching an inflection point. Does the company that dominated in the past suddenly seem less important? Does it look as though another company is about to eclipse it? This may be a sign of a shifting balance of power. Similarly, Grove calls for a major rethink when one of the competitive forces in an industry changes and becomes a "10x change": that is, it has become ten times what it once was. In a 10x change a company can lose competitive advantage and there is an opportunity for outsiders to enter the market.

21st-century leadership

What is leadership? The answers to this deceptively simple question vary widely. Although the most significant aspects of leadership may be disputed, one fact is clear: leadership is an essential skill for anyone developing or implementing a business strategy. It is important, therefore, to understand how to lead people so that they achieve the strategy. There may be differences in emphasis and priority, but there is a consensus on the essentials of leading people.

A study of several surveys conducted in North America and Europe found that successful leaders tend to share a broad range of characteristics. This has been confirmed by successive pieces of research from business schools (such as IMD), professional institutions (such as the UK Chartered Institute of Personnel and Development), business consultancies (such as McKinsey) and writers.[6] These include:

- determination combined with drive and a strong desire for achievement and results;
- a general curiosity and desire to learn, together with an ability to learn from adversity;
- an entrepreneurial, opportunity-spotting spirit, capable of taking chances when they come along.

Other personal qualities of leaders include:

- strong self-control and moderate risk-taking;
- a well-integrated set of values, including integrity, independence, initiative, empathy, affinity for people and ability to inspire trust;
- clear personal and work objectives and a well-organised approach;
- a high degree of dedication and motivation for the work itself rather than external rewards;
- a positive, pragmatic and successful approach to problem solving and decision-making – someone who tries to improve and is not afraid to make a considered decision;
- strong people skills – notably the ability to communicate and influence;
- awareness at three levels – self-awareness, an understanding of the immediate situation, and an appreciation of the wider environment;
- a high degree of innovative ability;
- a strong sense of purpose and vision.

These characteristics provide a sound basis to start considering the essentials of leading and implementing a strategy. Whatever you think of them, they show the importance of one underlying issue: attitude. Leaders have something within them – usually their attitude – that encourages and engages others. Ask yourself one question: why should anyone be led by you? When you come up with a convincing answer, you will have the confidence and attitude to lead.

Leadership is universally valued, but there are several skills that are essential for senior managers who are developing strategy or making strategic decisions. These include the ability to:

- coach people and help them develop their skills;
- engage with people and encourage them and others to change;
- inspire trust;
- delegate;
- innovate;
- solve problems;
- make decisions.

Coach

To help individuals understand and implement the strategy requires coaching skills. There are four main phases:

- Goals – setting goals for both the overall coaching relationship and the individual session.
- Reality – exploring the current position of the learner, the reality of their circumstances and their concerns.
- Options – generating strategies, action plans and options for achieving goals.
- Will/what – deciding what is to be done, by whom, how and when, and ensuring there is the will to succeed.

This is known as the GROW model, and the central element is that responsibility for setting the goals lies with the learner. Goals set by others are more likely to be wrong, inappropriate, too high or too low, and to lack the commitment of the learner. The main objective of the coach is to help the learner, mainly through a questioning approach rather than instruction or reminiscence. The goals established should cover both the long term (what the learner hopes to achieve in the next 12 months) and the short term (what can be achieved in the current session).

Questioning is central to coaching and it can also be used for self-coaching. To resolve any issue, ask:

- What am I trying to achieve?
- How will I know when I have achieved it?
- Is the goal specific and measurable?
- To what extent can I control the result? What sort of things won't I have control over?
- Will achieving the goal stretch or break me?
- When do I want to achieve the goal?
- What are the milestones or key points on the way to achieving my goal?
- Who is involved, and what effect could they have on the situation?
- What have I done about this situation so far, and what have been the results?
- What are the major constraints in finding a way forward?
- Are these constraints major or minor? How could their effect be reduced?
- What other issues are there at work that might affect my goal?
- What options do I have?
- If I had unlimited resources, what options would I have?
- Can I link my goal to some other organisational issue?
- What would be the perfect solution?
- What will I do to ensure success? (Be as specific and detailed as possible, and give commitments.)

Inspire trust

Trust is fundamental because the task of a leader is to work through others, enabling and empowering them to help develop or implement the strategy and succeed. This can occur only if there is trust. Good communication establishes and builds trust with colleagues, customers and other stakeholders. Trust is essential to a leader's credibility, so it is useful to know what attributes people look for when deciding to trust someone. Research among employees in Europe, the US and Asia found that the most common attributes are:[7]

- fairness;
- dependability;
- respect;
- openness;
- courage;
- unselfishness;
- competence;
- supportiveness;
- empathy;
- compassion.

Understanding and delivering these qualities is crucial if trust is to be developed and maintained. How will you build trust? How will you establish credibility? How well do you display the qualities of a trusted leader?

TABLE 11.1 **Characteristics of a trustworthy leader**

Characteristics of trustworthiness	Signs of untrustworthiness
Always displays the highest standards of behaviour, and encourages this in others	Often compromises personal integrity and ethical behaviour (for example, when placed under pressure)
Builds and inspires the confidence of all stakeholders	Infrequently takes steps to build and maintain the trust of stakeholders
Acts as a role model for corporate values	Occasionally contradicts colleagues and corporate values
Behaves fairly and consistently, and makes sure this underpins business conduct	Occasionally behaves unreasonably, inconsistently or with a lack of respect
Resolves issues positively and with integrity, and encourages trust between the business and stakeholders	Occasionally undermines trust

Show moral courage

Leadership is synonymous with consistency and moral courage. Although this may mean different things to people at different times, it implies an ability to do and say what you mean, especially when facing adversity. Moral courage also requires a capacity to take risks, to be constant and determined, to admit mistakes and to stand alone when necessary. Courage is a universally respected quality; even if we do not agree with a particular idea or approach, we admire bravery and associated qualities of integrity, conviction and determination. Moral courage – the courage of our convictions – is present in those we choose to trust.

Develop emotional intelligence

Emotional intelligence (EI) is the ability to understand your own emotions and the emotions of others, and then apply that knowledge to be more successful and fulfilled. This is important when getting people to change (the process of leading change) and ensuring that employees understand and actively support the strategy.

Daniel Goleman, a psychologist and writer, popularised his view of emotional intelligence in his book *Emotional Intelligence: Why It Can Matter More Than IQ*.[8] Building on the work of two EI researchers, Howard Gardner and Peter Salovey, Goleman proposed that EI can be observed in five areas:

- knowing your emotions;
- managing emotions;
- motivating others;
- recognising emotions in others;
- handling relationships.

He recognised that emotions are critical in determining a leader's success. In times of change, pressure or crisis, the leaders who possess superior EI have the edge. This is because success is achieved by being able to recognise, understand and deal appropriately with the emotions that we experience. For example, we may all feel anger but EI enables us to know what to do with it to achieve the best possible outcome. EI is valuable because it enables us to sense and use emotions. It helps us to manage ourselves and achieve positive outcomes in our relationships with others, in handling situations and when making decisions.

Emotional intelligence can be learnt. Each of the five areas listed above highlights aspects of EI that are essential to leading people successfully:

- Knowing your emotions, or self-awareness. Although our emotions and moods run in parallel to our thoughts, we rarely pay sufficient attention to the way we feel and the impact of those emotions. This is significant because previous emotional experiences provide a context for our decision-making and will, therefore, affect the decisions we make.

- Managing emotions. Effective leaders learn to manage their emotions, especially the big three – anger, anxiety and sadness. Managing emotions is a decisive leadership skill.

- Motivating others. To motivate others, leaders need to know how to create a supportive, enthusiastic environment; to be sensitive to the issues that affect the enthusiasm of others; and to provide the right approach to move and guide people in the right direction.

- Recognising emotions in others, or showing empathy. As well as being self-aware, it is important to develop the ability to understand emotions in others and act accordingly.

- Handling relationships, or staying connected. Emotions are contagious. There is an unseen emotional transaction between people in every interaction, making them feel either a little better or a little worse. Goleman refers to this as a "secret economy", and argues that it is crucial in motivating people.

Goleman believes that these emotional areas build on each other in a hierarchy. At the bottom is the ability to identify one's emotional state; then knowledge of each emotion is needed to move to the next level.

Develop self-awareness

The isolation of a leader's role makes it easy to lose objectivity. Decisions may need to be made with insufficient information, and poor decisions are more likely if leaders lack insight into their own reactions. To guard against this, you should develop self-awareness. This can be done through, for example, using structured self-assessment, setting time aside to reflect on what is happening and your reactions, or using a coach to help analyse the reality of the situation.

There are three potential pitfalls when assessing your own skills and behaviour (as well as improving your own self-awareness, this will allow you to help others overcome them):

- Regarding a personal failing as a situational problem. Even experienced leaders may believe that problems are a result of a situation rather than a consequence of their own inaction or failure. Attempting to resolve a situational problem is seen as more acceptable than overcoming a personal shortcoming, so this is where many people focus, blaming the situation rather than themselves. This is a mistake and will perpetuate the problem. To avoid this pitfall, ask: do these difficulties result from the situation or from my attitudes and approach? If the answer to this is to be of any use, strive to be ruthlessly honest, methodical and analytical.

- Avoiding the new and unfamiliar. Leaders, especially when they are new to a role, are often attracted to tasks they are comfortable with, avoiding those in unfamiliar areas. This may result in opportunities being missed simply because they are outside a leader's comfort zone. What matters is tackling the right issues, not simply acting.

- Suppressing doubts and acting with certainty. A frequent response to the demands of a new or challenging situation is to suppress doubts and uncertainties by acting with certainty and in a commanding manner. Although it is important to project a confident image, the need to be seen to be in control can lead leaders to suppress their opinions, resulting in weak or flawed decisions.

It is also possible to develop self-awareness by focusing on four specific areas:

- Learning. What are your priorities for learning? How are you learning? Is the balance between learning technical and leadership skills appropriate?

- Influence. How well are you influencing the groups of people, internally and externally, that are most influential when it comes to the business strategy? What coalitions do you most need to build?

- Execution. What progress have you made in assessing priorities, opportunities and challenges – and in advancing them?

- Self-management. Have style issues been a problem? If so, what can you do about it? Are you using advice effectively?

Adopt the seven habits of highly effective people

In his book *The Seven Habits of Highly Effective People*, Stephen Covey outlined a set of activities and attitudes that promote good leadership skills:[9]

1. **Be proactive.** This means being determined and working as hard as possible to find the best approach to a situation – for example, the best way to implement a specific aspect of the strategy. It is important that you control your environment rather than it controlling you.

2. **Begin with the end in mind.** This is essential for personal success and when leading others. To achieve your strategy, keep in mind the big picture – the end result – so that you do not get drawn down different paths and go off on distracting tangents.

3. **Put first things first.** To achieve your strategy, concentrate only on those activities that are most relevant. This will help you avoid distractions and be more productive and successful.

4. **Think win-win.** Leadership requires good interpersonal skills, as achievements often depend on the co-operation of others. Covey argues that win-win is based on several assumptions – there are enough resources for everyone to benefit, business is not a zero-sum game, and success tends to follow a co-operative approach rather than the confrontation of win-or-lose.

5. **Seek to understand first and then seek to be understood.** This is a powerful tool. Covey argues that for good communication you need to "diagnose before you prescribe".

6. **Synergise.** Not a great word, but Covey's point is that leaders need to understand how to co-operate creatively. Based on the principle of the whole being greater than the sum of the parts, creative co-operation uses each person's strengths to achieve a desired outcome. Covey argues that creative co-operation requires us to see both the good and the potential in the other person's contribution.

7. **Sharpen the saw, or self-renewal.** Self-renewal (or continuous learning and development) strengthens the other habits. Covey divides the self into four parts – spiritual, mental, physical and social/emotional – all of which should be developed to become a highly effective leader.

The seven habits are a simple set of rules for good leadership. Although interrelated and mutually supportive, each one is powerful and worth adopting in its own right.

Convey a clear vision

People respond best when they understand what they are doing and why they are doing it. A decisive leader must create and communicate a convincing vision for the business and a strategy that can be sustained through good times and bad. Not only does this inspire, but it also provides a clear focus on a desired outcome, as well as building confidence, teamwork and consistency.

Provide security and support

Although it is always worth considering contingency measures and fallback positions, it is important to remain committed to a decision or strategy. Successful leaders give people a sense of security and support; and for people to succeed a certain level of support is essential. Commitment, enthusiasm and success usually engender support, as people respond well to the infectious nature of enthusiasm.

Be open and guide people

People value open and honest discussions based on mutual trust. This is especially true during difficult or challenging times. Differences or varying views about the strategy should be openly discussed. Honesty and integrity are essential to effective leadership.

Moreover, progress cannot be achieved without guidance and control. Once the vision and strategy are clearly defined and implementation has started, controls are needed to monitor progress towards achieving the objectives. Guidance and a measure of control are indispensable parts of empowerment, as people need specific roles and responsibilities, as well as a clear vision and clear objectives.

Ruthlessly prioritise

One of the first leadership challenges when developing and implementing strategy is to prioritise. It is essential to set priorities and remove distractions so that people can get on with serving customers, thus increasing profits and the value of the business. Invariably, tough action is needed to make things happen and this can sometimes interfere with other priorities the business may have. The only way forward is to be ruthless about setting priorities. To do this, ask:

- What are the current priorities?
- What should be the priorities, goals and objectives for the business, the team, your direct reports and yourself? (It may help to ask this question for short-term and longer-term goals.)
- What needs to change?
- Are these end goals (objectives) or performance goals (continuing aims)? For example, "we will sell x units of our new product in the first year" is an end goal; "we will develop a coaching culture where people routinely receive feedback and support" is a performance goal.

Build collaboration

Another challenging task is to deal with the tensions caused by handling multiple goals. For example, moving out of a downturn may involve balancing long-term strategy with decisions needed to benefit customers and the business today. Such challenges are not incompatible but they are demanding, so collaboration – especially mutual support, consistency and sharing best practices – is crucial.

Working collaboratively can be achieved by managing the five Ms:

- Meaning – make sure that there is a shared understanding, passion and sense of purpose, with everyone in the business working in the same direction.
- Mindset – make sure that everyone understands and makes the changes in behaviour that are needed.
- Mobilising – find out about, and develop, the resources your business needs to achieve its strategy.
- Measurement – use measurements to assess and drive performance at the individual, team and organisational level. These should focus on achieving future goals, not simply measuring against past performance.
- Mechanisms for renewal – avoid complacency and make sure that performance continually improves and momentum is maintained. The best way to do this is by consulting and communicating well with colleagues.

Ignore the myths of leadership

It is important to ignore the myths of leadership. There are several that are particularly flawed and counter-productive:

- Leadership is a rare skill. This is untrue, as almost everyone has leadership potential. Leadership abilities and opportunities are within the reach of most people.
- Leaders are charismatic. Some are, some are not. There may be times when charisma helps, but it is not a prerequisite for strong leadership.
- Leadership exists only at the top of an organisation. This is also untrue. Leaders at the top may have a broader span of control and authority, but managers further down the hierarchy also have their teams and goals. Arguably, the most significant leaders are those in the middle of an organisation or those

dealing with customers, as it is their decisions that determine an organisation's success.

■ The leader controls and directs. This is a common misconception. The challenge in leadership is not the exercise of power but rather the empowerment of others. Leaders work with and through people; they succeed by engaging and inspiring, not by dictating. The best leaders enable people to use their own initiative, experience and individual skills.

■ Leaders have permanent teams. Increasingly, leaders are in charge of a temporary team for a specific project or activity. When this is completed the leader moves on to another task and role, not necessarily that of leader. This makes leading more complex and changeable, and means that effective leadership skills are essential for success.

Developing your leadership style

Leadership requires an understanding of your own style: how you behave and the implications for others around you, both inside and outside the organisation.

Leadership style is situational, and you should adjust your style to match each specific challenge. For example, an approach that works well with one group of people may not work well with a different group. Deciding which approach is best involves taking into account:

■ the kind of people you are managing;
■ the type of tasks they are completing.

Once these have been assessed you will have a better understanding of which leadership style is suitable. Different styles are appropriate at different times, as outlined in Table 11.2.

Strategic decision-making relies on using the right leadership style at the right time. This situational leadership draws on four management styles: directing, coaching, supporting and delegating. What matters is adapting your approach to suit each situation.

Each style is effective at different times. A directional approach is most appropriate when the leader needs to tell people what to do, perhaps in a crisis or when dealing with difficult personnel issues.

TABLE 11.2 **Management styles**

Management style	Characteristics
Directing (telling)	
Structure Control and supervise One-way communication	This approach is effective when the team is new, temporary or forming. The leader is hands-on, decisive and involved with the needs of the task and the team, directing the team and stressing the importance of tasks and deadlines
Coaching (engaging)	
Direct and support Teach skills	This style is often preferred when the team has worked together for some time and has developed understanding and expertise. It works when a balance is needed between short- and long-term aspects. The leader needs to monitor the achievement of targets, but longer-term elements, such as communication networks and decision-making processes, are also important
Supporting (developing)	
Praise, listen and facilitate development	This is suitable when a team continues to function well. The leader has delegated and empowered staff and is no longer involved in short-term performance and operational measures. The longer term is more important, with the leader focusing on individual and team development, planning and innovation
Delegating (hands-off facilitation)	
Delegate responsibility for routine decisions	This hands-off style works best with a highly experienced, successful team which functions well with little involvement from the leader. The leadership role is often to work externally for the team, developing networks, gaining resources, sharing best practice and expertise. The leader may intervene in the team, if requested, to help define problems and devise solutions or if a problem arises

These characteristics are based on the theory of situational leadership developed by Paul Hersey and Ken Blanchard.

This should be used only in exceptional circumstances. Delegating, supporting and coaching styles can be seen as a democratic approach, with the leader seeking consensus and engaging the team. This works best when you need to get your team to commit to a course of action.

Developing empathy

Leaders need to understand the feelings of others if they are to influence and engage with them. This is especially important with team members, as empathy enables the leader to get people to work productively and realise their potential. It also ensures that the leader stays in touch with developments and does not become isolated; this is crucial if the leader's decisions and actions are to work. Empathy underpins activities such as innovating, setting strategy and leading change. It is generated simply through thinking of others – but this is not easy or routine for everyone. Empathy can be enhanced by asking:

- How do you feel about this?
- How might that person or group react, and why?

Taking personal responsibility

The greatest leaders are characterised by a restless desire to learn, develop and improve. This keeps their skills and outlook current, relevant and flexible. Closely linked is the fact that leaders need to take personal responsibility for delivering the strategy. It is clear that the business environment and prevailing conditions, including the effectiveness of team members, are likely to change. The solution is to be engaged, positive and constructive, finding ways to manage the situation to achieve the results you want by:

- understanding reality;
- remaining open, flexible and determined;
- working through others.

Decision-making and problem solving

A defining skill of any leader is the ability to make strategic decisions: judgments that balance a rational approach with intuition. In other words, it is necessary sometimes to use analysis and hard data and sometimes to use personal perception and judgment. Both are valuable; what matters is knowing when to use a specific approach.

Steps in the decision-making process are as follows:

- Assess the situation. Start by asking whether the decision relates to a permanent, underlying or structural issue or whether it is the result of a one-off event. Some decisions are generic and are best addressed with a consistent rule or principle, whereas others are best resolved when they arise. Of course, what may appear to be an isolated event may be an early indicator of a generic problem. Product-quality problems usually fall into this category, with a specific failure traced back to a faulty process or poor morale.

- Define the critical issues. These include understanding who is affected, likely developments, the timescale involved and sensitive issues, as well as previous, comparable situations. It is important to focus on all the relevant issues; a partial analysis is almost as bad as no analysis at all, as it can lead to ill-founded overconfidence in the decision. A useful technique is "funnelling", which involves collecting as much information and data as possible and prioritising and eliminating themes to clarify a few critical issues.

- Define what the decision needs to achieve. Every decision should have a minimum set of goals – rules to comply with, a timescale for completion and a method of execution. Working through these will allow you to implement your final decision. Potential conflicts need to be clearly monitored and resolved.

- Make the decision. Decisions often involve compromise – sometimes the ideal solution is simply not attainable. Always have a clear view of the ideal decision and test it. If compromise is necessary, make sure it is made positively, with a clear focus on what needs to be achieved.

- Implement the decision. This is usually the most time-consuming and critical phase. You should understand the activities required and clearly assign responsibility for individual tasks. You should also communicate with the right people and manage resources, so that the people implementing the decision have everything they need to complete their task.

■ Monitor and make adjustments as necessary. There are two certainties in decision-making: first, the people who make and implement decisions are fallible; second, the context in which decisions are taken will change. As a result, you need to keep a close eye on the implementation so that you can make alterations as required.

To ensure that your strategic decision-making is effective it can help to step back from the process and consider your approach. Where are the strengths and weaknesses? What action is needed to improve and develop skills and abilities in this area? In particular, reflect on each stage in the decision-making process and decide where skills might be enhanced. This means knowing when a decision can be made independently and when support is needed from others. It also means knowing, for example, when to trust your instincts, when to gain further information and when to involve other people. Many other elements are significant: for example, when to apply principle and when to be pragmatic; when to compromise and when to be single-minded; when to be innovative and when to challenge; when to conform; and, above all, a sense of when a decision will succeed and when it will fail.

Through such an analysis the quality of decisions should improve and there should also be more consistency, making it easier for others to understand and emulate them. Furthermore, developing a clear and consistent approach to decision-making provides a fallback position, so that when pressure and/or complexity increase or urgency escalates, there is a reliable, tried-and-tested approach to fall back on, honed during less stressful or critical times. To misquote Kipling: if you can keep your head while about you others are losing theirs, it is just possible you haven't grasped the situation.

Leading people through change

The eight-stage process of creating major change was first outlined by John Kotter in his book *Leading Change*, in which he describes what the leader needs to do to ensure beneficial change is achieved.[10]

Establish a sense of urgency

As a leader, you should initiate or take control of the process by emphasising the need for change. The more urgent and pressing the need, the more likely people are to be focused. Usually, the leader's role is to stay positive and build on success. However, it can help to emphasise failure: what might go wrong, how and when, and what the consequences could be. You can also emphasise positive elements, such as windows of opportunity that require swift and effective change.

Create a guiding coalition

The guiding coalition needs to understand the purpose of the change process. Members should be united and co-ordinated, and carry significant authority. The coalition should have the power to make things happen, to change systems and procedures and win people over.

Develop a vision and strategy

The guiding coalition needs to create a simple, powerful vision that will direct and guide change and achieve goals. You need to develop a detailed strategy for achieving that vision. The strategy should be practical, workable, understandable, simple and consistent.

Communicate the change vision

Use every means available to communicate the new vision and strategies. This will build pressure, momentum and understanding, sustaining a sense of urgency. The guiding coalition should lead by example and act as a role model for employees' behaviour.

Empower broad-based action

The leader and the guiding coalition cannot achieve change in isolation; they need the commitment and effort of others. Provide a blame-free, supportive environment and empower your people by:

- removing obstacles;
- changing systems or structures that undermine the vision;

- encouraging risk-taking and non-traditional ideas;
- generating short-term wins.

These generate momentum and provide an opportunity to build on success. To do this you should:

- plan for visible improvements in performance, or "wins";
- create those wins;
- recognise and reward people who make wins possible.

Consolidate gains and produce more change

Once the excitement of the start-up phase has passed, success has been achieved and everyone knows what is needed, people may tire and problems may arise. The key is to move steadily, maintaining momentum without moving too fast. Use your increased credibility to:

- make sure people understand what is still needed;
- hire, promote and develop people who can implement the changes;
- reinvigorate the process with new projects, themes and change agents.

Establish new approaches in the organisation's culture

A danger in managing change is to finish too early. It is often best when change, development and continuous improvement become the norm. What matters is making sure that the changes are firmly grounded in the organisation. This requires the leader to explain the connections between the new behaviour or actions and success. It also helps to highlight what has been gained and where the process might go in the future.

Six principles for gaining commitment

The goal of employee engagement is to maximise performance and profit by putting the strategy to work. This will not happen if leaders do not have their people's commitment. Gone are the days when leaders simply informed others; now a dialogue needs to take place. People need to feel valued and listened to, and leaders need to inspire, win hearts and minds, and harness talent and potential.

Successful transitions depend on gaining commitment. Without it, companies underperform and strategy is harder to achieve. Developed by John Smythe, the author of *The CEO: Chief Engagement Officer*,[11] these principles engage employees, releasing creativity, raising productivity and promoting commitment and loyalty. They give people a compelling reason to work, to excel and to implement plans successfully. By listening, engaging, empowering and encouraging people to share ideas, you will build confidence, loyalty and camaraderie.

The six principles are as follows:

- Develop the right plan and make sure everyone agrees. Make sure that the senior team has explored all options and developed the best strategy. Although teams often agree on a plan, some people may have held back their ideas or disagreed with the majority. It is crucial to make sure that all senior managers are on board.

- Plan the transition process and prepare a timeline. When planning the timeline for implementation, consider the timing of the demands that you will make of people, including emotional and motivational aspects.

- Decide who is to be involved and how. Make sure that everyone is clear about who is involved or affected – and how and why. When people know what their role is and understand the strategy, they are more engaged, adaptable and committed.

- Set standards (including role modelling and measuring progress). Putting standards and timed goals in place enables people to measure progress. You need to win and maintain people's commitment, so any measures should motivate rather than demotivate them. When setting goals, consider the people involved. Ask yourself how they would respond.

- Connect with each person as an individual. Include opportunities for people to reflect, learn and enjoy working for your company. Implementing a new strategy should be enjoyable – emphasise the excitement, the potential and the opportunities. Include opportunities to celebrate past achievements; moving to the future without a nod to the past is discouraging.

■ Tell and sell the new strategy. Tap into people's desire to be part of something and interpret situations from their perspective. Empathy is an invaluable tool for generating enthusiasm and commitment. Remember that your version of change is not the only one people hear. Be honest, keep people informed and give a better, more inspirational and convincing explanation of events and strategy.

Lastly, it is helpful to remember that the role of the strategic decision-maker is often a pressured and lonely one, with lingering uncertainty as an occupational hazard as the decision plays out. Developing personal strategies to handle this pressure is important, but ultimately, delivering decisions that achieve success is immensely rewarding. It is worth remembering the words of Marie Curie, a pressured, unconventional scientist but an effective decision-maker: "One never notices what has been done, one can only see what remains to be done."

Key questions

■ What are your priorities? Have you set clear goals for yourself and your team? Are these specific, measurable, achievable, relevant and time-constrained? How will you know when you succeed?

■ How creative are you and your team? How could your team's creativity be developed further?

■ What gets measured gets managed – meaning that people focus on things that are being measured. What should you be measuring? What are the best measurements to use?

■ Which skills do you need to develop, and which skills and capabilities does your team need to develop? How will this be accomplished?

- Do you have the right people with the right skills and attitude? What are the people issues in your team, and how should they be addressed?

- Does your team have the right structure, processes and resources? How could the team's efficiency and structure improve?

- Do you have a clear vision of the future that guides the way people think and the decisions they make? How are decisions made and problems solved, and how could this be improved?

Other issues include:

- How do you want things to change?

- What are the priorities for action in the short and long term, for the business, team and each individual?

- What will success look like?

- Which specific leadership skills do you want to develop?

- Who is a leader that inspired you? What did they do and what can you learn from them?

12 Implementing business strategy

IN DEVELOPING A STRATEGY it is necessary to consider how it will be implemented. This requires leadership, employee engagement, the use of techniques such as the balanced scorecard and avoiding common pitfalls.

Leading change

A business strategy is dynamic: it involves choices, change and an ability to move the business (its employees and customers) from where they are now to where they need to be in the future. This is, by definition, a process of change, and there are several valuable points to remember when leading people through a period of change:

- **Vision.** A change programme should have a clear, compelling, guiding vision. People need to understand where they are going and the benefits of taking a new approach (see Chapter 10).

- **Communication.** Change often fails because it is seen and communicated as a single, fixed event when it is better compared to a journey, a destination or a process over time. Poor communication is often a problem, so it is important to identify how information should be cascaded down the organisation. Giving information gradually is risky – the grapevine may get there before the management message. Senior managers need to "walk the talk", to demonstrate the values, changes and behaviour espoused, but also to make sure that communication is two-way. This needs to be through open dialogue and regular feedback sessions.

- **Planning.** Planning and preparation are required. This means identifying the steps required to achieve the change and to avoid people suffering from tunnel vision – looking only at the result and not the intermediate events required to achieve the objectives.

- **Steady progress.** Goals should not be set too far in the future. Enthusiasm will not be sustained for a three- or five-year plan with no recognition of short-term wins. A single leap is rarely feasible; the journey of 1,000 miles starts with a single step.

- **Realism and practicality.** There is a need to overcome the legacy of previous change. Even if successful, years of streamlining, right-sizing and business development initiatives breed weariness and may well generate a sceptical, risk-averse culture that is not compatible with the innovative spirit required for change.

- **Participation.** People are inclined to support what they have helped to create and resist what is forced upon them.

- **Motivation.** Lack of confidence and fear of failure can waylay a change programme and need to be countered. This is true at every level of an organisation.

- **Overcoming resistance.** The greatest inertia may come, for example, from middle managers or supervisors with long service and limited employability but with hopes of time-served promotions or retirement in a few years. Resistance can be overcome by emphasising what people have to gain, or the advantages of losing the negative aspects.

- **Systems and processes.** Staff may also resist change and feel there is no incentive for them to change their behaviour when their efforts are continually frustrated by systems and processes that should be reviewed and revamped.

- **Training and support.** Any necessary training should be organised before initiating change, so people can quickly gain the confidence and ability they will need to succeed.

Successful change normally comes from planning the steps that should occur, setting clearly defined objectives and giving individuals accountability for the follow through: making sure the longer-term changes actually happen and the benefits are realised.

Achieving employee engagement

It has become increasingly accepted that if people are actively engaged with their work – not simply motivated, but valuing what they are doing and striving to do it better at all times – they will be more productive and likely to implement the strategy, as well as being more personally fulfilled.

The challenge, however, is to move from a position where people might (or might not) be simply happy and motivated to one where they are actively loyal, committed and engaged with their work.

Three useful techniques for developing employee engagement are:

- the employee–customer–profit chain;
- three-factor theory;
- questioning.

The employee–customer–profit chain

Employee engagement can be divided into two types:

- Rational commitment is when a job serves an employee's financial, developmental or professional self-interest. It is most often associated with traditional approaches to motivation, and the view that an important part of a manager's job is to create a motivating environment.

- Emotional commitment goes further than traditional motivation and is found when workers are not only content in their work, but also actively value, enjoy and believe in what they do. These "true believers" are of greatest value to the business and, consequently, go furthest in their careers.

A study conducted by researchers from Harvard University in the 1990s with Sears, a US retailer, found that emotional commitment has four times the power to improve performance than the average level of commitment found in most organisations. The researchers found that:

- 11% of workers demonstrate high levels of both types of commitment;

- 13% demonstrate little of either type of commitment;

- 76% are moderates – people who generally exhibit a strong commitment to one person or element of their job, but can take or leave the rest. According to researchers, this group neither shirks nor strives.

These percentages are likely to reflect the broad reality in all major corporations. The challenge, therefore, is to support and encourage as many moderates as possible to commit even further to their job for the benefit of everyone.

Sears: connecting employee practices with strategy

Sears provides a good example of employee practices connecting directly with strategy and business performance. The employee–customer–profit chain makes explicit the links between cause and effect. By enabling employees to see the implications of their actions, it can change the way people think and the results they achieve.

In the early 1990s, senior executives at Sears realised that performance was not going to improve simply by developing a different strategy or adjusting marketing plans. Following significant losses, executives focused on three issues:

- How employees felt about working at Sears.

- How employee behaviour affected customers' shopping experience.

- How customers' shopping experience affected profits.

Sears asked 10% of its workforce how much profit they thought was made for each dollar of sales. The average answer was 46 cents, whereas in reality it was 1 cent. This highlighted the need for employees, especially those at the front line, to better understand the issues determining profitability. Sears's approach was to develop the employee–customer–profit model (ECPM), making explicit the chain of cause and effect. Being better able to see the implications of their actions changed the way employees thought and acted and, in turn, this was reflected in bottom-line performance.

FIG 12.1 **Sears's employee–customer–profit model**

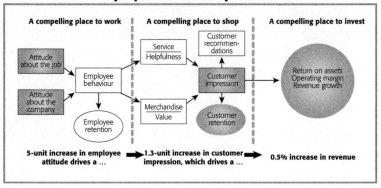

Note: rectangles are survey information, ovals are hard data, shaded areas are the Sears
total performance indicators.
Source: Sears

The Sears approach to creating an ECPM started by devising a set of measures based on objectives in three areas: making Sears a compelling place to work, a compelling place to shop and a compelling place to invest (see Figure 12.1).

For the top 200 managers at Sears, incentives are based on total performance indicators (TPI), which include non-financial and financial measures:

- one-third employee measures – attitude about the job and company;
- one-third customer measures – customer impression and retention;
- one-third financial measures – return on assets, operating margin and revenue growth.

As a result of the employee–customer–profit chain, managers at Sears are recruited, promoted and appraised on 12 criteria: customer service orientation; initiative and sense of urgency; business knowledge and literacy; problem solving; developing associates and valuing their ideas; teamworking skills; two-way communication skills; valuing diversity; empowerment skills; interpersonal skills; change leadership; and integrity.

Three-factor theory

Three-factor theory is based on the premise that workers have basic human needs that managers can and should work to address. Creating an environment in which these needs are met results in not just satisfied employees but also enthusiastic employees. During the last three decades of the 20th century, US-based Sirota Consulting surveyed 237 organisations worldwide across a range of industries about what employees wanted at work, receiving more than 2 million responses. This research suggests that there are three primary sets of goals for people at work (known as three-factor theory): equity (which means being treated fairly but not necessarily owning shares in the business), achievement and camaraderie. For most workers, no other goals are nearly as important. Moreover, these goals have not changed in recent times and they cut across demographic groups and cultures. Establishing policies and practices in tune with these three goals helps to create employee engagement.

Equity

This means being treated justly in relation to the basic conditions of employment. These are:

- physiological – such as having a safe working environment or manageable workload;
- economic – including pay, benefits and job security;
- psychological – being treated consistently, fairly, considerately and with respect.

Feelings of equity are influenced by perceptions of relative treatment. For example, am I being treated fairly in relation to my peers and colleagues?

Achievement

This means employees taking pride in their accomplishments by doing things that matter and doing them well, receiving recognition for those accomplishments and taking pride in the team's accomplishments. Sirota Consulting's research suggests that this sense of achievement has six primary sources:

- The challenge of the work and the extent to which employees can apply their skills and abilities.

- Acquiring new skills and the opportunity to develop, take risks and expand personal horizons.

- Ability to perform – and possessing the resources, authority, information and support to do the job well.

- Perceived importance of the job – knowing the work has a purpose and value, whether to the organisation, customers or society as a whole.

- Recognition for performance – non-financial as well as financial.

- Pride in the organisation – resulting from the organisation's purpose, success, ethics, the quality of its leadership, or the quality and impact of its products.

Camaraderie

Employees like to have warm, interesting and co-operative relations with others in the workplace. The most significant aspects of camaraderie are:

- relationships with co-workers;

- teamwork within an individual's business unit;

- teamwork across departments in a specific location;

- teamwork and co-operation across the entire organisation.

Equity is the most important factor in shaping employee engagement. When it is rated low, even if achievement and camaraderie are rated high, overall enthusiasm can be two-thirds lower.

Employee morale is a function of the way an organisation is led and the way that leadership is translated into daily management practices. Employee enthusiasm helps improve business performance, which helps improve morale and so on.

Questioning

The answers employees give to the following questions indicate how engaged they feel. The more positive the answers, the more engaged the employee is likely to be:

- Do you know what is expected of you at work?
- Do you have the materials and equipment you need to do your work properly?
- At work, do you have the opportunity to do what you do best every day?
- In the past seven days, have you received recognition or praise for doing good work?
- Does your supervisor, or someone at work, seem to care about you as a person?
- Is there someone at work who encourages your development?
- At work, do your opinions seem to count?
- Does the mission/purpose of your company make you feel your job is important?
- Are your fellow employees committed to doing high-quality work?
- Do you have good friends at work?
- In the past six months, has someone at work talked to you about your progress?
- In the past year, have you had opportunities at work to learn and develop?

The balanced scorecard technique

In their book *The Balanced Scorecard*,[1] Robert Kaplan and David Norton highlight several ways in which strategic decision-makers can increase the long-term value of a business. Their approach applies the concept of shareholder value analysis and is based on the premise that the traditional measures used by managers to gauge how well their organisations are performing, such as business ratios, productivity, unit costs, growth and profitability, are only a part of the picture. These measures are seen as providing a narrowly focused snapshot of an organisation's past performance and little indication of likely future performance. In contrast, the balanced scorecard offers a measurement and management system that links strategic objectives to comprehensive performance indicators.

The balanced scorecard approach generates objectives in four areas of business that will help to achieve the strategy. The scorecard then provides a way to work on each of these areas, with progress being regularly assessed.

The success of the balanced scorecard approach lies in its ability to unify and integrate a set of indicators that measure the performance of activities and processes at the core of an organisation's operations. This is valuable because it presents a balanced picture of overall performance and highlights specific activities that need to be completed. The balanced scorecard takes into account "hard" financial measures and three "soft", quantifiable operational measures, which are:

- customer perspective – how an organisation is perceived by its customers;
- internal perspective – those internal processes that the organisation must improve, which may include improving lead times, product quality, unit costs, employee morale or sales per employee;
- innovation and learning perspective – those areas where an organisation must continue to improve and add value.

The type, size and structure of an organisation will determine the detail of the implementation process; however, once the strategy has been defined, the main stages involved in applying a balanced scorecard approach are as follows:

- Deciding what to measure. Goals and measures should be determined for each of the four perspectives (finance, customers, internal processes, and innovation and learning). Some typical goals and measures are listed in Table 12.1.

TABLE 12.1 **Typical goals and measures**

Perspective	Goals	Measures
Financial	Increased profitability	Cash flows
	Share price performance	Cost reduction
	Increased return on assets	Gross margins
		Return on capital, equity, investments, sales
		Revenue growth
		Payment terms
Customers	New customer acquisition	Market share
	Customer retention	Customer service and satisfaction
	Customer satisfaction	Number of complaints
	Cross-sales volumes	Customer profitability
		Delivery times
		Units sold
		Number of customers
Internal processes	Improved core competencies	Efficiency improvements
	Improved critical technologies	Improved lead times
	Streamlined processes	Reduced unit costs
	Improved employee morale	Reduced waste
		Improved sourcing, supplier delivery
		Greater employee morale and satisfaction and reduced staff turnover
		Internal audit standards
		Sales per employee
Innovation and learning	New product development	Number of new products
	Continuous improvement	Sales of new products
	Employees' training and skills	Number of employees receiving training
		Outputs from employees' training
		Training hours per employee
		Number and scope of skills learnt

These goals and measures are based on the work of Robert Kaplan and David Norton in their book *The Balanced Scorecard*, Harvard Business School Press, 1996.

- Finalising and implementing the plan. Invariably, further discussions are necessary to agree the detail of the goals to be achieved, the activities required to achieve those goals and the measures to be used to assess the level of achievement. Once finalised, the plan needs to be communicated and implemented, with responsibility for the scorecards being delegated throughout the organisation (a variation on the old theme of managing by objectives for which responsibility was spread through the organisational hierarchy).

- Publicising and using the results. Everyone should understand the overall objectives, but deciding who should receive what information, why and how often, is also important. People want the information necessary to guide their decisions and actions. Too much detail can hinder clear thinking and too little hinders effective decision-making.

- Reviewing and revising the system. As with any management process, a final stage of review and revision is likely to be needed, and once scorecards have been introduced regular reviews of how they are working should take place.

One criticism of the balanced scorecard approach is that it is overly prescriptive and scientific, concerned with measurement and quantitative rather than qualitative issues. The counter to this is that first, it provides a structure for making decisions about the long-term value of an organisation, and these can be adapted later as necessary; second, it allows for qualitative measures to be included and recognises that the four perspectives are interrelated. However, as with any management tool or technique, the level of success achieved depends on the quality of the inputs and the way in which the system is implemented.

Avoiding pitfalls

Robert Reisner, a former vice-president of strategic planning for the US Postal Service, is well placed to talk about the pitfalls of organisational change. Amid soaring profits in 1999, the service attempted to technologically revolutionise its business to allow it to compete in a new wired era. Although this effort to better integrate into a technologically advanced society was met with initial optimism, it soon began to stall. In 2001, the company was facing a $3 billion loss, motivation was falling and the General Accounting Office described the turnaround as having a "high chance of failing".

Reisner identified several steps that caused the transition to stall. These provide lessons for anyone looking to implement a strategy:

- Do not miss your moment. Time your change initiatives to coincide with market opportunities and high morale among employees.
- Connect the transformation with the core of your business. Make sure employees understand how the changes are relevant to the mainstream operations of the company.
- Recognise the difference between incremental improvements and strategic transformation. Do not let temporary business success distract from the need for a strategic reinvention.
- Set realistic goals. Creating unrealistic expectations weakens motivation and distracts from the goals that can be achieved.

Although you can never guarantee that a major business transformation will proceed as planned, you can guarantee that you will be prepared to deal with the challenges it presents and to navigate your way around them. This can be achieved in various ways, several of which have been referred to in earlier chapters but which it is helpful to reiterate.

Communicate and influence

Observe body language – both yours and theirs – and ask questions to improve your understanding, test assumptions and show that you are listening. Maintain a professional demeanour and control emotions, and treat others as you would wish to be treated. Being critically aware when communicating requires a variety of skills, in particular:

- reacting to ideas, not people;
- focusing on the significance of the facts and evidence;
- avoiding jumping to conclusions;
- listening for how things are said and what is not said.

Build a team

Teams, not individuals acting alone, implement strategies, so an important aspect of leadership is building teamwork. Several useful actions will help:

- Choose the right people for the team based on their skills, experience and diversity, as well as the requirements of the role.
- Outline a clear vision and set the framework that team members will work within and make sure that they understand both.
- Encourage participation in decision-making. Make sure people are engaged and support each other.
- Empower team members within agreed and understood limits.
- Avoid or defuse conflicts by valuing different contributions and helping people play to their strengths.
- Explain the strategy and vision and demonstrate the standards and behaviour you expect from the rest of the team.
- Secure the resources needed and defend the team from external disruption.

Adopt a practical, flexible style of leadership

This may mean helping employees deal with the stress they face during the transformation, as well as taking advantage of people's contributions. List what needs to be done and communicate the priorities. This also means focusing on one initiative at a time – trying to do too much will overwhelm the organisation. Lastly, take control of the situation by asking productive, practical questions on how to make the strategy succeed.

Help people to embrace change

People need to be helped to move through the three stages involved in organisational change:

- the ending of the current situation;
- the transition to new circumstances;
- the new beginning (which may itself be evolving).

They also need to be comfortable with the pace of change, which may require a lot of patience and support from their managers.

Provide training and development

An inevitable result of the change process will be a need for training and development. People will not be doing what they were before or, if they are, they will be doing it better. To achieve this, some action will be required to increase their skills and ensure their personal development.

Check the organisation's systems

Systems such as human resources, finance and information technology (IT) need to be in line with the new strategy, providing the support that the new situation requires.

Confront problems early

Problems such as resistance to change rarely improve with age and frustration can spread quickly, particularly when people are working hard or facing the unknown. Tackle any difficulties as soon as possible (ideally pre-empting them). This will show commitment and determination, as well as inspiring respect and confidence.

Find ideas for improvements

This can be achieved by:

- talking to people in other areas who deal with similar issues;
- talking to friends in other companies;
- asking customers;
- exploring how things are done in another industry or country;
- reading books or articles by experts in the area;
- talking to creative people who know nothing about the area;
- brainstorming ideas.

Ask each member of the team to think of something they want to improve and use this list to generate ideas and priorities for action.

Key questions

- Can you identify, prioritise and explain the changes needed?
- Do you understand the concerns of major stakeholders, notably employees, shareholders and customers? How will these be addressed?
- Do people encourage colleagues to change by showing them how to do things differently? How can you foster an open, constructive and supportive approach?
- Are you actively overcoming the constraints (for example, bureaucracy or procedures) that are blocking or threatening to block action? What is being done to make sure that all parts of the business support the changes?
- Where are the strategy's potential pitfalls and how will these be overcome?
- Is there a plan with clear milestones for implementing the strategy?

13 Strategic innovation

INNOVATION PLAYS A LARGE PART in the strategies of organisations that want to move to a new, better position where they are more profitable and valuable. That innovation may be in terms of the products and services they sell or it may be in the way they are organised and the way they do things.

Understanding innovation

?What If!, a UK company, shows organisations how to be more innovative. It challenges people to see things differently by stepping out of their comfort zones and risking ideas that may seem to make little sense. Two important, but separate, processes are needed for innovation:

- Idea building, where people propose ideas and then develop and nurture them.
- Idea analysis, where these ideas are tested and evaluated.

Companies that struggle to be innovative often do so because ideas are stifled by a rush to judge and analyse them. Having the right processes for generating ideas is important, but so too is having a culture that values and fosters innovation.

Research by the Talent Foundation in the 2000s identified five catalysts for successful innovation:[1]

- **Consciousness.** Everyone knows the strategy and believes they can play a part in achieving it.

- **Multiplicity.** Teams and groups contain a wide and creative mix of skills, experiences, backgrounds and ideas.
- **Connectivity.** Relationships are strong and trusting and are actively encouraged and supported within and across teams and functions.
- **Accessibility.** Doors and minds are open; everyone in the organisation has access to resources, time and decision-makers.
- **Consistency.** Commitment to innovation runs throughout the business and is built into processes.

A survey of innovation literature highlights several challenges and lessons for innovators.[2] Foremost among them is the need to protect existing revenue streams while simultaneously developing new ones. In addition:

- Not every innovation has to be a blockbuster. In sufficient numbers, small or incremental innovations can be highly profitable.
- Innovation does not only mean product development. Great ideas can come from any business function (for instance, human resources, marketing, production or finance).
- Successful innovators often use an "innovation pyramid" with several big ideas at the top that receive most of the investment, a wider array of mid-range ideas in the test stage and a broad base of early-stage ideas or incremental innovations. Ideas and influence flow up and down the pyramid.
- Business processes and controls can stifle and block innovation. These most often include budgeting and review processes.
- Innovative businesses allow deviations from the plan. They do not simply reward people for doing what they are committed to; they also have the flexibility to allow people to seize opportunities and act as circumstances suggest.
- Although formal controls may need to loosen or increase in flexibility, connections between innovations and the rest of the business need to strengthen.

- Radical innovations often cut across established channels (such as hierarchies, departments, management reporting lines) or combine existing ideas in new and different ways.

- Strong leadership skills (notably relationship-building and communication) are essential for all types of innovation, even the most technical.

- Members of innovation teams often keep in close contact with each other through the development of an idea, even if the company moves them to another role.

Innovations need connectors, people who can combine things, either conceptually or in practice, and make things happen. For this reason, innovation flourishes where collaboration is encouraged.

21st-century innovators

Google and Apple are highly regarded innovators – valuable, global businesses that lead their sectors and consistently use technology to provide distinctive, popular and profitable products. Whereas Apple's approach is to give customers what they do not yet know they want, Google prefers to work closely with its customers as it develops new products and ways of working.

Apple: reinventing itself

Apple is an iconic and rare business, a technology company that not only is able to generate genuine passion among its customers but also has come roaring back since near disaster in 1997. The renowned developer of the Apple Mac reinvented itself as a consumer electronics firm with the iPod and iPhone and is consistently ranked as one of the world's most innovative firms. The story of its rise has several lessons for aspiring innovators.

Network innovation

Apple uses an approach known as network innovation: the process of acquiring good ideas from outside the business as well as from within. For example, Apple has been described by *The Economist* as:[3]

An orchestrator and integrator of technologies, unafraid to bring in ideas from outside but always adding its own twists.

The iPod was conceived by an external consultant recruited to manage the project. It was designed to work with Apple's iTunes software (which was itself acquired from outside and then overhauled) and a prototype was developed in-house. Network innovation is achieved by cultivating external expert contacts, constantly searching for new ideas and avoiding the "not-invented-here" syndrome.

Simplicity

Next, Apple emphasises simplicity, chiefly by designing a product around the needs of the user. When introducing technology, the temptation is to overcomplicate, often with experts including technical enhancements that appeal to them. This introduces a layer of cleverness and complexity that may seem ingenious in theory but leaves customers cold. The iPod was not the first digital music player but it was the first to make buying, transferring and organising music fun. Similarly, the iPhone was not the first mobile phone to include a music player, web browser and e-mail facility, but it was the first to be simple and highly appealing.

Understand customers

Apple's approach relies on its ability to understand customers. This is much more than "user-centric" innovation or simply listening to customers. Apple believes that from time to time it is necessary to ignore what customers say they want today. This is hazardous, but the risks can be reduced by understanding what customers value, how they typically work, what they want to achieve and what they will enjoy. It is crucial to understand customers better today to predict what they will want tomorrow.

Fail wisely

This is another hallmark of Apple's approach to innovation. Failure is disappointing but it is also an opportunity to learn and, significantly, it is inevitable. Everyone fails at some time so view failure positively. The alternative is, at best, staleness, timidity and incremental improvements; at worst, it can turn into blame, recrimination and a cycle of despair. For example, the iPhone sprang from the failure of Apple's original music phone developed with Motorola. Apple learnt from its mistakes and tried again. The leadership challenge is to overcome the concerns that successful, talented employees may have about failure and to make sure that failure is not stigmatised. Instead, employees should persist with new ideas, secure in their own expertise and ability to learn, and improve with the support of colleagues.

Google's remarkable rise

Google dominates the market for online searching and advertising. At times it is hard to discern which aspect of its business is most innovative: the ambition and ability to organise the world's information or the commercial ability to make money from its services. At the heart of Google's success is the use of simple, clear directives such as the principle that information should be organised by analysing users' intentions.

Several other factors underpin Google's remarkable rise.

Develop an infrastructure that is "built to build"

Google has invested billions in its internet-based operating platform and its proprietary technology. This enables the business to be consistent about its service levels, respond to searches in fractions of seconds and swiftly develop new services while making sure that all things Google are easy to use. These advantages result from its infrastructure, which has the following attributes:

■ Scalability. The business shares information globally to meet customers' changing demands. It also has a further characteristic of world-class businesses: a willingness to take risks and invest heavily in proprietary technology (including around 1m computers) to meet customers' needs.

■ A fast product development cycle. Google engineers quickly develop prototypes and beta versions of products; those that are popular with users are then given priority, with Google's enormous computing capability making room for them. Testing and marketing follow and are almost simultaneous. This creates a close relationship with customers, who, in effect, become part of the development team.

■ Support for mashups (web applications that combine data from more than one source into a single integrated tool) and new developments. Google has a flexible infrastructure described as "an innovation hub" where third parties can share access and create new applications incorporating Google's functionality.

Google's can-do attitude and the way that resources are gathered, shared and organised has made it successful, not simply its technology, and that success has allowed it to invest heavily in infrastructural development.

Control your world

Google dominates its industry, which gives it the ability to control its world. People come to Google because it is the market leader and Google responds by involving these third parties and customers in its business.

Make time for innovation

Technical employees are required to spend 80% of their time on the core search and advertising businesses and 20% on technical projects of their choosing. New ideas are often generated from the bottom up by employees at Google. Their time is specifically allocated for innovation; the improvisational, empowering, can-do culture positively demands it.

Improvise and improve

People at Google have the authority to act on their own initiative and are encouraged to make improvements and to work on new developments. This means the company is able to attract and retain driven people who enjoy improving and developing things and who value their freedom and autonomy. This becomes a self-sustaining cycle: autonomy and empowerment lead to success, which attracts more talented people who are then encouraged and empowered to succeed.

Recognise the value of failure and chaos

It can be argued that this is Google's greatest strength. It is shown, most notably, by an approach to product development whereby a wide range of products are developed with the expectation that at least some will become blockbusters. This way of working provides valuable insights that can then be fed back into future developments. This strategy may not be sustainable or even desirable in the long term, but it is creating an impressive array of new products and enhancements. Google's product development process has been described by *The Economist* as "frenzied and low friction". The creative frenzy also has the indirect benefit of building a culture that is not only innovative, but also dynamic, well-informed and determined.

Building a culture of innovation

There are several ways to encourage innovation.

Ask why and what

Nothing develops an innovative, creative approach as simply as a well-timed question such as: why have sales of this product stopped growing or what would make this product more appealing to customers?

Generate hotspots

Lynda Gratton, author of *Hot Spots: Why Some Teams, Workplaces, and Organisations Buzz with Energy – and Others Don't,*[4] believes that hotspots (where people in an organisation co-operate across business or geographic boundaries to improve the way they work, gain new insights or become more innovative) are a valuable way to develop innovation, creativity and ideas. They emerge where the conditions are right and where there is encouragement throughout the organisation. They cannot be formally imposed, although the conditions can be created by senior management, who can encourage them to arise naturally. Some of the characteristics needed for hotspots to develop and thrive are described below.

A co-operative mindset

People have to want to share not only their explicit knowledge or the information they hold (which is relatively easy) but also the tacit knowledge in their heads. To create a co-operative mindset organisations should:

- consider relationships when selecting staff;
- emphasise the need for co-operation in the induction processes;
- provide mentoring;
- emphasise collective rewards over individual ones;
- establish structures that facilitate peer-to-peer working;
- develop a genuine sense of shared responsibility.

A co-operative mindset results from a company's practices, processes, behaviours and norms, and the behaviour of top management is a significant factor.

Boundary spanning

This is the opposite of the silo mentality where businesses or functions remain separate from each other, unconnected, territorial or even competitive. To create a successful hotspot requires people who are good at spanning boundaries. This means that they must:

- be undeterred by physical distance;
- welcome a diverse range of ideas, insights, experience and people;
- be willing to explore issues together – starting as strangers is an advantage as the process of getting to know each other helps to build creativity and innovation;
- be good at networking – boundary spanners are good at introducing people to others with whom valuable co-operation might develop;
- use different levels of co-operation – for example, strong ties between people who share a similar background, experience and emotional concerns means that trust can be developed quickly; weak ties, which use less time and emotion and may be more numerous, can be organised into new combinations to generate new insights.

A sense of purpose

Developing a sense of purpose is best achieved by posing a question that invites the exploration of a range of options around a specific intention or issue. The value of such questions is that they can help to engage people.

Productive capacity

This is the key to sustaining innovation. The first three steps (developing a co-operative mindset, boundary spanning and developing a sense of purpose) lead to a practical outcome: the development of greater innovation. However, ensuring that the culture of innovation takes root relies on the ability to build productive capacity. This can be achieved by:

- understanding and appreciating the talents of others;
- obtaining practical, public and explicit commitments among participants;
- harnessing the creative energy that results from problem solving and decision-making;
- synchronising time, especially where different time zones have to be accommodated or where there are different attitudes to time;
- ensuring that pressure is neither too high, where people burn out, nor too low, where they lose interest;
- recognising when things need to change.

Bottom-up and top-down innovation

The word innovation conjures up the image of a process that is spontaneous, unpredictable and unmanageable. There are many stories of serendipitous discoveries and independent-minded champions doggedly pursuing an idea until they hit the jackpot. Often – as the stories stress – inventors worked in secret against the will of management. The archetypes of such innovators are Art Fry and Spence Silver, the 3M chemists who turned a poorly sticking adhesive into a billion-dollar blockbuster: Post-it notes. In these cases, innovation comes from the bottom up, with ideas and the drive to see them through originating in labs or marketing outposts, not from the top of the organisation. However, to ensure consistent and high-quality innovation, the role of management is crucial in initiating and spurring innovative developments, as the development of the credit card illustrates.

In 1958, the Customer Services Research Department at the Bank of America, with the remit to develop potential new products, created the first credit card, and bankers at Citibank later added such features as merchant discounts, credit limits and terms and conditions.

This development emerged because people within the banking business used their knowledge of customers, information and forecasts about economic and social trends, experience with similar product ideas (such as instalment loans) and knowledge about new developments in technology. Top-down innovation in financial services has since resulted in automated teller machines (ATMs) and telephone and internet banking. With top-down innovation senior management take the initiative in getting things approved and then provide whatever support is needed.

Deep-dive prototyping

Originally developed by IDEO, a design consultancy, and described by Andy Boynton and Bill Fischer in their book *Virtuoso Teams*,[5] deep-dive prototyping is a technique that encourages creative thinking and is used to develop, test and refine ideas swiftly. It is based on the belief that collaboration and rapid prototyping are the best ways to learn. It includes the following stages:

- Defining the challenge.
- Building the team using internal and outside experts.
- Brainstorming, generating as many ideas as possible and voting on the best ones.
- Rapid prototyping follows, with results that are as clear, tangible and specific as possible.
- Frenzy. This is the defining characteristic of deep-dive prototyping and involves team members presenting the prototyping to others, gathering feedback as well as stealing and building on new ideas (this stage may lead back to the brainstorm).
- The final recommendation.

Value innovation

Value innovation is based on the premise that what matters to companies is not simply the need to compete, but rather the need to redefine the market in ways that generate distinctive new benefits for the customer. When companies compete they tend to become locked in a process of incrementally improving a combination of costs, product and service. Value innovators break free from the pack by identifying a new market and developing products or services for which there are no direct competitors.

A concept of business school professors W. Chan Kim and Renée Mauborgne,[6] value innovation involves challenging and defying conventional wisdom either to redefine or to create a market. For example, for many years, US TV networks used the same format and the same schedules for news programmes and competed on the popularity and professionalism of their presenters and their ability to report and analyse events. This changed in 1980 when CNN launched real-time 24-hour news from around the world for only one-fifth of the cost of the networks. Similarly, in 1984, Virgin Atlantic defied convention when it eliminated first-class seats on its flights. Prevailing wisdom suggested that growth relied on more, not fewer, market segments, but Virgin focused on business-class passengers. It used the money saved from first class to provide a range of popular innovations, from better and different lounges to improved in-flight amenities.

Value innovation relies on the ability to redefine a business based on an understanding of what customers will respond to. Several techniques can help:

- Challenge industry assumptions by questioning them and asking how customers would react if things were different.

- Be ambitious. Monitoring competitors is necessary but avoid the trap of competing with them on their terms. Something different may be more valuable to the customer.

- Avoid segmentation. While segmentation may provide greater understanding of customers, value innovators build scale by focusing on what unites customers in order to appeal to as many as possible.

- Don't be constrained by existing resources. What matters is not what you can do with current assets and capabilities but what you could do if you had different or additional resources.

■ Think laterally by cutting across industry divisions and finding ways to improve the offer to the customer.

Avoiding pitfalls

When innovation is a cornerstone of business strategy there are several potential pitfalls.

Premium-position captivity

One of the dangers of being a market leader is that of complacency, thinking that the level of innovation that has worked in the past will ensure future success. This has the capacity to destroy once great businesses. This is sometimes known as "premium-position captivity", as described by writers such as Jim Collins, Clayton Christensen, Donald Sull and others. More accurately, the term refers to the inability of a firm to respond satisfactorily to new, low-cost competitive challenges or to a significant shift in customer views of a product. The term "captivity" is used because it suggests how management teams can be hemmed in by a long history of success. A company that solidly occupies a premium market position remains insulated for longer than its competitors against changes in the external environment. It has less reason to doubt its business model, which has historically provided a competitive advantage, and once it perceives the crisis, it changes too little too late. The towering strengths of a firm are transformed into towering weaknesses. Xerox, Polaroid and Bethlehem Steel are notable examples.

Breakdowns in innovation management

A frequent problem for businesses is a breakdown in innovation management. This is when a problem arises in the management of internal processes for updating existing products and services and creating new ones. This can occur in any part of the innovation process, from basic research and development to product commercialisation. The solution is to carefully manage, monitor and measure innovations. Are they proceeding well? Where are the potential challenges and how are these being addressed?

Abandoning a core business

A further cause of decline in revenue or innovation is a failure to fully exploit opportunities in the core business. Signs that the business is falling into this trap include acquisitions or growth initiatives in areas that are relatively distant from existing customers, products or channels. Leaving a core business can result from a mistaken belief that core markets are saturated or that there are circumstances that make other markets easier or more attractive.

A shortfall in talent and skills

Firms frequently fail to innovate because they lack people with the necessary skills. What stops innovation dead in its tracks is not merely a shortage of talent but the absence of required capabilities. Internal skills gaps are often self-inflicted, the unintended consequence of promote-from-within policies that have been too strictly applied.

Failing to understand the market

Failing to understand the market and how it is changing is another reason innovation fails and business strategy stalls. The underlying assumptions supporting the strategy need to change in line with the external environment. Again, a questioning approach is a way to make sure a business is market aware of everything from "Who are our customers?" to "What ten things would you never hear customers say about our business? Which firms have succeeded by breaking the established 'rules' of the industry and what conventions did they overturn?"

Ten signs that innovation is weak or weakening

- People laugh at new ideas.
- Someone who identifies a problem is shunned.
- Innovation is the privileged practice of a special few.
- The phrase "you can't do that because we've always done it this way" is often used to counter new ideas.
- No one can remember the last time anyone did anything really radical.

- People think innovation is about R&D.
- People have convinced themselves that competing on price is normal.
- The organisation is focused more on process than on results.
- There are few people younger than 25.
- After any type of surprise (product, market, industry or organisational change) people sit back and ask: "Where did that come from?"

Key questions

The six Rs approach is especially valuable in identifying opportunities for improvement. Identify something you want to improve and use the list below to generate ideas:

- Research – what can you learn from people or organisations that do this activity well?
- Reframe – what is a completely different way of thinking about this?
- Relate – what ideas can you borrow from another activity or field?
- Remove – what can you eliminate?
- Redesign – what can you do to improve this activity, process or procedure?
- Rehearse – what can you do to be certain you have a good idea?

To identify improvements, have you:

- Asked your customers for ideas?
- Talked to people in other areas who deal with similar issues?
- Talked to other companies and explored how things are done in another industry or country and thought about ideas you can borrow, adapt or combine?
- Talked to creative people who know nothing about the area but who may have different perspectives?
- Gathered a group together to brainstorm ideas?

If you are faced with a specific problem or challenge, have you considered the following:

■ If this problem was solved, what would the solution look like?

■ What would radically change what you do?

■ How you could reverse the way you think about the problem?

■ How you could build on the current pluses and eliminate the minuses?

14 Competitiveness and customer focus

SENIOR MANAGERS SET OBJECTIVES and are guided by an overall strategy, but competitive pressures can influence their strategies and decisions. Most businesses either focus too much on their competitors' activities or ignore them because they feel unable to control them.

Competitiveness is closely linked with customer focus. Understanding customers and market developments leads to customer-focused decisions, which, in turn, provide the most certain route to profitability.

This chapter explains how to:

■ understand the nature of competition so that it can be reflected in strategic decisions in a balanced way;

■ build competitiveness using practical techniques;

■ develop customer focus so that it routinely guides major decisions.

The nature of competition

Being competitive enables you to sell more goods or services, but it also means gaining greater flexibility in the market. A business must be competitive because this enables it to undertake activities central to its strategy. They include:

■ Developing customer loyalty. Customers will be more inclined to remain with you because they know you best.

■ Increasing sales to existing customers, either selling more of an existing product or selling additional products.

- Enhancing the strength and value of your brand. The need to compete brings discipline to your business, for example by forcing you to manage costs, which may also enhance profitability.

- Developing new products and product extensions. These will enjoy a good start because of your existing reputation and customer base.

- Increasing market effectiveness, as competitive businesses are better able to deter new competitors from entering the market. They can also enter new markets themselves from a position of strength and better resist the challenges and difficulties that may arise.

Michael Porter of Harvard Business School has identified five forces affecting competition in an industry:

- **Industry rivalry.** The cola wars between PepsiCo and Coca-Cola are a prominent example.

- **Market entry.** Never underestimate the competitive threat posed by new entrants to a market. Always consider who has the resources, technical skills and ingenuity to develop a more attractive product offer than yours and when it might happen. (This can be developed through scenario thinking – see Chapter 5.)

- **Substitutability.** Businesses with a product or service for which customers might choose an alternative face a competitive threat, especially if the alternative is cheaper. For example, a bookstore may face competition from an online retailer or a supermarket chain, such as Walmart. A company may need only to redefine its business in slightly broader terms to become a competitor. This was highlighted by Theodore Levitt, a business writer, who warned of the dangers of marketing myopia – seeing your business in simple, narrow terms, rather than from the perspective of the market. The key is to view the business in broader market terms and, invariably, to add an element of service. For example, bookstores are developing into cybercafés and coffee shops.

■ **Suppliers.** Suppliers can damage your competitive position if the item they provide is scarce or if there are only a few suppliers. One response is to build close relations with important suppliers to secure delivery and control prices. In the long term, the solution may be to move into the supplier's industry to safeguard supplies.

■ **Customers.** Leaders need to appreciate the power of customers as a source of competition by assessing:

- how dependent the business is on individual customers;
- the ease with which customers can move to an alternative supplier;
- the customer's knowledge of competitors' prices, quality and overall offers.

The internet has made prices much more transparent, showing where and by how much they differ. This became a crucial strategic issue for businesses when the euro zone adopted a single currency.

The impact of competition

Companies in the same industry are the most obvious and prominent source of competition.

Fighting the Cola wars

In 1975, PepsiCo attacked its long-term competitor, Coca-Cola, with the "Pepsi Challenge", claiming that in taste tests people preferred Pepsi. Coke's market share fell substantially in the face of competition from Pepsi and from new beverages such as diet drinks, citrus flavours and caffeine-free colas. Indeed, to combat this new source of competition, Coca-Cola was itself marketing many of these new products. However, Coke's shrinking lead in the cola market convinced the company that it needed to act. Brian Dyson, a former CEO of Coca-Cola, told the *New York Times*:

> *There is a danger when a company is doing as well as we are ... to think that we can do no wrong. I keep telling the organisation, we can do wrong and we can do wrong big.*

In December 1984 the company decided to reformulate Coke with a target launch date of April 1985. Technically, it went well, but before they had tasted the new recipe, millions of Americans reacted emotionally and angrily to the new Coke. Many were not even Coca-Cola drinkers, simply consumers disappointed that an iconic American product had been changed.

By mid-July, the pressure was such that the company decided to reintroduce the original Coke. On the day the decision was announced, Coca-Cola's hotline received 18,000 calls – people were positive, glad that their voices had been heard and that change had been aborted.

Against all expectations, the original Coca-Cola rebranded as Coke Classic outsold the new Coke, and sales overtook Pepsi's early in 1986. New Coke's market share shrank to 3% and Coke Classic began selling with renewed vigour.

One senior executive told the *Wall Street Journal*:

> *It's kind of like the fellow who's been married to the same woman for 35 years and really didn't pay much attention to her until somebody started to flirt with her.*

The lesson for competitors

Coca-Cola had focused too much on what a competitor was doing and on its own market research (designed in the light of PepsiCo's campaign). It had lost sight of its brand's strength and of the customer's unpredictability. The launch of new Coke was based on the erroneous assumption that flavour mattered more than image. The information gathered built upon this flawed notion to confirm that the original Coke needed replacing. But it was not what customers wanted. Their goodwill towards the original cola was so strong that it triggered its revival as consumers realised how much they appreciated it, or else tried it for the first time.

Techniques for building competitiveness

Action in several areas will help make sure that the strategy remains popular, relevant and distinctive and thus competitive.

Know when competition will intensify

Be aware of factors that can increase competition (and increase its significance). These include:

- When the market is expanding or new (as in online marketing over the past 20 years or the mobile phone industry since the mid-1990s).

- When the stakes are high and big profits can be made, notably when there are few competitors in a large market (as with cola).

- When the market is set to change, perhaps as a result of changes affecting patents and intellectual property rights (for example, when the patent for a drug expires) or as a result of political or legal change (such as privatisation).

- When there is overcapacity in an already shrinking market (for example, steel production or shipbuilding).

Develop market awareness

Keep abreast of what your competitors are doing, how they are perceived by customers, and why. When making major decisions, especially those affecting customers, take into account:

- pricing policies and product offers;
- brand reputation, recognition and strength;
- customers' perceptions and expectations;
- product quality and service levels;
- product portfolio;
- organisational factors such as size, economies of scale, type of employees, training, expenditure on product development and distribution channels;
- staff loyalty;
- promotional campaigns and the timing, nature and channels used;
- customer loyalty;
- financial structure and cash reserves.

This will help to identify competitors' strengths and where they are vulnerable. It can also help in analysing sources of competitive advantage.

Build and exploit sources of competitive advantage

Staying ahead of the competition requires acquiring and developing resources that will make the business competitive (see Chapter 7).

Assess the organisation's competitiveness

Any strategy is vulnerable to a competitor's actions. To be robust, decisions need to take account of potential competitive threats, so develop worst-case scenarios. Assessing an organisation's competitiveness is a complex, demanding and continuous task. What matters is the ability to make sure the organisation senses market developments and signals, and is able to act on them.

Be a SWOT

SWOT (strengths, weaknesses, opportunities and threats) analysis is most effective when it is part of a wider management audit. It can be done from the top, or at departmental or divisional level, and the results can be assessed alongside a larger picture of the market that takes into account current and potential developments for the whole organisation. Strengths and weaknesses are typically found within an organisation and opportunities and threats most often come from the outside. Some factors can be sources of both strength and weakness. For example, a large number of older employees may denote a stable organisation with a wealth of experience; it may also signal that it is too conservative.

Choose a market position

First movers define the product, set standards and, most valuably, gain market share and brand awareness. However, there are difficulties in being a pioneer. They include spending too much time and energy building market share, with the likelihood that achieving the position will be too consuming, either distracting the business leaders or constraining them. The lack of an existing best-practice example is a weakness: there are no lessons for the first mover to learn and no empirical knowledge of where the pitfalls lie.

There are no easy solutions to these problems, but successful first movers such as Dell, eBay and Amazon demonstrate several features.

These include the importance of listening to customers and building and entrenching market share swiftly, while constantly innovating to provide a stream of new products or services in the market.

Early challengers to first movers can learn from their mistakes and focus on the most profitable or promising market segments or product niches, or add features to the new product or service that will defeat the first mover by moving to the next level for the customer. However, potential customers will compare the early challenger with the first mover: every aspect of its offer and its relative strengths and weaknesses will be scrutinised. Furthermore, the early challenger is attacking an entrenched market position and targeting customers who may be pleased with – and loyal to – the first mover. Lastly, price competition will mean that margins for the early challenger are unlikely to match the first mover's.

One way to address this is to target those areas where the first mover is weak or where it is not meeting customers' needs. A second approach is for the early challenger to stress clearly to customers its competitive advantages – not only against the first mover but also against other potential market entrants. Early challengers can often succeed by improving quality and cutting prices, both of which involve understanding customers but are often achieved by establishing efficient processes, value chains and supplier relations ready for fighting the (almost) inevitable price war.

Followers are able to analyse trends, best practices and business opportunities, but often several followers rush into a market (if they do not, that is at least as worrying). Their problem is to find a sufficiently distinctive product offering. The most effective approach is to focus on meeting the needs of specific, tightly defined market segments and not deviating from that market. Another is to exploit cost advantages or economies of scale by growing the business out of an existing business, effectively leveraging current resources.

On entering a market, a business needs to deter further new competitors through sustained market focus, innovation and constantly developing sources of competitive advantage. This will depend on the nature of the business, the culture of the organisation and the competitiveness of the market.

Avoiding problems with competitors

To protect your business from becoming uncompetitive, you need to:

- Understand who your major competitors are. This may mean taking a view beyond traditional channels and types of competitor to see how the market is developing and where competitors may come from.

- Understand their strategies – assess how they are competing on price, quality, reputation, or in any other way. It may not be sensible to counter in certain ways, for example on price, if their cost base is much lower than yours. Find another way to compete.

- Understand exactly what products or services competitors provide, not only the product features but also the benefits to customers. Update this information regularly by visiting your competitors' websites, interviewing their former employees and speaking to customers.

- Focus on your strengths. Make sure that you give customers reasons to stay with you – and reasons to avoid going to your competitors.

- Make sure your marketing activities are tightly focused so that you appeal more deeply to narrower segments of the market than your competitors, who may have a broader general appeal to more people but a less compelling offer to specific segments of the market.

Food for thought: Pret A Manger

A good way to increase customer focus is to use customers to give you an instant guide to what is working – and what is not.

Julian Metcalfe and Sinclair Beecham founded the Pret A Manger chain of sandwich shops in the 1980s. Initially they ran an off-licence, but although takings were high, the profit margin was not. Beecham says: "We decided there was more scope in low-priced, high-margin foods like sandwiches." They succeeded by listening to clients and being bold enough to drastically alter the customer offering.

In 2001 McDonald's bought a 33% non-controlling stake in the US branch of the company. Pret A Manger then expanded to New York (ten stores) and Hong Kong (ten stores), although 85% of its trade remains in London. Unlike other fast-food outlets, Pret A Manger refuses to franchise. In February 2008 it was sold for £345 million to Bridgepoint, a private equity firm, and Goldman Sachs, an investment bank. However, the management team and the co-founders retained a 25% stake in the business.

Pret A Manger's experience suggests several lessons for businesses seeking to improve their customer focus and competitiveness:

- Don't expect to achieve a flawless formula instantly. There are always lessons that can be learnt only on the shop floor.

- Don't be discouraged by problems. They are invaluable opportunities for learning. Analyse why they occurred, their significance and impact.

- Be prepared to make drastic changes. A formula may have to be altered or even discarded for a more profitable alternative.

- Combine abstract learning with hands-on experience; they are not mutually exclusive.

Achieving customer focus

Customer focus underpins the health of a business. Being customer-focused means gathering facts, data and knowledge about customers – current and potential – to find out what they want and how they perceive the business's products and services. This enables the business to meet customers' requirements and secure its long-term survival, growth and profitability. Customer focus can be strengthened through:

- market sensing;
- market segmentation;
- data mining;
- product development.

Market sensing

The key to being competitive is not to base your strategy on broad generalisations but to know what each customer wants. Technology is a valuable tool in bonding with customers, building loyalty to products and brands, and improving customers' knowledge of products and services. It can also increase understanding of market developments: market sensing.

Supermarket loyalty schemes or airlines' frequent-flyer programmes generate individual-level purchase data and can benefit both the business and the customer. The data they provide can help to determine the most effective strategy by, for example, highlighting which customers account for the greatest proportion of profit.

Individual-level data are valuable when introducing a new product. Aggregate sales figures show whether the product is an initial success, but an analysis of trial rates (the percentage of customers who have bought the product once) and repeat rates (the percentage of those who have bought it more than once) reveal its longer-term prospects.

Market sensing should be used in making customer-focused decisions:

- Use market research objectively. Market research needs to be well designed, executed and interpreted. The best approach is to use it to refine and update your understanding of customer groups.

- Use research insights to identify unique qualities. Insights should provide a source of competitive advantage (a scarcity value) that competitors are unlikely to have realised. The research should be cross-referenced and enriched with accumulated knowledge and understanding to provide real insights.

- Be in touch with customers at a senior level. Decision-makers must meet customers. Customers usually welcome the opportunity to have their voice heard.

- Anticipate the future. Managers should use scenario thinking to help predict the future (see Chapter 5).

■ Involve employees. The organisation's structure, climate and practices should allow everyone to share their knowledge of customers and use these insights to improve customer service. Customer focus is not for the few, it is an essential prerequisite for everyone.

■ Use information systems. Information systems need to be developed so they provide a clear and coherent understanding of customers' preferences and actions. Surprisingly, some global businesses cannot easily identify their 20 largest clients as measured by sales or profitability.

Market segmentation

Market segmentation involves profiling a target market in order to understand, in as much detail as possible, how best to sell and deliver customer service. It enhances product development and aids understanding of customers and their buying habits, making marketing plans relevant, targeted, well-implemented and cost-effective. Segmentation also influences pricing strategies.

Conventionally, segmentation breaks information such as income, location and consumers' ages into sections relevant to the target market to provide tightly focused information. Using the internet helps decision-makers define the shape and composition of the market, target potential customers, build the loyalty of existing customers and analyse information to improve marketing efficiency. As the internet provides access to markets that are global, diverse and complex, market segmentation allows greater focus and simplicity.

Markets can be segmented into any group. The most appropriate divisions depend on factors such as the size and nature of the market and product, as well as the reason for segmenting the market. The following categories are common:

■ Commercial markets. Categories are commonly divided into standard industry classification (SIC) codes. For example, customers may be given a range of SIC codes that are used to target subgroups (such as all project managers in the oil industry in Scotland with a company turnover of more than £10 million).

Useful segments include location, type of organisation, job title, size of organisation and purchase data.

■ Consumer markets. The most common segments are location, product benefits, lifestyle and social groupings. Others include occupation, income, nationality, sex and age. The internet can help identify the segment that will value a product the most.

Data mining

Computer systems can record and analyse every part of a transaction between businesses and their customers. To gain maximum benefit:

■ Decide what information to collect.

■ Decide how best to collect the data.

■ Keep it as simple as possible.

■ Test the effectiveness of data collection.

■ Put yourself in the customer's place.

■ Apply common sense.

■ Make sure information is kept up-to-date.

■ Analyse the information. What are the most significant features? What are the trends and implications (opportunities as well as threats)?

■ Use the information to improve products, service and profitability.

Time for a change: Swatch

In the 1980s, the Swiss watch industry was at a crossroads. It enjoyed a reputation for premium quality but was losing the popular end of the market to Japanese companies. They were using technology and reliable, low-cost production techniques developed with other products (from cars to domestic appliances) to squeeze Swiss manufacturers into an ever-diminishing niche at the top end of the market. The Swiss found their craftsmanship was counting against them: potential customers perceived them as outmoded in the age of mass-produced quartz crystal watches.

In response, Swatch launched a range of watches aimed at a youthful mass market and backed them with a massive marketing campaign that caught the public imagination. Its watches became fashion icons and Swatch styling has since been applied to other industries. For example, Daimler consulted Swatch when developing the Smart car.

Unusually for a single firm, Swatch helped to redefine the market. For example, there are now watches for leisurewear and sports use as well as traditional styles.

Swatch succeeded because it was willing to throw away the rulebook, understand the changing market and then attempt to lead it. By understanding who it was targeting – younger, sporty people looking for style and reliability – and aggressively marketing its concept, the popularity of the new product range was so great that it gained a larger share of the market more quickly than is usual for a firm entering a new market. The launch turned the previously sedate world of watches on its head.

Product development

New product development can be fast or slow, reactive, adaptive or proactive, but it is always hazardous.

Product-development decisions are based on market trends, competitors, customer needs and the size – and priority – of available opportunities. Internal factors include the company's strategic goals, the strength of its reputation and product portfolio, and the resources available, especially cash.

Market issues

Understand the market as clearly and accurately as possible:

- Define customers' needs and identify which features of the product will be most appealing.
- Determine, in as much detail as possible, who the product appeals to and why.
- Consider market trends, including price, customer expectations and technological developments.

Innovations can arise from experience, creative genius or by collaboratively adapting the work and ideas of others. Learn by considering how everything from market research to developing customer loyalty has been addressed in other markets and industries. Understanding the current and future sources of competition will also guide development decisions.

Product issues

Assess how a new product fits with existing ones and how well it supports the organisation's overall strategy. For example, is the organisation positioning itself as a high-value provider of premium services, or it is more concerned with high volumes and low costs?

Resource issues

Issues relating to production, personnel and operations often receive less attention during development decisions than external factors relating to customers and competitors. However, it is essential to consider such questions as:

- Are the processes, skills and resources in place to develop and sell the product?
- How can viability and in particular the profit margin be enhanced?
- How can the level of risk be reduced and the return on investment increased?

Techniques to ensure customer focus

Strengthen customer relationships

Consider how each member of your team or organisation can build relationships with customers by helping them and spending time with them. Role-play a customer complaint scenario. You should also:

- Review your team's roles and responsibilities. Are the needs of customers being adequately addressed?
- Assess your team's skills and development needs. Do people have the skills and experience needed to serve customers?

■ Review information systems. Do you have the right information about customers and is it flowing to the right people at the right time? How could it be improved?

■ Include customer issues as a regular agenda item at meetings and implement a customer service "suggestion" scheme, rewarding staff who make helpful suggestions.

Build personal relationships by listening to people

Find out what people's concerns are – both business and personal – and find ways to show that you care about customers and colleagues. Be prepared to take tough short-term decisions to build stronger relationships and:

■ encourage people to learn;

■ publicly acknowledge outstanding performance;

■ encourage people to work together across teams and internal divisions;

■ encourage people to constantly improve quality;

■ set a personal example of what being customer-focused means;

■ seek feedback from the front line.

Use expertise from other businesses to benefit customers

Identify other businesses (either internal or external) that have implemented successful customer initiatives, and consider what they did, how they did it, the resources needed (and costs), the potential pitfalls and the results and benefits.

Encourage others to value customers

Three ways to encourage others to value customers are:

■ setting an example;

■ giving positive feedback;

■ debriefing.

Seek regular feedback from customers

This can be done formally or informally. Use interviews and focus groups to collect feedback and develop an action plan to address the issues raised. Then tell your customers what you are doing to address the issues. Useful techniques include:

■ Asking customers about the one thing they want above all else. Get them to paint their ideal picture. These aspirations can be very different from what you might find using hard data alone.

■ Assessing the extent to which different customers have different needs. Can you differentiate your market and deliver different services?

■ Finding out what improvements customers want in existing products. How will your customers' needs change in the future?

If you don't work directly with customers, spend time dealing directly with them to make sure you understand what drives their sense of value.

Identify your most profitable customers

Customer profitability can be measured by analysing customer revenue and customer costs, including defection and retention costs.

Key questions

Competition and competitiveness

■ What are the main sources of competition (industry rivalry, substitutability or something else)?

■ How effectively are competitors monitored?

■ Who decides how and when to respond to competitors, and how effective have those responses been in the past?

■ How competitive is your industry, and what is the trend (more competition or less)?

■ How competitive is your organisation, and, most importantly, how does it compare to others in the eyes of the customer?

Understanding your customers

To understand your customers – both internal and external – ask:

- How often do I communicate with my customers? Is it enough?
- Do I know my customers' business?
- What do my customers want to achieve? Have I asked them?
- What are my customers' long-term goals and how can I help achieve them?
- What do my customers perceive as added value? Have I asked them or am I making assumptions?
- What do I do to add value for the customer?
- How do I exceed my customers' expectations?

Monitoring and assessing market developments

Assessing market developments (market sensing) highlights where and how the organisation can improve. For example:

- To what extent does an informed, dynamic view of the market guide managers' actions?
- How effectively does customer information flow around the organisation?
- Is there an accurate, consistent and shared understanding of customers – who they are and what they want?
- Is there an overemphasis on gathering and measuring data at the expense of action? (The danger of data infatuation.)
- Is market data used merely to justify predetermined courses of action?
- Are the customer insights influencing the organisation unique or are they easily available to competitors?
- How comprehensively are competitors' actions monitored?
- How creative is the organisation in responding to customer data? What would improve it?

Segmenting your markets

■ Do you segment your markets? Are your market segments clearly focused and simple, or do they need to change?

■ To what extent are customers and competitors considered when making decisions? Could this be improved?

■ Does your organisation collect, analyse and use all the available data? Is information kept up-to-date?

■ Are customers contacted regularly and are senior managers actively involved?

■ Are information systems capable of providing a clear understanding of customers?

Developing new products

■ What will make the product unique or valuable to customers?

■ Which benefits will be used to sell the product? How, where and by whom will the product be sold?

■ What is the pricing strategy?

15 Sales, marketing and brand management

SALES MATTER; every business is only as strong as its order book. There are many examples of organisations that failed to make the right decisions about sales, marketing or brand issues and withered as their customers went to competitors. Sales and marketing are crucial functions as product differentiation has become less clear, prices have become more transparent and customers have become more fickle and assertive.

This chapter explains how to meet customers' needs profitably, building on techniques outlined in Chapter 12. It explains how to make successful decisions about:

- pricing;
- selling;
- internet sales;
- brand management;
- customer loyalty.

Pricing

Several factors affect pricing. They include antitrust legislation, supply and demand, and price elasticity – how the volume of demand is affected by changes in price.

Successful pricing requires a clear understanding of the specific needs and nature of the target market – what the customer wants and expects. It also depends on the culture of the market; if a particular pricing structure is common, strategies will often follow it. If the market is mature with relatively few new customers, pricing should concentrate on taking customers from competitors as well as retaining market share. However, if the market is new and growing, the aim must be to build and gain market share as rapidly as possible. Conversely, if it is in decline, price cuts may be needed to attract the dwindling number of customers.

Where there are few direct competitors there may be a greater degree of latitude on pricing, especially if some of them are vulnerable to price cuts because their costs prevent them lowering their prices. Other competitors may be open to claims of poor value or quality; if so, a higher price backed by appropriate advertising could reinforce perceptions of your product's premium value and quality. Target one competitor or one group of competitors, attacking them with the most appropriate pricing strategy.

Lastly, a product's costs are fundamental to pricing, as are the benefits and value it offers the customer. Many companies use break-even analysis when setting prices (see Chapter 17).

Pricing strategies

These include the following:

- Loss leading. Selling a product at less than cost to remove competitors or establish market share. It can be dangerous if the product becomes trapped with a low price.
- Penetration pricing. Combining a low price with aggressive sales techniques to break into the market and rapidly gain market share. This works best in highly competitive markets.
- Price differentiation. Charging different prices for the same product in different markets based on what customers will pay.
- Milking. Charging a premium price for high-quality versions of an existing product. This works best when selling in an affluent market.
- Target pricing. Targeting the level of profit the organisation is seeking, estimating sales volumes at a specific price and then confirming that price. This common technique relies on accurate sales estimates and ignores competitors' actions.

- Average cost pricing. Calculating the total costs and the desired profit margin divided by anticipated total sales. This popular approach relies on accurate sales estimates and stable costs.

- Marginal cost pricing. Calculating the extra cost of supplying one more item (for example, a printer may quote a run-on price for extra copies).

- Variable pricing. Cutting prices to stimulate business or raising them to control demand. This is an extreme measure. The problem lies in explaining to customers why prices are fluctuating when the product is unchanged.

- Customary pricing. Charging the same price but reducing the product's specification (for example, changing its size). Customers may find this misleading and resent a reduction in value.

- Barrier pricing. Reducing prices aggressively – usually temporarily – to deter or remove competitors. This is similar to loss leading and requires both the will and the money to support it over time. It is common in retailing.

Deciding the right price

When making pricing decisions:

- Calculate costs. Add together the direct costs of goods or services and the sales and marketing of them, and add an appropriate amount for overheads.

- Estimate sales volumes and assess the company's competitive strength. Take into account customer needs, market maturity, sales techniques, the culture and expectations of the market and the ability to sustain the price and the product portfolio.

To make sure pricing decisions are realistic, consider:

- customer perceptions;
- whether issues of timing or seasonality affect the price;
- how easily the price can be sustained – once set, a price strategy needs to be perceived as consistent (even if the price changes) otherwise customers may become confused or resentful;

- the likely response of competitors;
- how the pricing decision relates to other aspects of strategy, including brand management, product profile and the development of the business.

Selling

One wrong move can hand the initiative to competitors and customer perceptions can be difficult to alter. Sales decisions must be based on an understanding of customers, a commitment to service and a focus on profitability, but applying these principles can be difficult.

There are several ways to keep sales decisions on track:

- View the situation from another perspective – ideally that of your customers. Tailor your offer to suit their needs and priorities.
- Prepare a plan of action that will deliver success.
- Avoid basing decisions about customers on assumptions. Sustaining a dialogue with customers offers greater insights of a higher quality.
- Share information and insights about customers throughout the organisation and with others involved (such as agents) to better co-ordinate activities and decisions. Success is more likely if decisions are based on the same information and perceptions.
- Highlight the product's benefits, not just its features, and highlight where it compares favourably with competitors' products.
- Consider cross-selling additional products to existing customers and focus on increasing the value derived from each client. Don't offer discounts and special offers to everyone: they are most effective when targeted at specific clients or groups of customers.
- Build customer loyalty and respect for your brand. Satisfied customers are easier to keep and sell to repeatedly. To achieve such satisfaction, consider what matters to each customer – as far as possible – and bind customers to the product through initiatives such as loyalty schemes.

- Consider using a range of incentives such as discounts or easier payment terms to close the deal, but make sure payment will be made on the terms agreed.

- Develop uniqueness – either unique insights into customer needs that competitors do not possess or innovative features in the product or sales process that are distinctive and popular, or both.

- Act quickly and decisively to impress or reassure customers. To do otherwise may be interpreted as a lack of concern.

- Manage and update information systems to ensure a supportive approach to customers.

Ryder: helping customers to buy

In the early 1990s, Ryder, the world's largest truck-leasing business, suffered a steady decline in sales as its customers went elsewhere. Ryder's main response was to use information more effectively to benefit customers in a three-pronged approach:

- To help customers buy. For example, Ryder produced a truck-comparison chart, highlighting its competitive features and reassuring potential customers. It also printed brochures explaining the advantages of Ryder's damage insurance and to offer accessories.

- To help the customer use the service. Ryder offered a free guide to moving home to current and potential customers, published in Spanish and English. The company understood why customers used its trucks and used this advantage to help them.

- To help customers adapt their usage. Ryder introduced new services such as providing information about the advantages of using its towing equipment and details of longer-term discount rates to attract customers back.

The effect of these measures was monitored through a customer satisfaction survey form placed in each cab. As well as checking that customers were satisfied, this highlighted Ryder's renewed commitment to service.

These measures helped Ryder to revive its business during a recession and regain its position as the industry leader.

Customer loyalty is crucial to the success of a business and requires:

- measuring the profitability of customers so that you focus on keeping the most profitable loyal;
- developing a customer's lifetime value.

Emphasise your selling points

Every product should have an effective, direct and easily summarised selling point which appeals to the customer and is not shared by competitors. Yet surprisingly few businesses employ this concept, either meeting an industry standard without surpassing it or relying solely on market momentum for profitability. This approach was rejected by Tesco, a UK retailer, when it decided to achieve market superiority by remaining open 24 hours a day, becoming the first UK supermarket to do so. Tesco also introduced a number of other unique selling points (USPs), including the promise to open an extra checkout if more than one customer was queuing and providing a complimentary bag-packing service.

USPs can be emotional as well as offering the customer a practical benefit. This enables businesses to differentiate themselves and their products by using marketing techniques to trigger emotional reactions in prospective clients. For instance, although Mercedes-Benz cars are functional, the company has succeeded in selling them to people with a limited knowledge of cars who want to project a certain image.

Constant striving for selling points that make a firm stand out from its competitors drives businesses forward, preventing stagnation, benefiting consumers and increasing profits.

The following techniques help to develop product competitiveness:

- Recognise that your selling points may need to change quickly. If they are successful, competitors will mimic them. Innovate to find new selling points and remain ahead of the competition.
- Find out what your customers value most, what they lack and what they will pay for it. This may be the product's benefits to them, its price or the service they receive.

- Offer the highest quality to make sure your product has both practical and emotional, status-oriented selling points.
- Offer the widest choice. This can involve specialising and segmenting your market.

Internet sales

Selling on the internet offers many advantages, not just connecting with more potential customers across a wide spectrum. However, the internet is also a source of strong, hidden undercurrents that can blow plans off course or drown them in technology. The benefits are:

- increasing sales both to current and potential customers;
- reducing sales costs;
- satisfying more customers so that they return and generate market share and competitive advantage by reinventing whole industries.

Above all, internet activities must be integrated into the whole business.

Reducing sales costs and improving efficiency

The internet provides the latest details about products, testimonials, special offers and customer or market intelligence. It is especially valuable when in-depth product information is needed, as this can be made available directly to distributors as well as the sales force.

The internet allows products to be evaluated quickly and without assistance, which can be helpful with complex products or in rapidly evolving markets. Product and technical experts can be used to greater effect, and complex, customised quotations can be prepared without sales people intervening. This has several advantages: providing an immediate response to customers' enquiries; reducing the lead time for sales; ensuring accurate transmission of order details; and saving time and effort. In effect, doing it better, more quickly and more cost-effectively.

Lastly, the internet can cut inventory costs when products are made to order.

Building customer loyalty online

The internet makes it easier for customers to do business with you. It satisfies them, it encourages them to come back, and it cuts sales costs through increasing customer loyalty.

The elements to building customer loyalty online are as follows:

■ Customers will return to a website if they believe it is relevant to them.

■ The website must be easy to use. Customers must feel that it is responsive and provides what they want without irritatingly directing them along a predetermined course.

■ The website should be accurate and immediate, offering the chance to question or change choices before confirming details without raising fears that the order will go wrong.

■ The website needs to offer an element of service that is unique and options that are likely to suit the target customer.

If these elements can be included in an organisation's website, it is likely that returned shipments, adjustments and dissatisfied customers will decrease, combining cost reductions with increased customer loyalty.

Boosting internet sales

Seven decisions can help to drive sales online:

■ Generate participation, ownership and commitment throughout the business so that a co-ordinated, cross-functional approach is taken that increases value for the customer and reduces costs.

■ Make sure that the online sales strategy enhances existing activities and benefits from experience.

■ Simplify the customer's experience so that the sales process is streamlined with barriers to purchasing removed.

■ Make customers want to remain at the site when they arrive and then return time and again.

■ Focus on flexibility and personal service so customers are able to buy exactly what they want and how they want it.

■ Don't waste money, as so many firms have done. Avoid a complicated, high-cost solution when an effective, low-cost alternative is available.

■ Be realistic about what an internet sales strategy will deliver over time so that the organisation avoids investing too much, too little, too late or too soon.

The best online sales decisions blend experience and existing resources with the dynamism and invention of the internet. The internet's flexibility is a useful tool in effectively testing decisions and ideas, allowing one approach to be tried for a short period before making enhancements.

Ten critical Cs

Ten issues affect the success of online business activities:

■ content;

■ communication;

■ customer care;

■ community and culture;

■ convenience and ease;

■ connectivity (connecting with other sites and also with users);

■ cost and profitability;

■ customisation;

■ capability (dynamic, responsive and flexible);

■ competitiveness.

Each of the above influences the success of online activities. Some will be more important than others, depending on the organisation's stage of development, brand strength and competitive position. Some such as capability and convenience are always crucial, whereas others can be more significant at a particular time. For instance, competitiveness, while always in the background, may suddenly be relevant.

Viral marketing

The term viral marketing was invented to describe Hotmail's practice of including its own advertising message in outgoing e-mail from users. The concept is that if the advertisement reaches a susceptible user, that person will become "infected" and will then infect other susceptible users. As long as each infected user contacts, on average, more than one susceptible user, the number of infected users seeing the message will grow quickly.

The Hotmail strategy is simple. It provides free e-mail addresses and services with a tag at the bottom of every message: "Get your private, free email at http://www.hotmail.com." As people send e-mails to their friends and associates, more and more people see the message and sign up for the free e-mail service. This creates an ever-increasing circle of contacts, like a pebble creating ripples in a pond.

To succeed viral marketing must:

- Give away valuable products or services to attract attention. Viral marketers may not profit immediately, but if they generate interest from something "free" they soon will.

- Be easy to transfer or transmit. The medium that carries the marketing message must be easy to transfer and replicate, for example e-mail, website or software downloads. Viral marketing works online because instant communication is easy and inexpensive.

- Be simple. The most effective marketing messages are simple and compelling. Viral marketing messages must be simple enough to be transmitted easily and without confusion.

- Exploit people's motivations. People want to be connected, popular and understood, and they are self-centred as well as well-intentioned. Consequently, they produce blogs and forward e-mails and web addresses. So, design a marketing strategy that builds on common motivations and behaviours for its transmission.

- Use existing networks. Network marketers have long understood the power of human networks, both the strong, close networks as well as the weaker networked relationships. Use these networks to communicate your message.

■ Benefit from others' resources. Creative viral marketing plans use other people's resources to communicate. For example, affiliate programmes place text or graphic links on websites; and authors write free articles or establish web links.

Brand management

Brands are complex assets with distinguishing features. They help customers to understand what they are being offered or buying.

A popular method of managing a brand is to view it as having a personality. For example, Rolls-Royce cars are known for high quality and luxury and Walmart has a reputation for convenience and low prices.

A strong brand identity:

■ Commands a substantial price premium for a product, exceeding the extra production and marketing costs. The added value comes from the trust the brand enjoys.

■ Reinforces the product's appeal. For example, Rolls-Royce cars are associated with craftsmanship, tradition and prestige while Volvo is known more for safety and functionality. These values reinforce each brand's appeal to specific market segments. When markets decline, however, brand identity can become a handicap, linking the product to an unfashionable past.

■ Builds customer loyalty. Customers can identify preferred brands easily, becoming repeat purchasers. In the earlier days of computers, the adage that "no one ever got fired for buying IBM" was very powerful in sustaining the market dominance the company enjoyed before it fell to earth only to later reinvent itself.

■ Gives new products a flying start by exploiting the strengths of an established brand. Cherry Coke and Diet Coke were aided by being associated with one of the world's strongest brands. The new products reinforced the Coca-Cola brand strengths by attacking the competition, adding a new dimension to the brand (innovation) and developing new markets (diet cola).

- Helps the product extend its geographic market and spreads the brand's popularity. For example, coffee shops such as Starbucks grew during the 1990s in the US north-west and then spread throughout the US and Europe.

- Extends the life of a product. Lego producing toys linked to films is an example of this.

- Provides a market-oriented focus around which companies can organise. The brand manager is often directly responsible for what the product offers as well as how it appears to the customer.

Building a strong brand

Building a brand is complex, expensive and time-consuming. Sometimes it is seen as a natural by-product of building a successful business; sometimes it is made a priority in its own right. Either way, the successful development of a brand depends on making good decisions.

Decide the brand's purpose

A crucial question is: how will the brand be used? Is it to provide reassurance, to enable a premium price to be charged, or to create a desire to buy? What benefits can the brand offer customers? How reliable and trustworthy is it? Is it credible in the eyes of the customer? Is the market value of an established brand increasing or declining, and what is affecting its success?

Emphasise the brand's values

Understand what the brand means to customers, or what it is intended to mean, and then find ways to reinforce this appeal. This can be achieved by considering all aspects of the brand – for example, to whom does it appeal? Does the tone of voice reflect the brand's values, target market and any existing perceptions? If you had to describe the brand as an entity, what would you choose and why?

Use the brand

Understanding how the brand differentiates a product from its competitors is central to deciding which attributes to focus on and how to attack competitors. What makes it exceptional? How special is the brand and how easy would it be to replicate? Ideally, there should be sufficient barriers to replication to make sure the brand remains strong and distinctive. A brand audit will help to show how strong and credible it appears to customers, as well as giving guidance on how far the brand can be stretched into new markets and the values that could help (or hinder) that process. Lastly, consider whether there is enough investment in the brand and how it can be strengthened.

Customer loyalty

A popular way to build repeat business is to have a customer loyalty programme. It can provide insights into the brand values of the company as well as the threat they pose to competitors. For example, to reduce the time it takes to get new customers, in its early days Virgin Atlantic offered a free companion ticket to any British Airways frequent flyer who had accumulated 10,000 air miles. This directly challenged a large competitor and reinforced perceptions of the Virgin brand as being dynamic, bold and original.

Building customer relationships

There is a misconception that to sell successfully you must be aggressive. This leads to inappropriate behaviour. For example, sales people can become evasive, pushy and aggressive, or overly talkative. Influencing people to buy depends on getting behaviour right, balancing openness and assertiveness with warmth and competence. Combined with a strong product or brand, this goes a long way towards building customer loyalty.

Harley-Davidson: building customer loyalty

In the 1980s, the sales of Harley-Davidson, a famous US motorcycle brand, fell dramatically as a result of competition from affordable, high-quality Japanese machines. In response, Harley-Davidson improved its quality using just-in-time production techniques (see Chapter 17).

The next challenge was to win back and maintain market share. Knowledge of customers' needs and appealing to their emotions helped Harley-Davidson build customer trust. Managers meet customers regularly at rallies, where new models are demonstrated. Advertising reinforces the brand image and the Harley Owners Group (HOG) entrenches customer loyalty, with two-thirds of customers renewing their membership. Significantly, Harley-Davidson makes sure that customers receive the benefits they value. Now 90% of its customers join the HOG or make repeat purchases, or both.

This trust is used to develop stronger bonds and greater profits in a virtuous circle. Rich Teerlink, a former chairman of Harley-Davidson, commented:

Perhaps the most significant program was – and continues to be – the Harley Owners Group … Dealers regained confidence that Harley could and would be a dependable partner… [And] capturing the ideas of our people – all the people at Harley – was critical to our future success.

To make sure decisions benefit customers and improve long-term sales and profits:

- be competitive;
- deliver a consistent (ideally branded) experience each time a customer deals with your business;
- make a customer's experience as simple and enjoyable as possible;
- be clear about the value proposition – what you are offering customers;
- provide incentives for new customers to return and reorder;
- reward loyalty from established customers;
- reassure customers with a reliable service and product offer;
- continuously improve the process, based on customer feedback;
- deliver reliability by working with partners and investing in resources.

Key questions

Sales, marketing and brand management decisions are crucial, complex and change quickly, so approach them thoughtfully and regularly.

Pricing

- How elastic are product prices? Could they be increased without reducing revenue?
- When is the next price rise planned? Could it happen sooner?
- Are there forces driving down prices in your market? What are they and how can they be countered?
- Who sets prices in your organisation? How do they do it and could the process be improved?
- Are discounts targeted at the right sectors, or are they needlessly eroding profitability?
- Could pricing be used more aggressively?

Market entry

- What are the barriers to entry in your market? How high are they? Could you make it even harder for competitors to enter the market?
- When is the best time to enter or leave the market? What can be done to discourage and reduce the effectiveness of competitors entering?
- If you are planning to enter a new market, what makes your offer distinctive and likely to succeed?
- Are other firms entering the market? If not, why?

Selling

- Do people in the organisation view sales from the customers' perspective?
- How well does the business know each individual customer? Could more data be gathered and assessed?

- Do people in the organisation share information and insights about customers?
- Are product benefits (not just product features) highlighted?
- Could you sell more to existing customers?
- Does the organisation act decisively and swiftly to reassure and impress customers?

Internet sales

- Does the organisation take a co-ordinated approach to selling online?
- Is buying online from you an easy and worthwhile experience for the customer? How could it be improved?
- Is your website attractive, practical and relevant? Can it be improved?
- Is the organisation ready for the changes that may result from greater internet sales?

Brand management

- What is the purpose of the brand? What values does it need to emphasise to customers?
- How can the brand be used to greatest effect?
- Is sufficient attention given to building and publicising the brand?
- Is the brand used consistently?

Product positioning

- Is the product in the right part of the market?
- What is the best way to appeal to customers? How should the product be sold?
- Are you confronting the market leader? Are you in danger of waking a sleeping giant?
- Is a simple, consistent and compelling message being used to sell the product?

Customer loyalty

- Do you measure the profitability of customers?
- Are you targeting, attracting and retaining the most profitable customers?
- What plans are in place to keep customers loyal? Are they appealing to customers and difficult for competitors to copy?

16 Managing knowledge and information

KNOWLEDGE AND INFORMATION are essential for making effective decisions, so it is crucial to develop a leadership style and a simple, robust system that allows information and expertise to flow freely to where it can be used by those who need it.

Knowledge and information can affect:

- the way people act, their responsibilities and the work they do;
- status, training needs, accountability and the level of control;
- how people delegate, manage time, recruit, communicate, lead others and make decisions.

Making successful strategic decisions requires being open and transparent and sharing information. Yet many organisations pay insufficient attention to the valuable knowledge accumulated over years and stored in their employees' heads, relying instead on technology or data flow for information.

The strategic value of knowledge and information

Information is objective; knowledge includes elements of interpretation and understanding. Technological developments have sparked an explosion in the scope and depth of information and knowledge available to decision-makers. What sets successful organisations apart is their ability to develop and use them creatively.

Knowledge and information have to be collected, protected and effectively managed if they are to guide and inform every stage of decision-making. There is increasing recognition of the benefits of using not just some but all employees' knowledge. When information is withheld or poorly managed, it often causes suspicion, frustration or resentment. However, introducing systems to control and direct information can be disruptive, causing additional work and pressure.

There are several significant ways in which knowledge and information can benefit a business's strategy:

- Costly mistakes can be avoided by recording events and using this to understand why decisions were made and to avoid repeating the failures of the past.
- Greater flexibility and faster response times can be achieved by combining knowledge in interdisciplinary teams.
- Products and services can be improved by monitoring product failures and customer views and by sharing ideas and experiences.
- Customer service is enhanced and customers are attracted and retained because identifying and disseminating information about best practices will help improve customer service.
- The financial value of an organisation increases as people develop and share insights and assets, helping the business to improve and grow.
- Greater teamwork and higher levels of engagement stem from sharing information and knowledge, fostering an open, supportive exchange of ideas and making decisions based, as far as possible, on consensus.

Reading between the lines: Amazon

Information can be used to save costs, provide a tailor-made service to individual clients and to sell more – often using the internet.

Amazon, an online retailer that has moved from selling just books to selling all kinds of products, uses information in three ways. It:

- analyses information from millions of customers to see how and when they purchase, enabling it to reduce the level of risk;

- cuts costs by using technology to control how it manages its stocks and suppliers;
- uses information to add value and help customers by offering reviews of books and other free downloadable information and by making its website an individual shop window for each customer. For example, it tailors lists of suggested titles the customer may enjoy based on previous purchases.

It is not what information exists but how it is used to build competitive advantage that matters. Many other retailers have followed Amazon's lead; for example, Apple's iTunes and iStore apply the same principles to their music retailing. These include:

- Treating each customer as an individual. iTunes tracks each customer's purchases and provides a customised web page to suggest other products the client might like.

- Using the internet to provide information on individuals (even if your business does not carry out its primary operations online). By collecting customers' e-mail addresses, a business can develop an intimate marketing strategy.

- Enabling employees to research in-depth information about each client. This can be organised into an accessible database with subheadings covering areas of relevant information.

If your organisation has difficulties in tracking consumer trends, use incentives such as free products to encourage customers to volunteer information. Similarly, offer a reward to customers for agreeing to receive information about your organisation – the marketing should be entertaining, lively, appropriate and relevant.

Techniques for managing knowledge and information

There are various techniques for effectively managing knowledge.

Undertaking a knowledge audit

This is designed to uncover the breadth, depth and location of an organisation's knowledge, and has three components:

- Defining what knowledge assets exist, especially information or skills that would be difficult or expensive to replace.
- Locating those assets – discovering who keeps or "owns" them.
- Classifying them and assessing how they relate to other assets. This may lead to opportunities being found in other parts of the organisation.

Increasing knowledge

The results of a knowledge audit allow an organisation to use and develop its knowledge and information to support the business's strategy. The challenge is to increase the knowledge base, which can be done by:

- buying knowledge by hiring staff, forming alliances and partnerships or outsourcing;
- renting knowledge by hiring consultants or subcontracting work;
- developing knowledge through training and continuous learning.

Visiting websites and talking to others in similar businesses is a good way to help build a dependable knowledge base.

Maintaining knowledge

Knowledge gaps make an organisation vulnerable to competition. There are many examples of the dangers of downsizing that highlight the dangers of getting rid of people with expertise and experience in the pursuit of short-term cost savings. It is crucial to identify and then capture, codify and store people's expertise and tacit knowledge.

Protecting knowledge

Knowledge is a source of competitive advantage, so it must be protected. It falls into two categories: explicit knowledge, such as copyright or information in handbooks, systems or procedures; and tacit knowledge that is retained by individuals, including learning, experience, observation, deduction and informally acquired knowledge. Explicit knowledge can be protected through legal procedures. Tacit knowledge can be partially protected by legal methods (such as non-compete clauses in employment contracts), but it is sensible to record tacit knowledge and make sure it is passed on.

Establishing information systems

An efficient information management system will co-ordinate and control information and aid planning. There are three main stages in developing a system:

- Decide what information is needed, perhaps preparing a wish list of what will help improve decisions and achieve objectives. Information can be categorised by type, such as customer information, financial details and staff information. Some information may fall into more than one category.

- Understand when information is required and who needs it. Too much data produced too frequently can create information overload, making it harder to spot trends or relevant detail. Knowing who requires each piece of information involves assessing how information flows through an organisation. Information that flows according to status, from the top to the bottom, along the channels of the organisation chart, has inherent weaknesses – some people may require more data, or more time with it, than others.

- Display the information to maximum advantage. It must be clear and accessible; too much information is distracting but too little is inadequate.

You must also:

- Secure the information. Confidential data should be secure and all information should be backed up to prevent it being lost. Back-up files or documents should be kept at a different location.

- Manage costs and provide the necessary support. To gain maximum value from investments in information technology, list the functions and features that are required (including price and support) to ensure that minimum requirements are met.

■ Make data available for shared use throughout the organisation. Resolve any problems or concerns that may prevent this from happening.

■ Be aware of legal requirements and their implications, particularly relating to data held about customers, suppliers and employees. These requirements are increasing in scope and complexity.

■ Establish rules to prevent misuse or misinterpretation of data.

Managing the flow of information

To maximise the usefulness of any information system, understand how information flows, what it is used for and the ways in which it can be applied.

Understanding information requirements

To identify information requirements and make information routinely, consistently and reliably available, ask:

■ What information is needed?

■ How should it be presented (online, in writing, occasionally, informally, in meetings, by memo)?

■ When does it need to be supplied (timing and frequency)?

■ Where does it come from? This can affect the quality of information, as well as relevant details that put the facts into context.

■ What restrictions are there? Is some or all of the information confidential?

■ Which decisions and activities will it support? It helps if people understand why the information is needed.

Acquiring the right data

Information should be reliable and relevant if it is to be useful. There are many techniques for acquiring it, including surveys, telephone calls, meetings and interviews, as well as libraries and information centres. Customer surveys can be carried out online, and used discerningly the web is a source of regularly updated information. The skill lies in deciding which is the most appropriate technique for your purposes.

Reviewing and analysing information allows options to emerge and their effectiveness to be assessed. The quality of a decision depends on judgment, but quantitative statistical methods will highlight trends and anomalies, and scenario planning, modelling and simulation can help generate and assess information (see Chapter 5).

Storing and retrieving data

Information should be clearly labelled and categorised, and there should be criteria for adding information and discarding (or archiving) old, irrelevant details. The system and processes for storing and retrieving information should be cost-effective.

Using information

Three practices are useful when using information:

- Monitor decisions. See how well a decision is being implemented and assess whether new decisions are necessary and the implications for future choices.
- Act methodically. If the method is flawed, so may be the resulting decision.
- Manage constraints and other pressures. Keep a firm eye on objectives even if the deadline is tight.

Information orientation

Despite the billions of dollars invested each year in software and hardware, research indicates that most managers do not know what they must do to make sure these investments improve an organisation's profits.

Donald Marchand, professor of strategy and information management at IMD, a business school in Lausanne, Switzerland, and William Kettinger, professor of information systems at Moore School of Business at the University of South Carolina, conducted research that identified three factors critical to using information successfully. These factors combine to provide an overall measure of information orientation (IO),[1] which is being used increasingly by international companies as a guide when building their IT capabilities.

It is often said that you cannot manage what you cannot measure. Marchand emphasises that you cannot measure what you cannot see, and how managers see the world defines their actions and what they are able to achieve. Unfortunately, many managers see the use of information only within the narrow context of technology. However, technology and information in isolation do not create sustainable competitive advantage.

This view is potentially toxic for suppliers of customer relationship management (CRM), enterprise resource planning (ERP) and other software systems, which are often promoted as the technological panacea for whatever ails an organisation. According to CIO *Magazine*, in the early 2000s up to 70% of CRM projects would not produce measurable business benefits.[2] Anecdotal evidence from a number of consultants, business schools and corporations suggests that although this figure has fallen, there is still a lot of work to be done to ensure that CRM projects routinely and significantly produce measurable business benefits.

The three capabilities of information orientation

Research by Marchand and enterpriseIQ, a business analytics company of which he is chairman, involving more than 4,000 managers from 130 companies in 71 countries and 27 industries demonstrates that three information capabilities exist: the organisation's information behaviours and values; its information management practices; and its IT practices. The three capabilities contain 15 competencies (see Figure 16.1).

The three capabilities combine to determine how effectively information is used in decision-making:

- Information behaviours and values. This is the capability of an organisation to instil and promote behaviours and values for effective use of information. Managers should promote integrity,

FIG 16.1 **The Information Orientation Maturity Model**

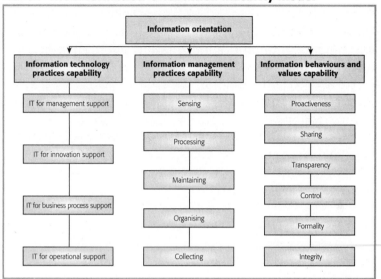

Source: Donald Marchand

formality, control, transparency and sharing, removing barriers to information flow and promoting its use.

■ Information management practices. Managing information involves sensing, collecting, organising, processing and maintaining information. Managers set up processes, train their employees and take responsibility for the management of information, thus focusing their organisations on the right information. They take care to avoid (or at least minimise) information overload, improve the quality of information available to employees and enhance decision-making.

■ Information technology practices. IT applications and infrastructure should support decision-making. Consequently, business strategy needs to be linked to IT strategy so that the IT systems and applications really do support operations, business processes, innovation and decisions.

Marchand and Kettinger found that companies with multiple

business units do not always build the same levels of IO across the entire company.

Avoiding disorientation: information orientation at work

Several companies have successfully implemented big IT projects. For example, Banco Bilbao Vizcaya Argentaria (BBVA) transformed its failing branch-based retail banking business into one of the most successful banks in Spain. It did so by getting the right information to people in the branches, which enabled them to successfully cross-sell their products. BBVA kept its new customer relationship project simple by giving branch staff:

- an easy-to-use and intuitive IT system;
- clear information about customer segmentation, sales targets and company performance information;
- team-building incentives, to create an open culture emphasising teamwork and action.

Similarly, Cemex used IT to transform its commodity business in Monterrey, Mexico, into the world's largest cement group (see Chapter 18).

Managing information so that decisions are as effective as possible depends upon how people use the information and systems, how they share their knowledge with others and how motivated they are to use information to innovate and create value. It also depends on the processes used to manage information and knowledge. The technology itself is just a tool. The IO measure, with its broader, rigorous assessment of the information capabilities in an organisation, provides a framework for managing all aspects of information effectively.

Organisational learning

New ideas are essential to improving an organisation. They may come from flashes of creative brilliance, from other industries or from analysis of new information. Ideas are central to making the right decisions, solving problems and adding value for customers. This can be achieved by efficiently applying knowledge and information. Companies that do so are learning organisations, defined as:[3]

An organisation skilled at creating, acquiring and transferring knowledge, and at modifying its behaviour to reflect new knowledge and insights.

It is in this last part of the definition – the need to modify behaviour – that so many organisations fail. Those that match the full description have made huge improvements in overall performance, largely by transforming the way in which knowledge is used. They include Honda, General Electric, Corning and General Motors' Saturn Division.

Organisational learning is a powerful technique for improving performance, especially in turbulent times. In business, learning is used in the context of attempts to improve efficiency and effectiveness and to be more innovative in uncertain market conditions. The greater the uncertainty, the greater is the need for learning. Arie De Geus, who worked at Shell for many years before becoming a business academic, says that in the long run survival depends on decisions displaying a sensitivity to the environment and being flexible. This is embodied in an organisation's ability to learn, to experiment, to continually explore new opportunities to create new sources of wealth and value, and to change its behaviour to fit what is happening around it.

David Kolb, a management writer, says that the learning process consists of four stages: experiences, reflective observation, abstract conceptualisation and active experimentation.

It begins with observing what has occurred, reflecting on what has been observed and assessing the underlying structures that drive the behaviour observed. From this we can develop a theory about what is happening that influences the development of a decision. These actions create an expectation, which will usually differ from reality. This triggers the next phase of the learning cycle: reflection, conceptualisation and mental model building.

Learning is a continuous process. Reflection and action combine to produce learning. Without action there can be no learning because all

FIG 16.2 **The cycle of learning**

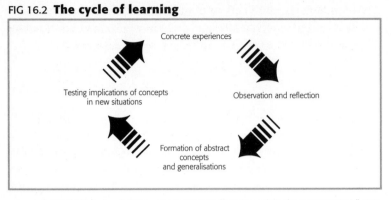

Source: Kolb, D., *Experiential Learning as a Source of Learning and Development*, Prentice Hall, 1984

that we can then reflect on is our previous reflections. Kolb's learning cycle is illustrated in Figure 16.2.

Organisational learning occurs when people reflect on their experiences, collectively develop new theories based on observation and then act together. In the process of joint reflection, individual views are shared and create a shared understanding. Without joint action, organisational learning cannot occur.

A tendency to act without first reflecting can be reinforced by organisational cultures and reward systems. Managers must be seen to be doing things. Sitting and thinking is seen as being idle, even though spending time thinking about how to build competitive advantage and profits is essential. Action and reflection are therefore essential for organisational learning.

Changing an organisation's culture and the way it functions takes time, but the following steps will help turn an organisation into a learning one:

■ Foster an atmosphere conducive to learning. Give managers time to pause and reflect, to use their knowledge to generate new insights and ideas, and, above all, to learn. This process of learning can be compromised by pressures and stress.

■ Stimulate the exchange of ideas by reducing bureaucracy and boundaries. In most organisations, structures, hierarchies and boundaries inhibit the flow of information, keeping individuals and groups isolated and reinforcing preconceptions. Emphasising communication and opening up the organisation lead to fresh flows of ideas, competing perspectives and insights. Jack Welch, former CEO of General Electric, says "boundarylessness" is one of the most potent forces for change.

■ Create learning forums. Once managers are working within a supportive, stimulating environment, they can create opportunities to foster learning by letting people wrestle with new knowledge and consider its implications. A learning forum can be anything from a strategic review or benchmark report to visiting customers or a supplier.

These steps are just a start. Any action – such as using appraisals to engender support and enthusiasm for learning – that removes barriers to learning and promotes action-centred learning will improve an organisation's decisions and actions through better knowledge and understanding.

Key questions

■ Does useful information flow freely and easily through the organisation to the people that need it and can use it to greatest effect?

■ How well is information used for decision-making? Are there examples of failings that could have been mitigated with more effective use of knowledge and information?

■ Would your organisation benefit from a knowledge audit – a methodical assessment of where critical knowledge lies within the business?

■ Is the website adding to the organisation's knowledge base? How might information collection be improved?

■ How well does your organisation use it to support management, innovation, business processes and operations?

■ How successfully does your organisation sense, process, maintain, organise and collect information? Is this assessed, and could it be improved?

- Is information in your organisation shared, transparent, controlled and formalised, with its veracity and integrity protected?

17 Managing finance and risk

FINANCE IS THE LIFEBLOOD of a business, heavily influencing strategies and decisions at every level. J.K. Galbraith, a Nobel Prize-winning economist, said:

> There can be few fields of human endeavour where history counts for so little as in the world of finance.

Many managers find it difficult to get to grips with financial issues and, as the 2008 global financial crisis revealed, many lost touch with basic financial ground rules.

Profitability, cash flow, long-term shareholder value and risk all need to be considered when setting and reviewing strategy. This chapter provides practical guidance about financial decisions and explains how to:

- improve profitability;
- avoid pitfalls in making financial decisions;
- reduce financial risk.

Improving profitability

Entrepreneurial flair and financial rigour are as much about attitude as skill. Nonetheless, certain skills will ensure that decisions are focused on commercial success.

Variance analysis

Interpreting the differences between actual and planned performance is crucial. Variance analysis is used to monitor and manage the results of past decisions, assess the current situation and highlight solutions.

The process starts by breaking down substantial variances into their component parts, identifying exactly where and why the variance occurred. Although it is best to focus on the most significant difference first, seemingly small issues can have significant effects. For example, small variances in unit costs or unit prices can have significant effects on volumes and alter profitability. Using key performance indicators (KPIs) will identify significant variances.

Common causes of variances include inefficiency, poor or flawed planning (for example, relying on historically inaccurate information), poor communication, interdependence between departments and random factors. Every business should use variance analysis but in a practical and pragmatic and cost-effective way.

Market entry and exit barriers[1]

How easy or difficult it is to either enter or leave a market is crucial in strategic decision-making. Entry barriers include the need to compete with businesses that enjoy economies of scale, or established, differentiated products. Other barriers include capital requirements, access to distribution channels, factors independent of scale (such as technology or location) and regulatory requirements. When markets are difficult or costly for competitors to enter and relatively easy and affordable to leave, firms can achieve high, stable returns, while still being able to leave for other opportunities. Consider where the barriers to entry lie for your market sector, how vulnerable you are to new entrants, and whether you can strengthen and entrench your market position.

Break-even analysis

Knowing when a project or new business will break even will affect any decision to invest money, time and resources.

The break-even point is when sales cover costs, where neither a profit nor a loss is made. It is calculated by dividing the costs of the project by the gross profit at specific dates, making sure to allow for overhead costs. Break-even analysis (cost–volume–profit or CVP analysis) is used to decide whether to continue developing a product, alter the price, provide or adjust a discount, or change suppliers to reduce costs. It also helps in managing the sales mix, cost structure and production capacity, as well as in forecasting and budgeting.

For break-even analysis to be reliable, the sales price per unit should be constant, as should the sales mix. Stock levels should not vary significantly.

Controlling costs

To control costs:

- Focus on the big items of expenditure. Categorise costs into major or peripheral items. Often, undue emphasis is given to the 80% of activities accounting for 20% of costs.

- Be cost aware. Casualness is the enemy of cost control. While focusing on major items of expenditure it may also be possible to cut the cost of peripheral items. Costs can be reduced over the medium to long term by managers' attitudes to cost control and the effects of expenses on cash flow.

- Maintain a balance between costs and quality. Getting the best value means achieving a balance between the price paid and the quality received.

- Use budgets for dynamic financial management. Budget early so financial requirements are known as soon as possible. Consider the best time-period for the budget – normally a year but it depends on the type of business. Some larger firms have moved to rolling budgets, getting managers to forecast the next 18 months every quarter. Budgets provide a starting point for cash flow forecasts and revenues, and they also play an essential role in monitoring costs and revenues.

- Develop a positive attitude to budgeting. People need to understand, accept and use the budget, feeling a sense of ownership and responsibility for developing, monitoring and controlling it.

- Eliminate waste. For decades, leading Japanese companies have directed much of their cost-management efforts towards waste elimination. They achieve this by using techniques such as process analysis, mapping and re-engineering.

Routes to profitability: Harley-Davidson and Caterpillar

After several difficult years in the late 1970s, motorcycle manufacturer Harley-Davidson was bought out in 1981. Soon after that its senior managers visited Honda's motorcycle plant in Marysville, Ohio. They saw dramatic differences between that factory and their own in terms of layout, production flow, efficiency and inventory management. They realised that if Harley wanted to compete with Japanese motorcycle manufacturers, it would have to introduce a just-in-time manufacturing system they called MAN – materials as needed. This streamlined production, reducing the resources required for materials handling. Inventories the company received (and produced) too early were cut and the space required for manufacturing was reduced. This created space for additional production as demand for Harley's motorcycles grew.

Similarly, during the 1980s, Caterpillar, the world's largest manufacturer of construction and mining equipment, realised that its costs were much higher than those of its main competitor, Komatsu of Japan. Caterpillar was moving parts and partially finished products from one production area to another, but Komatsu was using a "flow" process. Caterpillar created its own flow process, which cut the distances between operations and reduced materials handling expenses, inventory levels and the cycle time for producing products. In some cases, the cycle time was cut by 80%.

Improving profitability

Some practical techniques to improve profitability:

- Focus decision-making on the most profitable areas. Concentrating on products and services with the best margin will protect or enhance profitability. This might involve redirecting sales and advertising activities.

- Decide how to treat the least profitable products. These often drift, with dwindling profitability. Turn around a poor performer (by reducing costs, raising prices, altering discounts or changing the product) or abandon it to prevent a drain on resources and reputation. The shelf-life and appeal of a product must be considered when deciding to continue or discontinue it.

■ Make sure new products enhance overall profitability. New product development often focuses on market need or the production process, with insufficient regard to cost, price, sales volume and overall profitability, which are inextricably linked.

■ Manage development and production decisions. The amount spent on research, as well as the priorities and methods used, affect profitability. Too little expenditure may increase costs in the long term.

■ Set the buying policy. For example, should there be a small number of preferred suppliers or a bidding system among a wider number of potential suppliers? Also, consider techniques for controlling delivery charges, monitoring exchange rates, improving quality control, reducing inventory and improving production lead times.

■ Consider how to create greater value from existing customers and products to enhance profitability. Ask:

   - How can customer loyalty (and repeat purchasing) be enhanced?
   - How can the sales proposition be made more competitive relative to the opposition?
   - How can existing markets, sales channels, products, brand reputation and other resources be adapted to exploit new markets and new opportunities?
   - How can sales expenses be reduced?
   - How can the effectiveness of marketing activities be increased?

■ Consider how to increase profitability by managing people. Successful leadership is a prerequisite for profitability (see Chapter 11). People need to be motivated and supported, and this implies rewarding them fairly for their work, training and developing them, providing a clear sense of direction, and focusing on the needs of the team, the task and the individual.

There are many techniques for assessing the likely profitability of an investment. One of the most used is to apply discounted cash flows.

Discounted cash flow and investment appraisal decisions[2]

Discounted cash flow (DCF) is based on the principle that cash today is worth more than cash promised in the future. This means it is not worth investing $100,000 today for the promise of the same amount returned next year; more usefully, DCF can show that it may not be worth investing $100,000 today for the promise of $110,000 in three years' time and explains why.

There are three reasons:

- The organisation investing the $100,000 is bearing a market risk, and risk demands return. The greater the risk, the greater the compensation required.
- The investor is bearing an opportunity cost – it cannot invest the same money in another venture – and this cost also requires return.
- The value of the investor's money is being reduced by inflation, and this also demands a return. If annual inflation is running at 2.5%, an organisation investing $100,000 will need a yield after tax of $2,500 a year, just to compensate for inflation.

There are five steps in DCF analysis:

1 Project as accurately as possible the operations in which the money is going to be used, taking into account sales, costs and other relevant financial aspects. The projection should be broken down for each year of the investment.

2 Quantify positive and negative cash flows for each year of the projection, and the annual net totals of cash inflow or outflow.

3 Estimate the value of the cash flow for the final year of the

projection. It is prudent to assume that the final year's cash flow will continue forever.

4   Decide the percentage amount that will be applied to each year's cash flow. This is crucial because the higher the discount factor, the lower the overall valuation. Typically, two factors influence the level of the discount factor. The first is the level of business risk. If the risk is high (and the investment is unlikely to meet its projections), the discount factor should also be high. The second is often a compromise between the cost of borrowed money (such as 5% interest) and the return expected by the investor (for example, 15%); in this case, the discount factor would be 10%. It is wise to select a range of discount factors to cover optimistic, realistic and worst-case scenarios.

5   Apply the discount factor to the net cash flow for each year of the projection, and for the final value. This gives the present value contribution of each year's future cash flow; adding them provides a total estimate for the value of the investment.

Discounting cash flows helps to determine the potential of an investment and to compare different investment options. By applying DCF principles it is possible to calculate the net present value (the profit after funding costs are deducted) of an investment or its discounted payback (how long it will take to break even) or the internal rate of return (the interest rate at which a project will make neither a profit nor a loss).

Avoiding pitfalls

Many managers have financial responsibilities and their decisions will often be influenced by or have an impact on other parts of the business. The following principles will help avoid flawed financial decision-making.

Financial expertise must be widely available

Every manager needs to understand why successful financial management increases profits. People need to own their part of the financial control process, to have the information and expertise needed to routinely make the best financial decisions.

Consider the impact of financial decisions

Do not ignore or underestimate the wider impact of finance issues upon other departments and decisions.

Avoid weak budgetary control

Budgets are an active tool to help make financial decisions, not merely a way to measure performance.

Understand the impact of cash flow

Non-financial managers often ignore cash flows and the time value of money. Everyone should be aware of the importance of cash to the organisation.

Know where the risk lies

Identifying risks and how to reduce them is crucial to successful financial decision-making. For example, managers need to know not only where the break-even point is, but also how and when it will be reached.

Reducing and managing business risks

Reducing the risk inherent in business activity is best achieved by applying the principles and techniques appropriate to the situation.

Understand the nature of risk

The willingness to take personal and financial risks is a defining characteristic of the entrepreneurial decision-maker. A 1999 study commissioned by PricewaterhouseCoopers found that while in continental Europe strategies focus on avoiding and hedging risk, Anglo-American companies view risk as an opportunity and accept risk management as necessary to achieving their goals. In 2015 this relative attitude to risk among European and US companies remains broadly the same, the result of long-standing cultural experiences and history as well as more recent events.

Successful decision-makers make sure that the risks resulting from their decisions are measured, understood and as far as possible eliminated. They also go beyond the direct financial perspective and actively manage risk as it affects the whole organisation.

Accepting that risks exist is a starting point for the other actions needed, but the most important is to create the right climate for risk management. People need to understand why control systems are needed; this requires communication and leadership skills so that standards and expectations are set and clearly understood.

Consider the acceptable level of risk

An early step is to determine the nature and extent of the risks the business will accept. This involves assessing the likelihood of risks becoming reality and the effect they would have if they did. Only when this is understood can measures be taken to minimise the incidence and impact of such risks.

Identify and prioritise risks

Take the human factor into account. People behave differently and inconsistently when making decisions involving risk. They may be exuberant or diffident, overconfident or overly concerned. They may simply overlook the issue of risk.

It is crucial to identify significant risks both within and outside the organisation and allow these to inform decisions. This makes it easier to avoid unnecessary surprises. Examples of significant risks might be the loss of a major customer, the failure of a key supplier or the appearance of a significant competitor.

Risk surrounds us. As Harold Macmillan, a former British prime minister, once said: "To be alive at all involves some risk." When identifying risks it helps to define the categories into which they fall. This allows for a more structured analysis and reduces the chances of a risk being overlooked. Some of the most common areas of risk affecting business are shown in Table 17.1.

There is also an opportunity cost associated with risk: avoiding a risk may mean avoiding a potentially big opportunity. People can be too cautious and risk averse even though they are often at their best

TABLE 17.1 **Typical areas of organisational risk**

Financial	Commercial	Strategic	Technical	Operational
Accounting decisions and practices	Loss of key personnel and tacit knowledge	Marketing, pricing and market entry decisions	Failure of plant or equipment	Product or design failure, including failure to maintain supply
Treasury risks	Failure of commercial partners (such as licensees, agents, joint venture partners)	Acquisitions decisions	Infrastructure failure	Failure to develop new products
Viability of debtors and strategic suppliers	Failure to comply with legal regulations or codes of practice	Market changes affecting commercial decisions (due to customers and/or competitors)	Accidental or negligent actions (such as fire, pollution, floods)	Client failure
Fraud	Contract conditions	Political or regulatory developments	–	Breakdown in labour relations
Robustness of information management systems	Poor brand management or handling of a crisis	Resource-building and resource allocation decisions	–	Corporate malpractice (such as sex discrimination)
Inefficient cash management	Market changes	–	–	Political change
Inadequate insurance	–	–	–	–

when facing the pressure of risk or deciding to take a more audacious approach. Sometimes the greatest risk is to do nothing.

Understand why risks become reality

Once risks are identified they can be prioritised according to their potential impact and the likelihood of them occurring. This helps to highlight not only where things might go wrong and what their impact would be, but how, why and where these catalysts might be triggered. The five most significant types of risk catalyst are as follows:

- **Technology.** New hardware, software or system configurations can trigger risks, as can new demands on existing information systems and technology. In 2003 London's first directly elected mayor introduced a congestion charge for traffic using the centre of the city; the greatest threat to the scheme's success (and his tenure as mayor) was posed by the use of new technology. It worked and the scheme was widely seen as a success.

- **Organisational change.** Risks are triggered by, for example, new management structures or reporting lines, new strategies and commercial agreements (including mergers, agency or distribution agreements).

- **Processes.** New products, markets and acquisitions all cause change and can trigger risks. The disastrous launch of "New Coke" by Coca-Cola was an even bigger risk than anyone at the company had realised; it outraged Americans who felt angry that an iconic US product was being changed (see Chapter 14). That Coca-Cola eventually turned the situation to its advantage shows that risk can be managed and controlled, but such success is rare.

- **People.** New employees, losing key people, poor succession planning, or weak people management can all create dislocation, but the main danger is behaviour: everything from laziness to fraud, exhaustion and simple human error can trigger this risk. Note how Nick Leeson, a rogue trader in Singapore, sparked the collapse in 1995 of Barings, then the longest established merchant bank in London.

- **External factors.** Changes to regulation and political, economic or social developments can all affect strategic decisions by bringing to the surface risks that may have lain hidden. The economic disruption caused by the sudden spread of the SARS epidemic from China to the rest of Asia in 2003 highlights this risk.

Use a simple risk management process

The stages of managing the risk inherent in decisions are simple. First, assess and analyse the risks resulting from a decision by systematically identifying and quantifying them. Second, consider how best to avoid or mitigate them. Third, in parallel with the second stage, take action to manage, control and monitor the risks.

Risk assessment and analysis

It is harder to assess the risks inherent in a business decision than to identify them. Risks that lead to frequent losses, such as an increasing incidence of employee-related problems or difficulties with suppliers, can often be overcome using past experience. Unusual or infrequent losses are harder to quantify. Risks with little likelihood of occurring

FIG 17.1 **Assessing and mapping risk**

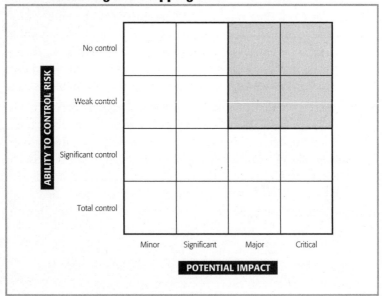

in the next five years are not important to a company focused on meeting shareholders' shorter-term expectations. Thus it is sensible to quantify the potential consequences of identified risks and then define courses of action to remove or mitigate them.

Each category of risk can be mapped in terms of both likely frequency and potential impact, with the potential consequences being ranked on a scale ranging from inconvenient to catastrophic (see Figure 17.1).

Risk management and control

Risk should be actively managed and given a high priority across the whole organisation. Risk management procedures and techniques should be well documented, clearly communicated, regularly reviewed and monitored. To successfully manage risks, you have to know what they are, what factors affect them and their potential impact.

If you plot the ability to control a risk against its potential impact, as shown in Figure 17.1, you can decide on actions either to exercise greater control over the risk or to mitigate its potential impact. Risks falling into the top-right quadrant require urgent action, but those in the bottom-right quadrant (total/significant control, major/critical impact) should not be ignored because complacency, mistakes and a lack of control can turn the risk into a reality.

Once the inherent risks in a decision are understood, the priority is to exercise control. All employees must be aware that unnecessary risk-taking is unacceptable. They should understand what the risks are, where they lie and their role in controlling them. To achieve this, share information, prepare and communicate clear guidelines, and establish control procedures and risk measurement systems.

Avoiding and mitigating risks

Start by reducing or eliminating those risks that result only in costs: the non-trading risks. These can be thought of as the fixed costs of risk and might include property damage risks, legal and contractual liabilities and business interruption risks. Reducing these risks can be achieved through quality assurance programmes, environmental control processes, enforcing health and safety regulations, installing accident prevention and emergency equipment and training people to use it, and taking security measures to prevent crime, sabotage, espionage, and threats to people and systems. Reducing a risk may also mean that the cost of insuring against it goes down.

Risks can be reduced or mitigated by sharing them. For example, acceptable service agreements from vendors are essential to reducing risk. Joint ventures, licensing and agency agreements can also be used to mitigate risk. To reduce the chances of things going wrong, focus on the quality of what people do – doing the right things right reduces risks and costs.

Risk management relies on accurate, timely information. Management information systems should provide details of the likely areas of risk, and the information needed to control the risks. This information must reach the right people at the right time so that they can investigate and take corrective action.

Create a positive climate for managing risk

Recognising the need to manage risk is not enough. The ethos of an organisation should recognise and reward behaviour that manages risk. This requires a commitment by senior managers and the resources (including training) to match. Too often, control systems are seen only as an additional overhead and not as something that can add value by ensuring the effective use of assets, the avoidance of waste and the success of key decisions.

Overcoming the fear of risk

Everyone accepts that taking risks is needed to keep ahead of the competition. Consequently, employees need to understand better what the real risks are, to share responsibility for the risks being taken and to see risk as an opportunity, not a threat.[3] Understanding how organisations manage risk effectively is important, but managing risk is only one possible strategy. Another approach is to look for ways to use the risk to achieve success by adding value or outstripping competitors – or both.

To do this, organisations need to stop taking the fun out of risk by controlling it in ways that are perceived as bureaucratic and stifling. Risk is both desirable and necessary. It provides opportunities to learn and develop and compels people to improve and effectively meet the challenge of change.

Key questions

Managing finance

- Are the most effective and relevant performance measures in place to monitor and assess the effectiveness of financial decisions?

- Have you analysed key business ratios recently? How useful are your performance indicators? What are the main issues? Are you measuring the right things?

- Is there a positive attitude to budgets and budgeting?

- Does decision-making focus on the most profitable products and services, or is it preoccupied with peripheral issues?

- What are the least profitable parts of the organisation? How will they be improved?

- Are market and customer decisions focused on improving profitability? Too often, attention is given to non-financial objectives, such as increasing market share, without adequately considering the financial risks and alternatives.

- How efficiently is cash managed? Do your strategic business decisions take account of cash considerations, such as the time value of money?

Managing risk

- Where are the greatest areas of risk relating to the most significant strategic decisions?

- What are the potentially dislocating events that could inflict the greatest damage on your organisation?

- What level of risk is acceptable for the company to bear?

- What is the overall level of exposure to risk? Has this been assessed and is it being actively monitored?

- What are the risks inherent in the organisation's strategic decisions, and what is the organisation's ability to reduce their incidence and impact on the business?
- What are the costs and benefits of operating effective risk management controls?
- Are the risks inherent in strategic decisions (such as acquiring a new business, developing a new product or entering a new market) adequately understood?
- At what level in the organisation are the risks understood and actively managed? Do people fully realise the potential consequences of their actions, and are they equipped to understand, avoid, control or mitigate risk?
- What review procedures are in place to monitor risks?
- To what extent would the company be exposed if key staff left?
- If there have been major developments (such as a new management structure or reporting arrangements), are the new responsibilities understood and accepted?
- Are management information systems keeping pace with demands? Are there persistent black spots – priority areas where the system needs to be improved or overhauled?
- Do employees resent risk, or are they encouraged to view certain risks as opportunities?

18 Making strategic decisions

THERE ARE MANY APPROACHES to taking the strategic decisions that affect the direction and performance of an organisation or team. This chapter examines the ideas, old and new, that benefit decision-makers. Some provide a ready framework for action and others offer insights that can be readily applied. Often a combination of methods is the best approach in dealing with the changing business environment.

Operational business decisions

Successful operational business decisions can be achieved by:

- managing knowledge and information;
- getting the corporate culture right;
- fostering creativity and innovation;
- focusing on continuous improvement;
- empowering and mobilising people;
- fitting operational decisions with the overall strategy.

Managing knowledge and information

Establishing systems that routinely provide accurate, reliable information is essential. Organisations need to exploit all knowledge, from information held on computers to the expertise and experience of their employees, to ensure that durable, effective decisions are made. Examples of businesses that manage to do this well include logistics firms, which provide customers with up-to-the-minute information about the location of their parcels, and online bookstores, which build up an understanding of their customers' reading tastes. However, not all knowledge systems need to be computerised. Law firms and professional practices generally are good at getting to know their clients, storing large amounts of useful information, usually in the heads of the partners, about their clients and their interests. This knowledge is certainly no less legitimate or valuable for being held outside a computer system. What matters is that it is shared and used, and this relies on the culture of the organisation.

Getting the corporate culture right

Corporate culture directly affects the quality and effectiveness of decisions, both what is decided and how it is implemented. The difficulty is that corporate culture is subject to innumerable different influences. As a result, it should be managed by:

- defining the vision and mission;
- setting the overriding values;
- leading by example;
- treating others as you would wish to be treated;
- building a positive, blame-free environment in which all issues can be discussed without ridicule or hostility.

Fostering creativity and innovation

Building competitive advantage is not only about doing your best to attract and satisfy customers; it is also about attracting and satisfying them more than your competitors do. This invariably requires decisions to be innovative, that is, cleverer than those of the competition. To do this, an organisation must encourage challenges to accepted norms and engage in direct dialogue with customers and other stakeholders. It should not rely on assumptions that have little evidence to support them. Having a corporate culture that encourages or allows this is essential. In reversal theory terms,[1] the rebellious motivational state, rather than the conforming state, needs to dominate.

Focusing on continuous improvement

Continuous improvement through a commitment to learning, development and investment will often help to keep operational decisions incisive and relevant. Past performance and areas of weakness must be regularly assessed. A commitment to developing individuals, training people and spreading best-practice techniques is also necessary. An organisation must be prepared to challenge established systems and processes, and to set new targets in its pursuit of improved performance.

Empowering and mobilising people

For decisions to be formulated accurately and implemented effectively, people must have the freedom to act and to be able to exploit their potential. This requires the removal of unnecessary bureaucratic or procedural constraints, giving people clear (and possibly expanding) areas of responsibility and authority. The quality and ultimately the success of strategic decisions will be profoundly influenced by people's level of motivation. Thus their efforts need to be mobilised and focused, and recognised and rewarded, in such a way that they tackle the important issues affecting the success of the business with commitment and determination.

Fitting operational decisions with the overall strategy

A strategic plan should guide actions and decisions, providing a sense of purpose, energy and direction. It should also offer a means of communicating, motivating and co-ordinating efforts throughout an organisation, helping to focus on areas for improvement or development. A strategic plan provides an opportunity to change an organisation's nature: its purpose, its activities and even its organisational culture, including values and the ways things are done. It can embrace a set of guiding principles as well as a practical framework for achieving its aims. It also offers a means by which performance can be measured and assessed. So how can strategic plans be made to guide and direct operational decisions? Some necessary steps are as follows:

- Subdivide the overall strategic plan into business plans for each operating unit, and then into objectives for each department, team and ultimately each individual. Always start by asking some basic questions such as: What business are we in? What is our purpose? Where are we now? Where do we want to be in the future? How will we achieve this?

- Consult widely to identify opportunities and decide priorities. Innovation and common-sense ideas come from employees at the lowest level as well as the highest and from customers and suppliers.

- Assess the organisation's competitive position. Current trends need to be taken into account to highlight strengths and weaknesses.

- Focus on the purpose of the organisation. What does it do? What makes it unique? Does it need to change? What will help to achieve success in the future? Take a balanced view of the opportunities. Too narrow a perspective may result in missed opportunities; too broad a canvas can make it difficult to focus, bringing risks and learning curves associated with diversification.

- Communicate a powerful vision. This should include a clear statement of what the organisation's business is, where it is going and how it will get there. A vision or mission statement must be inspirational and help win commitment. It must also be realistic, understandable and clearly understood by everyone in the organisation.

- Set time frames. Vision statements are concerned with the long term, but the strategic planning process must provide objectives that are attainable within a time frame of 1–5 years. Without short-term goals to aim for, it is difficult to maintain momentum and motivation.

- Set clear objectives. The most effective managers translate a vision into practical objectives, taking account of the strengths and weaknesses of the people they manage.

■ Make sure the plan is relevant. A strategic plan cannot be static. It must be adaptable to change and must reflect the process of continuous improvement and development within an organisation. To keep the plan relevant and realistic, it is essential to evaluate and modify it on a rolling basis, mindful of changing circumstances and new opportunities or problems.

Decisions involving legal issues

In dealing with legal issues, there are a number of guiding principles.

Identify vulnerabilities

It is important to assess the areas of greatest vulnerability, particular contract terms, employment or regulatory issues, laws relating to advertising and data protection, or whatever. Once these have been identified, the level of vulnerability should be assessed and then monitored closely, taking steps to establish necessary training and compliance.

Never ignore or trivialise legal action

A threat of legal action may be tactical, but it should always be taken seriously and, wherever possible, anticipated so that preventive measures can be taken. If the worst happens and the organisation is faced with legal action, even though, according to the International Bar Association, over 90% of cases never reach court, large amounts of time and money may have to be spent dealing with the matter. It may also mean that projects have to be delayed or products withdrawn from sale until the matter is resolved.

Seek legal advice and early resolution

Taking legal advice early on may save a great deal of time and expense later. It can also help to avoid undermining your case, either through ill-advised action or ignorance of the legal implications. Negotiating "without prejudice" allows all concerned to explore different options to resolve the situation, as any offers cannot subsequently be revealed in court. At this stage, gather the relevant documentation, in case the matter does go to court.

Prepare

If legal action ensues, review your options and consider any implications. The legal team should possess decision-making authority in internal and external commercial communication issues and technical legal decisions. It is important to define clearly the rights and wrongs of the case, identifying where the organisation is on firm ground and where it is weak. This can also help to identify where compromise is possible. Where it is not, endeavour to understand what the other party wants to achieve. Then negotiate with a view to settling the matter out of court.

Settling

Once a dispute is settled, taking time to reflect when the heat is off will help provide an understanding of what happened, and why, and how it can be avoided in the future. It is worth making a written evaluation to help inform future decisions.

Problem solving

A hidden trap within problem solving is the danger of overanalysis, when often what is really required is nothing more than a pen, paper and a period of quiet thought and discussion. The following points are important in all problem-solving styles:

- Identify the problem. What is the nature of the problem? What is its importance to your operations? Asking or answering these questions sets the tone for how the problem is tackled (for example, whether it is handled urgently or patiently, individually or collectively).

- Collect and process information. What information is needed to solve the problem, what data are available, and what extra information may be required? Too little information may make it difficult to come up with a solution. Too much information may make it difficult to see what the solution is.

- Generate possible solutions. Foster an exploratory tone in the problem-solving process. This will allow a range of potential solutions to be generated.

■ Assess options. Generate certain criteria (financial, time, organisational precedent and workability) against which different courses of action can be rated. This helps to determine which approach is best.

■ Make the decision and inform people. Once a solution has been determined, it should be communicated clearly to all those responsible for implementing it or to those affected by it to counter any confusion.

■ Implement the solution. Set a time frame for delivery and deadlines for each stage. After this, it is a matter of seeing that everything is done on time and that the inevitable glitches in the implementation process are overcome.

■ Verify the decision. When the plan has been implemented, its effects can be monitored to see if they are what was desired, or whether they have resulted in other problems that will need solving.

These steps are common to all forms of problem solving, but there are many ways to complete them. Some problems may need ingenious solutions that require the adoption of techniques such as ratio analysis and brainstorming. It is therefore necessary to differentiate between two types of problem: programmed and non-programmed.

Programmed problems are usually those that occur as a routine part of a manager's job. Even when they are complex, the solutions are often found by following organisational precedent and procedures. Examples include machine breakdown, salary and staff dilemmas, and budget issues. Linear programming, queuing theory and decision-tree techniques are methods that can be used to deal with such problems.[2]

Non-programmed problems are those for which there is no single system or procedure for determining the right course of action. They may involve anything from new-product development to the shape of a marketing campaign, and they are usually of fundamental importance to the success of particular product lines, even an organisation itself. The most common but not always the most effective technique for solving non-programmed problems is some form of creative problem solving, including brainstorming. Other useful techniques include cause and effect analysis and Pareto analysis.

Techniques for problem solving

Cause and effect analysis

When treating a patient, a doctor observes the symptoms to decide what the problem is. Similarly, in cause and effect analysis, the first step is to determine the effects of the problem in order to work out what the problem is and deal with it. To do this, it helps to take the following steps:

- Label the problem. Express its effects in detail so that others can also identify what it is. Labels should endeavour to connect effects to possible causes. For example, if the effect is a 10% increase in late deliveries of goods in the past month, connect this to all the causes of this problem, such as people, poor transport, inefficient order systems, limited product availability, or whatever.

- Identify the root causes of the problem. The most common are likely to be people, materials and equipment. For example, if late product delivery is because of poor communication, communications systems or bureaucracy might be the root cause. A flow diagram of work processes can help to illustrate the relationship between problems, their effects and their causes. Collect data on the causes of the problem. Asking the staff involved for their opinions should help pin down the cause or causes, which can then be dealt with.

Pareto analysis

Frequently recurring problems may be several different problems, all linked and with many causes. In such circumstances, Pareto analysis can be useful in organising the data so that the most significant factors are clearly illustrated. This is based upon the 80-20 Pareto principle: that 80% of problems are caused by 20% of possible factors. To tackle a problem, therefore, concentrate on the troublemaking 20%, and take the following four steps:

- Identify the overarching problem.
- Determine the factors causing it and how often they are to blame for the problem occurring.
- List the biggest factors contributing to the problem. Pareto analysis is most useful when few factors are involved.
- Develop a solution targeting each factor individually.

This approach has the potential to eliminate the biggest causes of a problem and often prevents it recurring or, at the very least, mitigates its effects. But it is less useful when a large number of factors are more or less equally responsible, as it is difficult and time-consuming to analyse each one and pointless to prioritise the order in which they should be tackled. Pareto analysis works best when only damage control is possible. For example, all organisations get customer complaints, but the biggest reasons for customer dissatisfaction can be attended to, thus reducing the incidence of complaints. However, the more complicated the problem, the less likely it is that Pareto analysis will help to find a solution. For complex problems, creative problem solving is required.

Kepner-Tregoe analysis

Sometimes all that is needed is to determine what is wrong and why it is wrong, and then to fix it. This approach is at the heart of Kepner-Tregoe (KT) analysis and its emphasis on solid, rational analysis makes it suited to hard rather than soft management issues. For example, it is used to explain deviations from the norm, quality or process problems (often in manufacturing), and how to repair machines or systems and to identify potential problems.

KT analysis is simple, methodical and powerful. The first stage is to define the problem in detail by asking the following questions:

- What is the problem or deviation?
- Where does it occur?
- When does it (or did it) occur?
- How does it occur? Specifically, how often does it happen, and how old is the process when it first occurs?

■ How big is the problem (how much is affected in real terms or as a proportion of the whole)?

The answers to these questions should allow you to define what the problem is, as well as what it is not. The next stage is to examine the differences between what should happen and what does happen, preparing a list of possible reasons for each difference and for the problem as a whole.

Techniques for creative problem solving

It is often said that in many organisations, too much attention is paid to norms, rules, procedures and precedents and not enough to creative thinking. However, many of the problems that organisations face today cannot be solved without a creative approach. Some of the most popular and effective approaches are described below.

Vertical and lateral thinking

Creativity can be divided into left-brain activities, those that are logical and analytical, and right-brain activities, those that are creative and integrative. A systematic approach to creativity is provided by Edward de Bono, a creativity consultant, who distinguished between vertical thinking, bounded by logic and linear thinking, and lateral thinking, which cuts across normal boundaries and processes. He claims that where traditional techniques are inadequate for solving problems, lateral thinking will generate new ideas and approaches that provide the answer. Lateral thinking combines ideas and concepts that have not previously been brought together. It removes assumptions, typically by asking "What if?" questions.

Why and why not

Questioning is a useful starting point for creative problem solving. Challenging the way that things are can lead to alternatives being generated. Although questioning alone may not provide breakthrough thinking, it is often an essential first step in breaking traditional thinking. In particular, it can help to question established logic, asking "Why?" as well as "Why not?". Questioning the limits of existing processes, systems or technology can also stimulate creativity. Identifying false assumptions is another valuable step.

Good ideas come from anywhere

Ideas are no respecters of status or salary. It may be true that in certain industries senior people have the best ideas, and this is probably a reflection of their experience or confidence. However, excellent ideas can be found in unexpected places: junior members of staff, competitors, other industries or historical legend.

Maintaining momentum and avoiding drift

For the process of innovation to succeed, it is necessary to avoid drift and the dissipation of ideas. This can be achieved by having a rigorous, focused approach and by setting tight deadlines. It can help to focus on issues such as customer needs and preferences, the strategic aims of the organisation, team and individual objectives, vision statements and goals that guide activities and progress, and information about competitors and other industries.

Removing constraints

Embracing radical change and re-engineering business processes can help to foster innovation. Experience is valuable, but it is not everything. Something may never have been tried before, but this does not mean that it can never succeed. Another way to remove constraints is to make further use of the resources that are available, notably data, IT and the knowledge and experience of others. Motivation is important in driving innovation, and this means rewarding innovators.

Planning the implementation of new ideas

New ideas often fail because of poor planning or execution, or because of a lack of communication and co-operation between the innovator and the implementer in making sure the vision is fulfilled but adapted as necessary according to practical and commercial considerations. Patient, critical analysis is more important in planning implementation of new ideas than it is for the initial process of innovation.

Brainstorming

One of the most popular methods of generating answers to problems is brainstorming, whereby those involved in the process come up with many solutions to a problem. Most will be inappropriate, but from the ideas generated a creative and effective solution may emerge. Brainstorming is a process in which a group employs all its creative talent. However, it is only through the adoption of several important principles that it is likely to work:

- Quantity matters. Generate as many ideas as possible. Quality is secondary to the quantity of ideas. The quality of each idea can be assessed later.

- Suspend judgment. Prevent criticism or evaluation until as many ideas as possible have been produced, so that participants feel free to contribute without fear that their ideas will be torpedoed by others.

- Freewheel. Encourage every idea, even ones that may seem wild and silly. The ideas that at first seem outlandish may be the ones of greatest brilliance.

- Cross-fertilise. Allow participants to build on each other's ideas and thus spawn new solutions that represent their collective thinking. This is how brainstorming becomes truly productive.

- Don't rush to judgment. Allow time between the generation of ideas and the evaluation process. A methodical process of elimination should be used to select the optimal solution. Set the criteria on which to rate the ideas generated. This helps to whittle down the ideas to a few promising solutions, of which one should be labelled front-runner and the others kept as back-up alternatives.

Mind mapping

This is an approach that organises thoughts and ideas into a clear form, from which patterns and new approaches emerge or crystallise. Mind maps help to clarify issues, as well as to share and communicate ideas. A starting point is to list the pros and cons of each idea. Grouping issues into specific categories can also be useful. A popular example of this is SWOT analysis, which identifies internal strengths and weaknesses, and external opportunities and threats. Lastly, displaying ideas in diagrammatic form can highlight relationships between ideas.

Heuristics

A heuristic system uses experience to guide future plans and decisions. It is characterised by flexibility and tentativeness rather than forcefulness or certainty, with decisions adjusted as events develop, guided by a specific set of values. Thus heuristic methods work best in situations where structured or systematic decision-making methods cannot be applied, perhaps because the situation is new. Heuristics are relevant to the world of business: core principles (such as meeting customer needs or being an effective leader) combined with experience can be applied quickly and flexibly to effect a solution.

Cemex: mixing analysis and intuition

One of the biggest difficulties when making strategic decisions is to balance intuition with reason. In the 1990s Lorenzo Zambrano, the chairman and CEO of Cemex, recognised that the Mexican cement company founded by his grandfather in 1906 could grow only by finding an approach that was different from those of its competitors. By reassessing what customers wanted, he transformed Cemex from a small commodity business in Mexico into one of the world's largest cement companies.

Cemex has outperformed its international rivals by changing from selling concrete as a product by the yard (the industry norm) to selling timely delivery of it. Zambrano realised that customers wanted the right amount in the right place at the right time, without workers waiting or the concrete spoiling. Cemex developed digital technology to manage the location and dispatch of its trucks and now uses global positioning technology to guarantee delivery of ready-mixed concrete within a 20-minute window. It uses IT to control temperatures in its kilns around the world from its headquarters.

Balancing intuition and analysis, Cemex understood its customers' priorities and transformed the service it offered. This can be done, for example, by sorting product attributes into three categories: basic, differentiated and exceptional. The next stage is to develop new advantages and strengthen existing ones to make your product exceptional. For Cemex, this meant changing how it measured performance to monitor and improve its service.

Implementing solutions

Before implementing any solution, other questions should be considered:

- Is there a problem at all and does it need a solution? People and organisations rush into changes, often assuming that some action is necessary because something has occurred or may occur. Even if it has, it can sometimes be easier and less costly to ride out its effects.

- Who is the best person to act? Important issues relating to shareholders or personnel are clearly the responsibility of senior managers. Many issues are cross-functional, which can complicate jurisdiction; and many are simply too complex to be addressed by one person alone. In any event, it is often useful to discuss situations with senior colleagues who are able to provide a different perspective or additional experience, even if their authority is not required.

- Who should be involved? Identify in advance people whose help is essential and those who can be called upon should the need arise, and enlist their support. If implementation means a significant organisational change, then as well as those who lead the process there need to be influencers who can help to gain support and commitment. Any solution will rely on the skills and commitment of people.

- What is the best way to plan, test and implement the solution? Planning is essential to ensure successful implementation. So is monitoring the implementation process, changing methods where necessary while still keeping the final goal clearly in mind. Contingency planning is valuable in overcoming any difficulties that may arise.

Developing problem-solving techniques

Problem-solving skills and processes, designed to prevent or overcome difficulties, should be improved during stable periods. If techniques have to be developed in the middle of a problem, the process will become complex, distracted and overly experimental, making it harder to succeed. It is essential that solutions are practical and attainable within the organisation's resources, otherwise they are unlikely to work and may lead to additional problems.

International business decisions

Why do businesses expand internationally? The answer may be simple: to exploit markets and the economies of scale that come with expansion. But expanding into new geographical markets successfully is not simple to do.

Reasons for international expansion

Consider this question from the chairman of one of the largest industrial groups in East Asia:

> How can our group of 20 diversified companies provide flexibility for each operating company to grow and innovate and, at the same time, reduce administrative overheads and employ information technology effectively across the group?

And this, from the president of the largest division of one of the world's leading elevator companies:

> Our business focuses on providing local services to customers in 22 countries. Will our biggest foreign competitor enter our region with a business infrastructure that relies on 22 country operations? No way!

The reason for international expansion is generally to pursue an opportunity for growth; it may also be because existing markets are saturated. But business history is full of examples of companies whose international ventures do not succeed as intended. For example, Marks & Spencer, a UK retailer, believed it could broaden its revenue base by expanding internationally, only to find that it did not work. It closed or sold most of its foreign operations and focused on its core UK market, and in a subsequent partial reversal of its policy, such as expanding into Shanghai, its progress has been disappointing.

Some firms expand abroad because their market as a whole is an international one, as it is for such industries as entertainment, publishing, pharmaceuticals and telecoms. Or it may be because the domestic market is too small, as it is for such industries as aerospace, shipbuilding and automotive manufacturing.

However, decisions to expand internationally are probably driven by less rational factors or by conjecture. International expansion may result from a desire to exploit a much larger market, which can then be justified with spurious interpretations of data. There is prima facie evidence of this from two sources. The first is the dotcom boom that occurred during the 1990s, when many entrepreneurs and their backers believed that a global market existed for whatever was being sold. The key was simply to get online, drive traffic to a website and gain market share. The internet came to be seen as a fast track to securing a strong global position. The second is the keenness of companies to expand into China during the 1980s and 1990s. Many saw China as the most promising market in the world, and many have so far been sorely disappointed.

Pursuing foreign markets is invariably much more complex than it may appear at first sight. It can also be largely untried. It has to be said that hubris may also play a part. If the opportunity exists for overseas expansion, a company's leaders may feel obliged to expand there. Not to do so may be a tacit admission of failure. Or an ambitious CEO may simply be bored with the current business and want a new challenge.

Succeeding with international decisions

Strategic decisions about international expansion must take into account all kinds of things, including market entry, product development and production, sales and service, marketing and distribution. Substantial costs and risk may be involved, and the following steps should be taken.

Define objectives

The first priority is to be clear about what your international strategy can and cannot achieve. There should also be clearly defined success criteria. Many companies stage the implementation of their international expansion, only committing additional resources when initial objectives have been achieved. A helpful question to ask might be: "What level of achievement would be acceptable to the business, regardless of how the market is perceived?" Other questions include:

- How does the international strategy help to achieve the overall aims of the organisation?

- What are the priorities (cross-selling or improving service for existing customers, attracting new clients, attacking current or potential competitors, reducing costs, gaining information and experience, or something else)?

- What are the options? For example, should the firm set up an overseas office or subsidiary, or would acquisition, a joint venture, franchising or licensing be better approaches?

- Where are the potential pitfalls and how will the risk be managed?

- Does the organisational structure need to be altered to take full advantage of the international operations? If so, how?

Understand the market

Many companies think they understand a foreign market when they do not. There are a number of examples of UK firms (Marks & Spencer and EMAP are two) entering the US market and getting it badly wrong. You need to understand how progress is made, how things are done and what the principal issues, including cultural ones, are. How will the organisation be perceived? Is everyone involved prepared for doing business in an environment that may be different? Cultural issues are particularly significant in cross-border mergers or acquisitions. One lesson from successful mergers is that it is often best to recognise cultural differences, show flexibility and compromise, and work hard at developing a unitary set of values. Common systems and integrated objectives can help achieve this.

Assess organisational issues

There are many areas where an overseas expansion can run into difficulty. Are employees prepared, motivated, trained and equipped to do business internationally? What practical difficulties and barriers to expansion are there in the short and medium term? Another area requiring consideration is the communication of the decision. How will existing customers, employees and shareholders react to the decision to expand overseas? Are there opportunities to raise the profile of the organisation and facilitate its entry into the new market?

To better understand such organisational issues, it makes sense to use external advisers with experience of the market. Government agencies and trade associations can also provide help and so, too, can other, non-competing businesses. Local personnel with expertise in the market can be recruited to advise on the best way of succeeding in a new market.

Establish operations abroad

Analysing the available options will highlight the best approach and inform the way in which it is executed. A strategy to expand internationally requires a champion, someone with dynamism and commitment, and ideally with local expertise or expertise in setting up a similar expansion elsewhere. Such a champion must be flexible enough to make adjustments as necessary to make the new strategy succeed, and must have (or have a subordinate who has) good project management skills to provide focus and prioritise actions and aims.

Structure international operations

It can be unproductive and a waste of resources to make a new international firm fit existing systems and procedures. But core management issues such as communications, structure and leadership are best resolved early. Managers must make sure that information and expertise flow freely throughout the organisation. In particular, best-practice information should be widely disseminated and available for everyone in the organisation. Deciding the degree of autonomy given to international business units is fundamental. Reporting structures, responsibilities and authority levels need to be clear. An organisation benefits from being integrated and cohesive and should be fair and consistent in its practices and with its employees. Local factors should be taken into account, but an organisation should be true to its values. Co-ordination and control are important; if left to drift, international operations may become disconnected from the rest of the organisation, even in conflict with it.

Leading and motivating people, setting direction and making decisions are all made more difficult across borders. Empowerment often provides a solution, enabling people to work within clearly defined areas of responsibility. Mentoring schemes can provide individuals with support and coaching, helping to integrate international business units into the organisation as a whole.

Ensure stability and efficiency

Multinational companies will want to reduce costs and maximise resources within a single, integrated structure. Things to consider when determining the best structure include:

- Political, economic and other factors affecting stability. If the operating environment is unstable, the best solution may be to provide direct support.
- Resources – human, financial and so on.
- The purpose, size and complexity of the operation. Generally, the more sophisticated and complex the organisation, the more autonomy is required. But good communications between local operations and overseas headquarters are always important.

Communicate

When building an international business, all those with a stake in the company, especially shareholders, providers of finance and employees, should be informed of what is happening, what the advantages are and what it means for them. Without an explanation, people often fear the worst. Without a convincing explanation, they worry that senior managers have not thought things through and may be making a strategic error.

Financial issues

The commercial issues associated with any major new undertaking include:

- Transfer pricing. The prices at which an organisation transfers goods between subsidiaries in different countries will affect local profitability and may have tax implications.
- Exchange-rate volatility. Changes in the value of currencies complicate cross-border business and can affect profitability. For companies operating within the euro zone, reducing this uncertainty is seen as a benefit of the single European currency. Companies can, of course, hedge their currency risks by buying and selling currencies forward, but the fewer currencies they have to work with the simpler is the administration.
- Taxation and accounting differences, and legal and other local requirements. These will affect the way the business should be set up and managed.

Avoiding pitfalls

Paradoxically, the more choices there are, the tougher life can be. Greater choice comes at a price: more time, more demands on your cognitive abilities, more confusion and paralysis resulting from indecision. Decision-making is littered with potential hazards. Understanding them is one half of the story; trusting yourself is the other half.

The way that people think, both as individuals and collectively, affects the decisions they make, and in ways that are rarely understood. John Hammond, Ralph Keeney and Howard Raiffa, writing in *Harvard Business Review*, described several traps in decision-making:[3]

- The anchoring trap – giving disproportionate weight to the first piece of information we receive. The impact of the first information and our immediate reaction to it are so significant that they drown our ability to evaluate a problem.
- The status quo trap – a bias towards not making changes, even when better alternatives exist, as a result of inertia or the potential loss of face if the current position were to change.

- The sunk-cost trap – perpetuating the mistakes of the past because the investment involved makes abandoning previous decisions unthinkable.

- The confirming evidence trap (confirmation bias) – seeking information to support a predilection, to discount opposing information, to justify past decisions and to support a current favoured strategy.

- The overconfidence trap – overestimating the accuracy of forecasts. Linked to confirming evidence, it occurs when decision-makers have an exaggerated belief in their ability to understand issues and predict the future.

- The framing trap – incorrectly defining a problem and therefore undermining the decision-making process. This may be unintentional.

- The recent event trap – giving undue weight to a recent, possibly dramatic, event or sequence of events. It is similar to the anchoring trap, except that it can arise at any time.

- The prudence trap – being overcautious when estimating uncertain factors. The tendency to be risk averse is likely to be strongest when the decision-maker feels that both the current approach and the alternative courses carry risks.

There are two other potential pitfalls resulting from an organisation's culture or environment:

- Fragmentation occurs when people disagree, either with their peers or with their superiors. Emerging dissent is disguised or suppressed and left to fester rather than being raised both clearly and formally. This hinders effective analysis and decision-making, and worsens when the views of one group dominate. It is also self-sustaining and difficult to reverse because any attempt to counter it is seen as an attempt to dominate.

- Groupthink is the opposite of fragmentation and occurs when the group suppresses ideas that challenge or do not support the direction in which the organisation is moving. It is caused by, for example, complacency or past successes generating a sense of infallibility. Groupthink may occur because the group is denied information, or because people are concerned about disagreeing, due to past events, present concerns or a fear of what the future might hold. This results in an incomplete survey of the available options and failure to assess the risks of preferred decisions. Groupthink can occur in organisations where teamwork is either strong or weak and is just as self-perpetuating as fragmentation.

Several principles and techniques can help avoid these pitfalls:

- Be bold and do not fear the consequences of decisions. People often overestimate the consequences of choice and discount their ability to make the right one. They fear that a loss will hurt more than a gain will please. Remember that the worst-case scenario might not occur, and even if it does, people will usually cope with it.

- Trust your instincts and emotions. Humans have evolved by making good decisions and implementing them. Sometimes, a quick decision works best precisely because you have identified the key pieces of information rapidly and then responded. Extra time can lead to information overload and other distractions.

- Be prepared to play devil's advocate. Searching for flaws and failings will strengthen your decisions and illuminate factors affecting them, such as biases.

- Avoid irrelevancies. Irrelevant information distorts your perception, as in the anchoring trap. Be ready to question the context of the information. What are you basing your decision on, and is it really relevant?

- Reframe the decision. View the issues from a new perspective. The sunk-cost trap highlights the tendency to stick with previous choices because too much has been invested. Don't do this – better alternatives may exist.

- Challenge groupthink. Find out what people really think and use that to inform decisions.

- Limit your options. Remove pressure and clarify your thinking by choosing the most promising options. Also consider whether to delegate the decision to someone better qualified.

- Take unpopular decisions when needed. To do this, you will need to prepare the ground (if possible) to minimise the surprise. Also:
  - provide an honest explanation and put the message over calmly and consistently;
  - explain the implications of not taking the decision;
  - involve those affected by the decision wherever possible;
  - keep people informed of progress;
  - paint clear pictures of the desired result;
  - avoid delay or signs of personal uncertainty.

- Achieve consensus by agreeing the purpose of the decision. Allow leaders to emerge and provide the resources they need to ensure success. Understand the group's expectations and act on them; involvement in the decision-making process usually generates commitment.

- Gather the facts and accurately define and understand the problem. Objective, unbiased analysis is best.

Other potential pitfalls include tiredness, laziness, lack of sensitivity, an absence of focus and direction, a lack of creativity or innovation and being too risk averse. Part of leadership is the willingness and ability to take calculated risks – and to show the way in controlling risk and managing the situation.

Key questions

Decision-making

- Is the organisation too bureaucratic for intuitive, flexible and swift decision-making?

- Are decisions made close to the action, or are they generally made some distance away? Has this – could this – cause difficulties?

- What are the most important decisions facing the organisation? How are they being resolved and who is responsible?
- What are the most significant decisions arising over the next three years? What planning is being done to resolve these?
- What do your customers, employees and shareholders think of the organisation's ability to make the right decisions? How do they feel the situation could improve?
- Do you or your colleagues:
  - give disproportionate weight to the first piece of information received?
  - seek to maintain the status quo?
  - pursue failing decisions in a forlorn attempt to recover past investments and credibility?
  - seek confirming evidence to justify past or present decisions?
  - display overconfidence?
  - display excessive caution?
  - incorrectly define an issue, often leading to a flawed decision?
  - give undue weight to a recent or dramatic event?
  - delay important decisions?

Problem solving

Use these questions to find information on the cause of a problem:

- What has caused similar problems in the past?
- What might be causing the problem to occur here and not elsewhere?
- What might be causing the problem to occur now and not previously?
- What precipitated the problem?
- What combination of factors might have caused the problem?
- If X is the cause, how does it explain all the facts?

The pitfall in problem solving is often "jumping to cause". If you make assumptions about the cause of the problem, you may fix the wrong thing. At best, you still have the problem. At worst, you cause more problems:

- Has your thinking been as creative as possible?
- Have you consulted widely and used as much information as possible in generating your solution?

To assess the strength of your solution, gather information to answer the following questions:

- What results do we want, need or expect?
- What money and time can we invest?

To evaluate alternatives, gather information to answer the following questions:

- Which alternatives meet the non-negotiable constraints?
- Which alternative(s) best satisfy the other criteria?
- What are the risks associated with our preferred alternative(s)?

Notes and references

1 What is business strategy?

1   Kim, W.C. and Mauborgne, R., *Blue Ocean Strategy: How to Create Uncontested Market Space and Make the Competition Irrelevant*, Harvard Business School Press, 2005.

2 What strategic thinking can achieve

1   Raynor, M., *The Strategy Paradox: Why Committing to Success Leads to Failure (And What to do About It)*, Crown Business, 2007.

3 The different views of strategy

1   Farnham, A., "The man who changed work forever", *Fortune*, July 21st 1997.
2   Taylor, F., *The Principles of Scientific Management*, Harper and Brothers, 1911. For a more recent analysis, see Taylor, F., *Scientific Management*, Harper and Row, 1948.
3   Ansoff, I., *Corporate Strategy*, McGraw-Hill, 1965.
4   Hamel, G. and Prahalad, C.K., *Competing for the Future*, Harvard Business School Press, 1994.
5   Six Sigma is a business management strategy, originally developed by Motorola, used to identify and remove the causes of defects in manufacturing and business processes. It uses quality management methods (including statistical techniques) and relies on a special cadre of people within the organisation who are experts in these methods. Each Six Sigma project follows a defined sequence of steps and has quantified financial targets.
6   Peters, T. and Waterman, R., *In Search of Excellence*, Collins Business, 2004.
7   Senge, P., *The Fifth Discipline: The Art and Practice of the Learning Organization*, revised 3rd edn, Doubleday, 2006.

8   Taleb, N., *The Black Swan: The Impact of the Highly Improbable*, Penguin, 2007.

4   Forces that shape business strategy

1   Edgerton, D., *The Shock of the Old: Technology and Global History since 1900*, Oxford University Press, 2006.
2   Naisbitt, J., *Global Paradox*, William Morrow & Company, 1994.
3   Waterman, Jr, Robert H. and Peters, T., *In Search of Excellence: Lessons from America's Best-Run Companies*, 2nd edn, Profile Books, 2004.

5   Scenarios

1   Collins, J., *Good to Great*, Random House Business Books, 2001.
2   Porter, M., *Competitive Advantage: Creating and Sustaining Superior Performance*, Free Press, 1998.
3   Van der Heijden, K. *et al.*, *The Sixth Sense: Accelerating Organizational Learning with Scenarios*, John Wiley & Sons, 2002.
4   Ibid.
5   Ibid.
6   Ibid.

6   Involving and engaging stakeholders

1   Benko, C. and Anderson, M., *The Corporate Lattice: Achieving High Performance In the Changing World of Work*, Harvard Business School Press, 2010.
2   Sobel, A. and Sheth, J., *Clients for Life: How Great Professionals Develop Breakthrough Relationships*, Simon & Schuster, 2001.
3   Maister, D.H., Green, C.H. and Galford, R.M., *The Trusted Advisor: How to Create Trust-Based Relationships with Your Clients*, Free Press, 2001.

7   Resources and strategy

1   Warren, K., *The Critical Path*, Vola Press, 2004. See also Warren's popular book *Strategy Management Dynamics*, John Wiley & Sons, 2007.
2   Coyne, K. and Subramaniam, S., "Bringing Discipline to Strategy", *The McKinsey Quarterly Anthology on Strategy*, 2000.

8   Strategies for growth

1   Bower, J.L., "Not all M&As are alike, and it matters", *Harvard Business Review*, March 2001.

9 Developing a business strategy and thinking strategically

1 Waterman, R.H., *The Frontiers of Excellence: Learning from Companies That Put People First*, BCA, 1994.
2 Drucker, P., *Managing in Turbulent Times*, Harper Publishing, 1980.
3 Grove, A., *Only the Paranoid Survive: How to Exploit the Crisis Points That Challenge Every Company and Career*, Doubleday, 1996.
4 Kotler, P., *Kotler on Marketing*, Free Press, 1999.
5 Porter, M., "What is Strategy", *Harvard Business Review*, November–December 1996.
6 Ohmae, K., *The Mind of the Strategist: The Art of Japanese Business*, McGraw-Hill, 1982.

10 Vision

1 Sorensen, T., *Counselor: A Life at the Edge of History*, HarperCollins, 2008.

Other useful publications

Collins, J. and Porras, G., *Built to Last: Successful Habits of Visionary Companies*, HarperCollins, 1994.
Jones, P. and Kahaner, L., *Say It and Live It: The 50 Corporate Mission Statements That Hit the Mark*, Doubleday, 1995.
Kakabadse, A.P., Nortier, F. and Abramovici, N.B., *Success in Sight: Visioning*, International Thomson Publishing, 1998.
Kouzes, J. and Posner, B., *The Leadership Challenge*, 3rd edn, Jossey Bass, 2003.

11 Leading people through change

1 Sull, D., *Revival of the Fittest: Why Good Companies Go Bad and How Great Managers Remake Them*, Harvard Business School Press, 2003.
2 Collins, J., *Good to Great*, op. cit.
3 Day, G.S. and Schoemaker, P.J.H., *Peripheral Vision: Detecting the Weak Signals that Will Make Or Break Your Company*, Harvard Business School Press, 2006.
4 George, B., *Seven Lessons of Leading in a Crisis*, Jossey-Bass, 2009.
5 Grove, A., *Only the Paranoid Survive*, op. cit.
6 Cox, C. and Cooper, C., *High Flyers: An Anatomy of Managerial Success*, Basil Blackwell, 1988.
7 For details of the research see Kourdi, J. and Bibb, S., *A Question of Trust: The Crucial Nature of Trust in Business, Work and Life – And How to Build it*, Marshall Cavendish, 2007.
8 Goleman, D., *Emotional Intelligence: Why It Can Matter More Than IQ*, Bantam Books, 10th anniversary edition, 2005.

9   Covey, S., *The Seven Habits of Highly Effective People*, Free Press, 1989.
10 Kotter, J.P., *Leading Change*, Harvard Business School Press, 1996.
11 Smythe, J., *The CEO: Chief Engagement Officer*, Gower Publishing, 2007.

12 Implementing business strategy

1   Kaplan, R.S. and Norton, D.P., *The Balanced Scorecard: Translating Strategy into Action*, Harvard Business School Press, 1996.

13 Strategic innovation

1   For details visit www.talentfoundation.com
2   This includes the following publications: *Growing Global Executive Talent: High Priority, Limited Progress*, Development Dimensions International and the Economist Intelligence Unit, 2008; *Overcoming Barriers to Innovation: Emerging Role of the Chief Innovation Executive*, Accenture and the Economist Intelligence Unit, 2008; Gratton, L., *Hot Spots: Why Some Teams, Workplaces, and Organizations Buzz with Energy – and Others Don't*, Berrett-Koehler, 2007; Christensen, C., *The Innovator's Dilemma: When New Technologies Cause Great Firms to Fail*, Harvard Business School Press, 1997; Deschamps, J.P., *Innovation Leaders: How Senior Executives Stimulate, Steer and Sustain Innovation*, John Wiley & Sons, 2008; Kim, W.C. and Mauborgne, R., *Blue Ocean Strategy*, op. cit.; Collins, J., *Good to Great*, op. cit.
3   "Something new under the sun", *The Economist*, Special Report, October 11th 2007.
4   Gratton, L., *Hot Spots*., op. cit.
5   Boynton, A.C. and Fischer, B., *Virtuoso Teams: Lessons from Teams That Changed Their Worlds*, Financial Times/Prentice Hall, 2005.
6   Kim, W.C. and Mauborgne, R., *Blue Ocean Strategy*, op. cit.

Other useful publications

Allan, D., Kingdon, M., Rudkin, D. and Murrin, C., *Sticky Wisdom: How to Start a Creative Revolution at Work*, Capstone, 2002.
Edgerton, D., *The Shock of the Old: Technology and Global History Since 1900*, Profile Books, 2006.
"Get Your Innovations to Market – and Keep Them There" (HBR Article Collection), *Harvard Business Review*, July–August 2006.
Glazer, R., "Meta-Technologies and Innovation Leadership: Why There May Be Nothing New Under the Sun", *California Management Review*, Fall 2007.
Goldenberg, J., Horovitz, R., Levav, A. and Mazursky, D., "Finding Your Innovation Sweet Spot", *Harvard Business Review*, March 2003.
Huston, L. and Sakkab, N., "Connect and Develop: Inside Procter & Gamble's

New Model for Innovation", *Harvard Business Review*, March 2006.

Kanter, R.M., "Innovation: The Classic Traps", *Harvard Business Review*, November 2006.

Kelley, T., *The Art of Innovation: Success Through Innovation the IDEO Way*, Profile Books, 2002.

Ogle, R., *Smart World: Breakthrough Creativity and the New Science of Ideas*, Harvard Business School Press, 2007.

Shrage, M. and Peters, T., *Serious Play*, Harvard Business School Press, 1999.

Skarzynski, P. and Gibson, R., *Innovation to the Core: A Blueprint for Transforming the Way Your Company Innovates*, Harvard Business School Press, 2008.

"The iPod Touch – Apple's Sleeper Device", *BusinessWeek*, March 13th 2008 (www.businessweek.com).

Utterback, J., *Mastering the Dynamics of Innovation*, Harvard Business School Press, 1994.

Victor, B. and Boynton, A.C., *Invented Here: Maximizing Your Organization's Internal Growth and Profitability*, Harvard Business School Press, 1998.

16 Managing knowledge and information

1 Marchand, D., Kettinger, W. and Rollins, J.D., *Making the Invisible Visible: How Companies Win with the Right Information, People and IT*, John Wiley & Sons, 2001.

2 "The Truth about CRM", *CIO Magazine*, May 1st 2001.

3 Garvin, D.A., "Building a Learning Organization", *Harvard Business Review*, July–August 1993.

17 Managing finance and risk

1 This concept was expertly outlined by Michael Porter in *Competitive Strategy: Techniques for Analysing Industries and Competitors*, Free Press, 1980.

2 There are many excellent books outlining in detail the financial techniques that can be applied by non-financial managers for decision-making. See, for example, Harrison, J., *Finance for the Non-Financial Manager: All You Need to Know About Business Finance*, Thorsons, 1989.

3 A guide to overcoming the fear of risk is provided by Jeremy Kourdi and Steve Carter in *The Road to Audacity: Being Adventurous in Life and Work*, Palgrave Macmillan, 2003.

18 Making strategic decisions

1 Reversal theory is a theory of motivation developed by Ken Smith and Michael Apter, two psychology professors. The idea is that our experience is shaped by alternative ways of seeing the world. Specifically, four pairs of opposite states have been discerned and we "reverse" between these opposites in our everyday life. Reversal theory recognises the paradoxes of human behaviour and suggests that all individuals are motivated:
   - to be serious and pursue goals, but also to play, take risks and look for excitement;
   - to conform, but also to challenge;
   - by issues of mastery (of people, processes and ideas), but also by notions of sympathy (caring, friendship and affection);
   - by interest and focus on themselves, but also on others.

2 Linear programming in business is a way of determining how to achieve the best outcome, such as maximum profit or minimum cost, using a mathematical model in a given set of circumstances (represented as linear equations). Practical problems in operations research, such as how items flow through a network, can be expressed as linear programming problems. Also used in operations research and management science are decision trees (for example, fishbone diagrams). These are diagrams designed to show how issues or events are connected, and they are used to help analyse how a complex series of decisions or alternatives affect each other. They are particularly helpful for mapping a path through a set of alternatives.

3 Hammond, J.S., Keeney, R.L. and Raiffa, H., "The Hidden Traps in Decision-making", *Harvard Business Review*, September–October 1998.

Other useful publications

Adair, J., *Decision Making and Problem Solving*, Chartered Institute of Personnel and Development, 1999.

Hammond, J.S., Keeney, R.L. and Raiffa, H., *Smart Choices: A Practical Guide to Making Better Decisions*, Harvard Business School Press, 1998.

Hayashi, A.M., "When to Trust Your Gut", *Harvard Business Review*, February 2001.

Jennings, D. and Wattam, S., *Decision-making: An Integrated Approach*, 2nd edn, Financial Times/Prentice Hall, 1998.

Lambert, T., *Key Management Solutions*, 2nd edn, Financial Times/Prentice Hall, 1997.

Vroom, V.H. and Yetton, P.W., *Leadership and Decision Making*, Pittsburgh University Press, 1973.

Index

JEREMY KOURDI is an executive coach, writer and co-founder of Entendéo (www.Entendeo.com). He has worked with many well-known organisations in the UK and internationally, including The Economist, IMD Business School in Lausanne and the Chartered Management Institute. He has an MA in International Relations and is the author of numerous business books and articles.

PublicAffairs is a publishing house founded in 1997. It is a tribute to the standards, values, and flair of three persons who have served as mentors to countless reporters, writers, editors, and book people of all kinds, including me.

I. F. STONE, proprietor of *I. F. Stone's Weekly*, combined a commitment to the First Amendment with entrepreneurial zeal and reporting skill and became one of the great independent journalists in American history. At the age of eighty, Izzy published *The Trial of Socrates*, which was a national bestseller. He wrote the book after he taught himself ancient Greek.

BENJAMIN C. BRADLEE was for nearly thirty years the charismatic editorial leader of *The Washington Post*. It was Ben who gave the *Post* the range and courage to pursue such historic issues as Watergate. He supported his reporters with a tenacity that made them fearless and it is no accident that so many became authors of influential, best-selling books.

ROBERT L. BERNSTEIN, the chief executive of Random House for more than a quarter century, guided one of the nation's premier publishing houses. Bob was personally responsible for many books of political dissent and argument that challenged tyranny around the globe. He is also the founder and longtime chair of Human Rights Watch, one of the most respected human rights organizations in the world.

·　　·　　·

For fifty years, the banner of Public Affairs Press was carried by its owner Morris B. Schnapper, who published Gandhi, Nasser, Toynbee, Truman, and about 1,500 other authors. In 1983, Schnapper was described by *The Washington Post* as "a redoubtable gadfly." His legacy will endure in the books to come.

Peter Osnos, *Founder and Editor-at-Large*